The **"Four Seasons Method"** is more than a metaphor or an analogy about life cycles. Simply, it is a method to assess and rebalance one's life. It is a reminder that life is full of numerous cycles from start to finish and renewal all over again. Applying Tobe's method allows one an opportunity to put his method into action for any aspect of our lives that may need improvement or change.

Tobe has done an amazing job tying **The Four Seasons Way of Life** analogy together with his story behind the seasons: Beginning with **Spring** as a time to plan, make decisions and commit. **Summer** as a time to nurture what you have planned or weed out the problems and move ahead with passion. **Fall** as at time to reap what you have sown; while accepting, learning and gaining closure on matters. Lastly, and perhaps most importantly, the **Winter** when you take the time to reflect upon what you have learned and appreciate your successes; while making an effort to maintain yourself and remember to recuperate and prepare for the next cycle.

Furthermore, Tobe has given an excellent primer on non-traditional medicine and its applications to health and wellness. I, as an MD and Family Physician, trained in the traditional ways of Western Medicine, never had the opportunity to learn nor understand the ways of Eastern Medicine. I always knew that there must be something to this as it has survived for over 5000 years, but I never understood it. The terminology of Meridians, Acupuncture and Acupressure points just did not fit into the education that I trained and practiced under. However, my education had often failed my efforts with my patients and I looked to other non-traditional approaches.

I was introduced to Tobe over 10 years ago and began collaborating on patients. His "HansOn Muscle Therapy" (HMT) has proven suc d anything I ever anticipated. In fact, I as well as m y members have been his patients over the y treatments he applies, but the "Method" he In essence The Four Seasons Method.

For those readers of Western Medical ., I suggest reading the appendix first as an essential b und education that will assist the reader in understanding some of the references to "Traditional Chinese Medicine". I too was a bit perplexed in the past when patients have come to me stating that their "Gallbladder" organ system was amiss after an evaluation from Tobe and I could find no such traditional medicine problem in the "gallbladder system".

Tobe educates us in his book about the 12 organ systems and how they manifest as a disturbance along an axis or meridian and how it will relate to symptoms and disorders which is not taken literally as a problem in that specific organ but rather along that organs associated tissues or functions.

Tobe's exercises to introspect and assess where one is at should not be overlooked. These are important lessons to learn from, and I would suggest reading and rereading these last sections of his book. I too learned that I am stuck in "Winter" at times as I don't usually know my own limits and try to meet the needs of others at the expense of myself. This has given me hope to renew and improve myself. To quote his book: "Life is a continuum of problems to solve and lessons to learn. Once you accept this truth, then the problem you're facing is no longer a problem but rather an opportunity to learn.

Congrats Tobe on writing this book and helping so many others. I am proud and honored to consider you a friend and fellow healer.

Béla S. Kenessey, MD
Diplomate, American Board of Family Physicians
Fellow, American Academy of Family Medicine

A session with Tobe is a journey into self-discovery. Utilizing his hybrid philosophy of The Four Seasons, Tobe views into the mental and emotional underlying causes of pain and why it persists.

Integrating 5,000 years of Eastern Wisdom with modern sensibilities, The Four Seasons Way of Life; Ancient Wisdom for Healing and Personal Growth brings together these aspects of a personal session with Tobe into a clear and easily interpreted philosophy for living. Based on the simple concepts of "living in balance" I try to integrate Tobe's teachings and wisdom from our personal sessions into every aspect of my life. When old pain recurs, rather than remit to it, or simply seek relief, I turn inward and examine where the imbalance lies within my life. As Tobe so clearly points out, living in harmony with our "seasons" brings healthy dividends, while resisting the natural order of the universe results in internal stress, fatigue, and eventually, ill-health.

Integrating Tobe's Four Seasons life philosophy into my own daily life helps me to find that balance and harmony, with the natural result of dissolution of stress and alleviation of pain. As someone who is always "doing, doing, doing" Tobe's explanation of my Winter imbalances assists me in learning to let it go and relax into the natural order of things. In truth, I'd have a hard time imagining my life without this knowledge, and I thank Tobe sincerely for his teachings and wisdom.

Everybody has something they can learn from these teachings. Whether you're experiencing chronic pain, stress, depression, anxiety, or any other physical or mental fatigue, there is tremendous value in learning the sources of our imbalances, and seeking the path towards harmony.

Todd Severin MD
www.healthgrades.com

Tobe Hanson has created a very inspiring and useful work. It is a very clear exposition of Chinese medicine, but it is much more than technical. This book is eminently readable. Readers will become engrossed in the aura of a true healer with a huge heart and great discerning wisdom. The clinical stories are impressive, and his wise advice based on sound principles are inspiring. The season-based checklist queries toward the end are especially valuable tools for personal growth. A must read for thoughtful inquiring people!

Bill Gray MD, Saratoga, Ca.
www.**billgrayhomeopathy**.com

The Four Seasons Way of Life

Ancient Wisdom for Healing and Personal Growth

Tobe Hanson

One Source Unlimited, Inc.
7090 Johnson Drive
Pleasanton, CA 94588
Phone: 1-925-400-9932
info@TheFourSeasonsWayOfLife.com

For more information visit:
www.TheFourSeasonsWayofLife.com

Read Tobe's latest book:

Athletes Way to Be - Way of Excellence:
Ancient Eastern Wisdom Revealing the Secrets to Modern Day Athletic Peak
Performance and How to Be in The Zone.
www.AthletesWaytoBe.com

Printed in the United States of America:

ISBN: 978-0-9990601-0-0 (sc)
ISBN: 978-0-9990601-1-7 (hc)
ISBN: 978-0-9990601-2-4 (e)

Library of Congress Control Number: 2017908681

Acknowledgements

First of all, I want to thank my wife, my love and best friend, Sue, for her endless support through hundreds of hours writing this book.

I want to thank Dr. Lars-Olof Berglov for introducing me to the healing arts of ancient Chinese Medicine. My desire to understand this knowledge to heal and to educate fellow humans put me on my path and has led to the culmination of this book.

A special gratitude to my friends Jay Sarkis, Chris (Smircich) Matthies, who were both truly godsends. Without all their help, I do not know how I could have finished this book.

Jay helped with illustrations, design, logos and formatting of the book throughout all the different versions of re-writing and re-designing. Chris helped in editing and formatting, as well as giving feedback on how to formulate ideas. She never ceased to amaze me in how fast she could return edited material to me.

A special gratitude to my friend Sam Awad for always being there willing to help at any time in spite of his own busy schedule.

I want to thank Todd Severin, Mary Owens, Evan Corstorphine, Tess Reynolds, Kevin Comerford, and Douglas Clay for their feedback and ideas during the writing and development of this book.

For the editing of the third edition of this book I am grateful for all the help from D'Anne Harp.

And finally I want to thank all my patients over the last thirty years for the privilege of letting me treat them and for everything taught me to make this book possible.

Disclaimer

To the best of my knowledge, the principles offered in the Four Seasons System are not in opposition to any religion, they are not intended to be dogmatic in nature, nor are they designed to create or support any form of cultist doctrine. I have seasoned my own conclusions and understandings of ancient Chinese philosophy, the Law of the Five Elements, and the Law of the Four Seasons with my personal interpretations of biblical scriptures and thirty years of practice studying the cause of stress, tension, and pain. In the later years I have incorporated some of the teachings of today's masters, such as Eckhart Tolle, Byron Katie, Dr. Scott Peck, Dr. Marshall Rosenberg, and Don Miguel Ruiz.

The Four Seasons System is highly adaptable and applicable to people from all walks of life, independent of religion, race, sex, age, profession, or education level.

When reading this book, do not make the mistake of focusing on what's wrong with your friends and loved ones. It is always easier to see flaws in others than in yourself. It is my sincere hope that you will use this material to take charge and responsibility for your own life. Look inside, not outside of yourself for the answers.

All the case histories given in this book are true stories told to the best of my recollection. Except for the cases where the patients have given permission for me to use their real names and ages, all names, ages, and circumstances have been changed to protect the identities of the individuals.

Any person reading this book who has a medical condition, or suspects that they have one, should always consult their licensed physician regarding the proper way to treat this condition.

Contents

Introduction

L IFE IS AN ONGOING CYCLE of change. Whether you're ready for it or not, the sun will rise tomorrow morning and set tomorrow evening. The same thing will happen the following day, and on and on. As the days pass, spring will shift into summer, and then summer will shift to fall. Earth spins and rotates, and as long as you're here on earth, it's going to take you with it. No one can stop this ongoing cycle; it is a fact of life.

The very definition of life is something that is alive; the continuum from birth, or germination, until death. To be truly alive is to be on a continuous journey of learning and growth that passes in cycles intrinsically linked to the cycle of life we see all around us in the natural world. Everything that is alive is growing. To grow, we have to be challenged, put to the test, and go outside our comfort zones. Life is therefore a continuum of lessons to learn or problems to solve.

Situations change. We encounter problems. These are as inevitable as the sun rising. Resistance to challenges and avoidance of problems leads to a stagnation of growth, which causes us pain and suffering. If we experience ongoing problems, pain, and suffering in our lives, it may seem like the world is spinning out of control. But for ages, we've seen the sun come and go; the cycle continues with or without us. We can resist change all we want, but if we continue to resist, we become miserable, miss unlimited opportunities to grow, improve and start fresh. A wise man or woman will welcome challenges and problems as opportunities for growth. Once we accept our challenges and problems, and learn to live in harmony with the cycle of our lives, our suffering will be gone. Once we accept the problem, it ceases to be a problem; it becomes an opportunity to learn and grow.

When we are young, we are typically more idealistic and full of dreams, passion, and life. As we get older, many people lose their dreams and passion for life. They find themselves stuck or in a crisis, filled with disappointments, suffering, and pain. Anyone who has lived a little has discovered that life does not always turn out the way we wanted or expected. Do you know how you got to where you are? Do you know what you need and how to get it? Are you still growing? Do you know what is alive in you? When you reflect on your life up to this point, do you feel as if you are a success or a failure? Are you still excited about life? Are you learning and growing? Are you alive and fulfilled in your relationships? Are you engaged with and enjoying your work? Are you healthy and fit? Do you have peace of mind? Don't worry if you can't answer all of these questions positively right now. Every patient I have ever met has issues in life that challenge him or her. By repeating an erroneous behavior, avoiding growth, or ignoring our problems, we bring pain and suffering on ourselves and carry the tension somewhere in our bodies and minds. This tension leads to injury or disease ("dis-ease") and affects the quality of our lives.

What's most important is that you realize you did not end up where you are for no reason. When we were young, it seemed as if we healed and bounced back from injuries and pain in no time. As we get older, the same types of injuries linger or reappear. Why is that? I firmly believe in cause and effect, or, "As you sow, so also shall you reap." Every action, or lack of action, has a reaction and consequences.

Your potential for health, well-being, performance, and happiness is in your own hands. This goes against popular thinking. In our modern society, it's common to blame someone or something other than ourselves for our pain and failures. As we stubbornly refuse to grow and to take responsibility for our reality, we are unable to learn the lessons life teaches us. The lessons or life problems do not go away. As we resist, more and more tension builds up, causing anxiety, depression, and pain. If you keep doing what you have been doing you will keep getting what you have been getting. When we are unable to see this for ourselves, we keep doing what we have always been doing, and wondering why we are still in pain or unhappy. Albert Einstein once said, "The definition of insanity is to keep doing the same thing over and over while expecting a different outcome." We can all read this quote and nod our heads in agreement, but it's ironic that we continue the same ineffective patterns in our own lives, over and over. No one has pain or an injury for no reason! The same is true for failure and unhappiness with life.

Cause and effect exist in everything. If an injury does not heal, there must be a continuous stressor present. Stress picks at the scab, and the wound - emotional or physical - will never heal. Most people don't see the big picture or the cause, because they focus too much on relieving the symptom. If we are depressed, we are taught to take antidepressant drugs. If we have heartburn or acid reflux, the TV commercials have conditioned us to take antacid medication to reduce the acid. If we have pain, we are told to take over-the-counter ibuprofen or stronger prescription painkillers. These are standard practices. However, when the warning light appears on the dashboard of your car, indicating that you are low on fuel, you do not solve the problem by covering it with duct tape or breaking it with a hammer. Anxiety, depression, heartburn, tension, inflammation, and pain are all warning lights indicating something is wrong. Not one case of back pain is due to a deficiency of ibuprofen in the body. Ibuprofen is an anti-inflammatory drug that removes or reduces inflammation but not its cause. If the cause is still there, the drug will only mask the symptoms, and prolonged use of these Band-Aid treatments can have side effects, including other injuries or even more pain. We have been conditioned to treat the symptom, injury, or the disease rather than the cause.

Why aren't more studies done to understand what healthy people do to stay healthy? Why don't we focus on strengthening the immune system rather than treating the disease? Why is it that two people can be in the same car accident, where one person is severely injured while the other walks away as if nothing happened? How can two people eat the same meal, but only one gets food poisoning? How can two people be exposed to the same bacteria or virus, but only one of them gets sick? We do not really have health care in our modern society; what we practice is "sick care". We believe the cure for our pain and suffering has to come from the "outside" in the form of a drug. If this drug only treats the symptom, we will become dependent on the drug. In the same erroneous way, we look externally for love and happiness. We believe other people are responsible for providing us with these feelings. We then become dependent on this significant other. Many people in today's society have been sucked into believing that happiness comes from material possessions, such as expensive cars, houses, clothes, or "bling." Happiness does not come in a pill or a drug. We can't buy happiness, and we can't buy health or peace of mind. But we can alleviate our aches, pains, diseases, failures, and unhappiness by changing the way we think, talk, and act. Happiness, peace of mind, and success are all in our hands.

The Birth of the Four Seasons System

SINCE 1983, I HAVE HAD over 100,000 patient visits. On each visit and with each and every patient, I studied the pattern of their tension, pain, suffering, and injury. I saw first- hand how these patterns affect function, performance, success, happiness, and peace of mind. This helped me develop a technique to alleviate the pain and tension. I feel blessed to have a purpose and such a fulfilling job. However, I began to notice that any time I needed to leave my practice, even just to go home at the end of the day; I felt pressure from patients who begged me to work longer hours so they could get an appointment. There were not enough hours in a day or week for me to see everyone who wished to be on my schedule! Many of my patients only needed an average of two to three visits to heal from one ailment. However, many others experienced great relief at first, but their symptoms kept coming back, and they kept coming back for more visits. This sometimes created a dependency, which is the opposite of what I desire. If I have to repeat the same therapy over and over to give them relief, an underlying problem must be causing their pain to return. You can keep a leaky boat from sinking by continually pouring out buckets of water. But unless the leak is repaired, the boat will never stay afloat on its own. In some cases, I was able to pour more water out than was leaking in, and the patient enjoyed longer-lasting relief. In other cases, if the patient came back for regular treatments, I barely managed to keep him or her afloat. In extreme cases where the leak was too big and the underlying problem had caused chronic or degenerative changes, my treatments couldn't provide any relief - it was too little, too late. In the cases where I could find and correct the underlying cause of my patient's pain (repair the leak), permanent healing was possible. I have no desire to serve as a drug for my patients and make them totally dependent on my therapy. As long as a patient is growing and moving forward by changing their ways, continued treatment is productive. I want them to take charge of their own lives and eliminate their own tension, pain, and suffering. I want to teach my patients how to fish, as the saying goes, rather than spoon-feed them the meal.

In 1985, I diligently started to search and pray for knowledge that would help me teach my patients how to understand the cause of their tension, pain, and suffering, as well as an application that would help them overcome and succeed. I thought that if my patients realized and understood the causes of their tension, failure, pain, and suffering, they could change their behaviors and feelings and eventually obtain success, healing, and peace of mind. Early on, I felt the answer to my quest lay in the ancient Eastern philosophies and the Law of the Five Elements. I had been fascinated with this 5,000-year-old philosophy since I was a student at acupuncture school. At first this philosophy seemed too esoteric to be understood and applied in today's society. I needed to find a way to explain a very complex ancient Eastern viewpoint in modern Western terms. As far back as 2697 B.C., Chinese philosophers talked about the interaction of five elements (sometimes referred to as five transformations), which comprised all things we know and the flow of life. They introduced the concept that everything in nature and in the universe was composed of "Chi" (energy). This Chi was described as being omnipresent and everlasting. Chi flows within the human body just as it does within all things around us. With Chi (energy), every action had a reaction. Too much or too little of any type of energy was considered potentially stressful, causing harm to our balance and well-being.

The Law of the Five Elements is a primary foundation of traditional Chinese acupuncture. It relates all energy and substances to one of the elements - wood, fire, earth, metal, and water - all of which are linked to the seasonal cycles of nature. The ancient Chinese acupuncture masters used the Law of the Five Elements to diagnose not only where the blockages of Chi (tension) were located but also to educate their patients in the causes of their ailments or failures in life. This age-old concept, that those five elements influence human health and well-being, originated with Taoist philosophers, who taught about transformations and interactions of Chi in nature and man in the Law of the Five Elements. This law described the way to live and grow in harmony with oneself, others, nature, and their circumstances, as well as the consequences when man failed to grow or to live in harmony.

The ancient Chinese said the human body is covered with a network of circuits or pathways called meridians. Each of the twelve meridians is related to one of the five elements, associated organs, emotions, mental actions, spiritual aspects, sense organs, a season, and all factors of life. Along the twelve main meridians, which correspond with organ systems in the body, are acupuncture points. In a healthy state, the Chi flows from point to point and all around the body without obstruction. This ancient theory is still the fundamental principle of traditional acupuncture and acupressure practiced today. I believe acupuncture points work as circuit breakers. When overloaded by any stress (cause), tension builds up and the vital flow of Chi stagnates (effect). Localizing the blockage and releasing the tension in a specific acupuncture point allows the body to heal and regenerate itself by restoring the circulation of life energy (Chi). If an individual understands the cause of the blockage, learns from it, and changes his behavior, he can defuse the stress and tension it caused. Freed from stress and tension, he can heal from an ailment and the physical and/or emotional pain and suffering. In a similar manner, if an individual understands the cause of a blockage, learns from it, and changes his behavior, the same individual can perform at his peak and live life to the fullest.

I recall one of the first times I unintentionally found the underlying cause of a patient's physical injury, pain, and suffering. It was in 1985, my first year after immigrating to the United States. I was working as an assistant to a chiropractor in northern California when a man in his late forties came to the practice because he'd been suffering with pain in his right shoulder for a year. The man was the stereotypical New Age, old hippie with a ponytail, a crystal around his neck, and Birkenstock sandals, and he was unable to lift his arm more than 45 degrees from his body. Based on the location of the pain and his complaints, I evaluated him using the ancient Chinese principles. The pain he described was located in his upper chest, anterior (front) shoulder, and his biceps muscle, all of which followed the lung meridian. So I started to treat acupressure points along the lung meridian, starting at his thumb and working up towards his shoulder and chest. While working, I told the patient what the lung meridian was associated with according to ancient Chinese medicine. I said, "The lungs are related to the ability to receive and let go, and disturbances along this meridian can be related to sadness, grief, and holding on."

"My wife passed away of cancer last year," he said without any show of emotion. I considered a possible connection between the death of his wife and his shoulder pain, but the man did not seem to be grieving his wife. And he could not recall any trauma or injury to his shoulder, just that the pain and range of motion had gradually worsened over the last year.

As I continued to work on his lung meridian, I kept talking to him and asking him to try to move his arm while I was releasing tension in one reflex point at a time. To his astonishment, he could lift the arm a little higher with each point released. The points were painful to touch but released gradually with my therapy. By the time I started working on his front shoulder, he could lift his arm about 100 degrees.

As I moved along his meridian and started working on the lung point in his upper chest, I asked about his wife and her death and learned that she had a very strong Christian faith. She had been in pain, but was calm and at peace with dying. I asked if her death was hard for him to accept. He seemed to be somewhat disconnected from his own feelings and said that his wife had asked him to promise to accept Jesus in his life. He was still moving his arm up and down while I massaged the chest-lung acu-point, and then he said, "Her only concern before dying was for my salvation." As he told me this, his voice got louder and emotional. To my amazement, I could feel the muscle and acu-point I was working on go into spasm. I had not increased my pressure, but the man yelled out, "I cannot accept that Jesus was anything more than a regular man." Then he screamed out in pain from my pressure as if I had stabbed a knife into his chest.

This incident scared me; I had goose bumps up my back. The man dropped his injured arm down to his side as he sobbed. The range of motion we'd gained only seconds earlier was lost; he was now unable to lift the arm more than 45 degrees. The man seemed shaken up by the incident, and I never saw him again. Afterward, I realized that, as the expression goes, I had "touched a nerve" or "pushed his buttons." What had happened? The acu-point and muscle clearly went into spasm as the man became emotionally upset. The same acu-point that had been almost pain-free from my therapy instantly became extremely painful without me changing the pressure or location. This sudden muscle spasm and pain coincided with the man yelling out what he was upset about. Had he internalized his grief to a point where the tension caused him physical pain? Was he upset with his wife for making him promise to do something he did not believe in? Was he angry with himself for promising his dying wife he would do something he did not believe in? Did he feel unworthy of healing due to guilt? Or was the man in pain because he could not accept or receive salvation? Obviously, he was stuck somewhere and so was the mobility in his shoulder. Why was the increase in pain-free range of motion instantly lost once he spoke about something that was upsetting him? He was clearly in pain but not only in the shoulder joint. Since this incident I have found that most people are more willing to accept physical pain and limitation rather than acknowledge and deal with the mental and/or emotional pain that might have caused it.

That was the first time I witnessed the cause and effect in a patient suffering physical pain and limitation from being mentally and emotionally stuck and avoiding a problem. Since that first incident, I have found more and more evidence that physical tension and pain are directly correlated with stressful emotions and thoughts. When working on patients and releasing their muscular tension with deep digital pressure, I literally feel the link between mental/emotional stress and physical tension. As I talk to my patients about their lives and they tell me about their stressful experiences, I feel the tension and tightness in their muscles increase under my fingers. At this point, the patients alert me that the pressure gets increasingly painful or in some cases, even unbearable. This increase in pain is brought on solely by the patient talking about something he or she experienced as stressful and without me changing the point or amount of pressure.

With this knowledge, I started using a systematic approach to applying the ancient Chinese Five Element philosophy when I inquire about my patients' symptoms, emotions, and life situations. Their answers usually reveal that they are stuck and keep repeating behavioral patterns over and over again. I started to believe that people experience unrelenting tension, pain, and suffering because they keep doing what they had been doing and aren't learning from their mistakes. They don't change their ways and hence, their growth is stifled.

While teaching and elaborating on ancient Chinese philosophy during a seminar in Toronto, Canada, in the fall of 1986, it all came together. I realized that I could explain the way behavior and thinking cause pain and suffering using a metaphor of the four seasons. This four season metaphor was derived from the ancient Chinese Law of the Five Elements; hence, the Four Seasons System was born. Now I use it every day in my practice on thousands of patients and still marvel at how it helps me pinpoint the causes of tension, suffering, and pain. Quite frankly, I have yet to discover an aspect of life where the system is not applicable.

The Message

ARE YOU GROWING OR ARE you stagnant? Are you at peace, or anxious and depressed? Are you healthy and feeling good, or in pain and suffering? Look at all aspects of your life, how you feel throughout your days. Perhaps you're in pain or you're unhappy, but at the same time you might be successful in your career, enjoy a great relationship with your spouse, or have acquired great wealth. Does that mean you're not growing? If you experience negative emotions, tension, or pain, then yes, something is missing! You may not immediately see what's missing, but you need to be whole, and if you're experiencing negative emotions, pain, or tension, you have needs that are not being met. You are not in harmony within yourself or within your surroundings. You need to strive for balance and growth at all times in all areas of your life; you must grow to stay alive, and to be present, complete, whole, and free of suffering.

If we get stuck, we stagnate and stop growing. If we stop growing, parts of us start to die: at first, that which is alive in our hearts, our dreams, desires, and passions. Then our physical bodies —our cells, systems, and functions—start to break down. Our emotions work as a feedback system that indicates when we are stuck or off course; when we're not doing well, we don't feel well about things. Anxiety, depression, or any other negative emotion is a warning signal that we have fallen off the path. Negative emotions cause tension. We start to experience aches and pains, followed by injury, degeneration, disease, and ultimately our death. Just as negative emotions are feedback that we are out of balance, so are tension, suffering, and pain. This book is an attempt to apply this ancient wisdom to understand the causes of pain and suffering in present-day life

The Four Seasons System is about timing and doing the right thing at the right time in harmony with our surroundings and circumstances.

This knowledge, when understood and applied, will show you how to defuse tension in your mind and body, as well as finding the way to health, performance, success, and peace of mind. Understanding the implications of cause and effect on our bodies and minds will guide us toward living our lives to the fullest. It forces us to take responsibility for how our lives are turning out and gives us the tools to change for the better. The Four Seasons way of life is to strive for a balance; to be present, honest, and clear on intent and direction; to be engaged, authentic, and passionate; to accept what life brings and learn from it; to approve of yourself; and to appreciate what you have and remember what you learned. This will keep you on a path of continuous growth and allow you to fulfill your potential. It will keep you in the present, in harmony and peace.

Where do you want to be? Are you unhappy with your life? Have you had enough of your aches and pains? Are you sick and tired of being sick and tired? Life will eventually come to an end for all of us. Life is precious; everyone has the ability to be alive, to learn, and to grow. The process outlined in this book shows you how to constantly question the results of your life—your actions and behavior—and learn from them. This learning assures a continuous growth. By following the steps outlined in the Four Seasons System, you essentially use the process of elimination to get closer and closer to meeting all the needs in your life.

My hope is that this book will help you, the reader, free yourself from tension, pain, and suffering by understanding the causes and effects of your own actions. I want this knowledge to help you reach your potential to live a more successful, healthy, happy, and fulfilled life. I wrote this book to show you how to find and repair your own leaks for successful sailing and navigation on your way through life. A thousand-mile journey starts with one step, and most importantly, the only thing you have any control over is always the step you take right now.

Overview of the Four Seasons System

"The spring energy gives birth; summer exemplifies flourishing or development; fall is representative of gathering in, and winter correlates with a time of storage or conservation."
Nei-Ching, the Yellow Emperor, circa 2000 B.C.

"And let us not weary in well doing; for in due season we shall reap, if we faint not."
(Gal. 6:9)

WHEN YOU CONSIDER THE NATURAL world, the changing of seasons is impossible to ignore. Spring, summer, fall, and winter—each phase is marked by characteristic changes that come and go in a cycle that repeats every year. Spring is the beginning or birth of a cycle, while winter is the end, a burial of everything that is dead and preserving that which will live on as the cycle of life continues into a new spring. Just as nature around us progresses through its natural sequence of change, so do we as individuals. In the world around us, spring suddenly explodes with shoots and leaves bursting forth with life. The same thing happens within us when we get a great idea or realize a new purpose or direction. In nature we find summer blooming and flourishing, but we also bloom and flourish when we authentically and passionately labor in what we love. On the outside, the world harvests in the fall, but also within ourselves we harvest by accepting and receiving what life bring us, learning and growing as human beings. Finally, in nature's winter, not only does life go into a state of stillness, rest, and recuperation, but we also see the farmer store the excesses of his harvest. As individuals we must also store knowledge, remember lessons learned, accumulate and exercise wisdom, appreciate what we have, and allow ourselves to rest and recuperate. As man progresses through the cycles of the Four Seasons, the seasons are echoed within us; each season is ever present and ever basic to our life.

However, the metaphor of the Four Seasons is not limited to the timeframe of a year, or any other timeframe for that matter. We typically think of the four seasons we experience in nature as something that aligns with the course of a calendar year. And when speaking of a single day (in the metaphor), morning is governed by spring, midday (noon and afternoon) by summer, evening by fall, and night by winter. But in life, depending on what you're talking about, the cycle can be much longer or much shorter. A cycle could complete in minutes - it could be as simple as making the decision to vacuum the floor (spring), pulling out the vacuum and using it (summer), emptying the dirt and putting away the machine (fall), and finally sitting down, resting, and appreciating a job well done and a clean home (winter). Theoretically, we could plant (spring) bean sprouts, watch them grow (summer) for a few days, and then harvest (fall) in a week or so. If, on the other hand, we planted (spring) apple seeds, it would take several years (summer) before the first harvest (fall) was yielded. Then if we maintained (winter) the soil and pruned the tree properly, we could continue harvesting fruit every year for the rest of our life. Each phase could last a minute, or it could last decades, depending on the harvest you're trying to realize. For our purposes, the Four Seasons metaphor describes one complete cycle of any duration of time.

The Four Seasons System is a way of living in balance. Within it lie the answers to a peaceful, fulfilled, healthy, and successful life. It is a metaphor explaining the passage of time and timing (doing the right thing at the right time). The Four Seasons is a navigational system for maneuvering through life and making the most out of it. All things experienced in life must pass through the four phases in order to arrive at completion. We do not always know with certainty during the planning stage of ventures and projects when the harvest will occur. However, if we follow the principles of the Four Seasons System faithfully, a harvest will always be realized.

The Four Seasons System has some similarities to what you might have learned from other self-help books about realizing your dreams and setting goals (which is spring), authentically engaging in life with positive expectation of a harvest (summer), being worthy to receive and accept what life brings you (fall). However, this system takes it a step further with winter, the phase in which you remember what you learned and appreciate what you have, to keep what you gained. In our modern disposable (gain and throw away) world, people tend to gravitate towards quick money, fast food, and rapid weight loss. But what good is accomplished by gaining prosperity, acquiring new knowledge, or losing excess weight, if we lack the wisdom to manage the money, use the knowledge, or maintain a lean body? Too often what we are then faced with is starting all over, having to experience the same life lessons again and again until we move fully through all four seasons.'

SPRING: fertilize/plant, intention, decision, and clear commitment.
SUMMER: water/weed, discernment, authentic action, engagement with passion.
FALL: harvest, acceptance, learning, closure, achieving and receiving.
WINTER: store/preserve, appreciation, maintenance, keeping and remembering.

The Four Seasons System applies in all aspects of our lives.

SPRING

In the spring the farmer spreads manure, collected over the year from his livestock, onto his fields. He turns the soil over to make the soil fertile. He examines the soil and the climate to find what seed will yield the largest crop, then takes his best seeds and plants them.

In Sports:

As he prepares himself for the new season, the Olympic high jumper must first view how his failures in the previous seasons can help him get a clear insight on what to do and what not to do, as well as what he needs and what he does not need. The successes are the harvest from the last season and the seeds for future harvest. It's out of the failures (manure) that a larger harvest can be reaped. He must prepare himself mentally by seeing how bad habits, bad technique, and any negative beliefs from the past can be used to get clear (fertilizing) on what good habits, techniques, and beliefs will serve him in future competitions. He must plan for the new season, set personal goals, and commit (planting) to a demanding training schedule and diet. He must be clear, committed, and assertive on his direction, as well as know what it will take to accomplish his goal and dream.

In Business:

In the beginning of a new business venture the businesswoman first frees herself from wasteful and destructive business partners, bad habits, limiting beliefs, and disappointing experiences (fertilizing). By doing so she realizes that everything she previously considered bad or wasteful will serve her as a fertilizer for future success. She then investigates her potential market, does her due diligence, establishes a business strategy, and finally makes a commitment by investing her capital into the most fertile project (planting). The successful businesswoman is dynamic and clear on what she intends to do and how to achieve her goal.

In True Love Relationships:

After a failed marriage I found myself with poor self-esteem, full of grief, sadness, regret, resentment, anger, and fear. Beat down and disillusioned, I questioned if I would ever find the right woman and experience true love in a committed relationship. I had to let go of and forgive the past: old pain, disappointments, stinking thinking, negative attitude, and wasteful belief systems from past relationships (fertilizing). The waste from the past became the fertilizer of my future. Once I realized I was fine, and even better off, without that relationship, I was able to get clear on how I needed to be, what I wanted from a relationship, and exactly how I wanted my life companion to be. Learning from the past and using it to help me get clear on what I really wanted prevented me from repeating the same mistakes over again. I made a list of qualities that I desired in a life companion and best friend, and as I wrote I realized many essential qualities that I had not been clear on before I met my ex-wife. I had grown older and wiser, and I had become clear on what was important and what I desired in a relationship. Each failed relationship in the past can help you see more clearly about what you want in the future. Once I was clear on what I desired, I committed to find this woman (planting).

In all three examples above, you see the people applying lessons from past failures, to change to a new approach, to get clear on exactly what they need (fertilizing), and to commit to what they want out of the future (planting). These are critical steps that create the foundation of the whole cycle. When we don't take these steps every time we begin something new, we leave the harvest of our future to chance and doom ourselves to repeat old mistakes over and over, limiting any potential success.

SUMMER

In the summer the farmer waters and weeds his fields, and inspects them daily with joy, because he anticipates a rich harvest.

In Sports:

As the high-jumper persistently trains for the next Olympics, he must not allow anything to deter him from his goal. In his mind, he visualizes performing the perfect jump repeatedly each and every day (watering). Fully engaged in his training, he has fun as he labors in love. He overcomes obstacles by focusing on solutions rather than problems (weeding). With a passion for his sport, he tracks his daily progress, anticipates success, and avoids socializing with people (even family members and friends) that do not support his training, diet, or positive attitude.

In Business:

Once the businesswoman has invested her money and has made her commitment, she knows there is no backing out of the project. She understands that she must engage and keep her co-investors enthusiastic and focused (watering). She must talk, think, feel, and believe in success. She must remain focused in the here and now and take necessary actions to counter obstacles (weeding).

In True Love Relationships:

As I sorted through profiles of potential dates on an online dating web site, I kept focused on my list of what I expected in a life partner and best friend. Every day I visualized this authentic woman, her character, her looks, her interests (watering), not wasting any time on pursuing dates that did not fit my list of essential qualities (weeding).

By being true to their hearts and anticipating what they desired (watering), the people in the three examples achieved something we all want at the deepest level: to be authentically engaged in all of our activities each and every day, experiencing joy and happiness in what we do. By staying on course with their goals and overcoming obstacles (weeding), they focus on the solutions (what they want) instead of the problems (what they do not want). They feel confident that nothing will stand in the way of a positive harvest.

FALL

In the fall the farmer is rewarded for his work as he accepts and receives his harvest.

In Sports:

The young high jumper performs to his expectations and accomplishes his perfect jump, and in so doing, he not only wins his Olympic gold medal but also sets a new world record (harvest). He had already accomplished the world record jump so many times in his own mind that the record was his before he even competed! He is humble and empathetic towards his fellow competitors, realizing that their efforts and disappointments are intimately linked to his success. Still, he understands success was not achieved without commitment, determination and hard work. He learned that without supportive family, friends, and coaches, his goal could not come to pass.

In Business:

The businesswoman receives the financial rewards she worked so hard to achieve (harvest). She knows and understands that her actions in planning, persistence of effort, and constant anticipation have resulted in success, and she feels she is deserving and worthy of that financial success and personal gratification.

In True Love Relationships:

After the second or third date with Sue, I realized that I had found my ideal woman and best friend. She was everything I had conceptualized in spring and visualized on a daily basis in summer. It was as if we were made for each other with so much in common, including life experiences, interests, morals, integrity, ethics, and diet. I was attracted to her looks and body type, and we both enjoyed spending time together as friends. I felt I was worthy and deserved her —my dream relationship had become a reality.

Harvesting what you want out of life means receiving the experiences and a sense of accomplishment. The three examples worked hard to get what they wanted, and they felt they deserved to get it. Understanding this, accepting and receiving the outcome will allow them to rest and reflect peacefully in winter.

WINTER

In the winter the farmer stores and preserves the excess from his harvest, so it will feed him and his family over the cold, unproductive winter. For him, it is a time to be still, to remember what he learned, and to appreciate what he has. It is a time for spending quality time with loved ones, maintaining equipment, resting, recuperating, and reflecting.

In Sports:

Our young high jumper takes time to rest and recuperate after a long, intense season of training and competition. This provides his muscles ample time to heal from the punishing, rigorous workouts he subjected them to on a daily basis. He also takes time to reflect and evaluate his season mentally (storing) to remember what he learned and appreciate what he has. He spends time studying videos of his techniques so he can improve for the next season, and he shows his appreciation to coaches, family, friends, and all who supported him, because he knows that he will require their support again in the future.

In Business:

The businesswoman has carefully placed a portion of her increased wealth in a saving account to serve as a form of security (storing) - taking the save-it-for-a-rainy-day approach. She also invests a portion of her financial reward back into her venture, enabling her success to continue working on her behalf. She buys assets in the form of savings bonds and low-risk mutual funds so that her money can work for her and secure her retirement. She reflects on her past cycle to remember what she learned. Evaluation of past experiences provides wisdom. She has capital stored to use as "seeds" for a time when the right opportunity or ideal financial climate arrives to begin a new venture (spring).

In True Love Relationships:

To maintain a romantic relationship and true love for a lifetime, one can never take his or her partner for granted. For our love and friendship to last, I must show appreciation, love, and respect every day at all times. Spending quality time together is essential—the more the better. We both enjoy spending time together and being each other's best friend. We are equally willing to have each other's back, to protect and keep each other safe. True love means you are loving even when you do not feel like it. I put in the work, effort, and will power to sincerely listen to my partner even when I am tired. Every day I appreciate Sue, I show her my love, gratitude and appreciation by spending quality time and sincerely paying attention and listening to her— showing her through quality time spent together, and telling her, in person as well as in text messages, how much I love and appreciate her throughout the day. This is how true love can last.

Rest, reflection, and appreciation for the harvest you've experienced bring the Four Seasons Cycle to a close. In each of the examples, a quest for a harvest has come to an end, and the person is preparing for the next beginning so the cycle can continue and they can accomplish even more. In each example, the person takes specific actions to ensure he or she completes that phase of the cycle in a way that readies them for what's coming in the future. Every accomplishment starts as a seed that is planted in fertilized soil. That seed is watered and obstacles to success are avoided by weeding. Then the hard work pays off in receiving a harvest, which is stored and appreciated while the person rests, recuperates, and prepares for what need (goal) he or she desires to meet next. Each phase builds upon the last, one activity leads to the next, to create success in life.

Cycles of Life

Life is a never-ending sequence of cycles. Each cycle of time can be divided into smaller cycles of shorter duration, and each cycle is part of a bigger cycle of longer duration. For example, the high jumper's completion of a cycle of setting a goal, working towards it, accomplishing the goal, and appreciating his Olympic gold medal can be broken into smaller cycles. It can be broken down into a four season metaphor of every month, every week, every day, and each and every individual workout or jump. So can the final jump in the Olympics be broken down to the Four Seasons phases as well.

The final jump's spring (clear and committed): As he is getting ready for the final jump that could win him the gold medal and give him the world record, the high jumper is calm, present, at peace, and assertive. He is clear on what he has to do. He visualizes one last time being in the zone and making the perfect jump. He sees it the way he wants it to be, as he has over a thousand times in his preparations for this moment. He is committed to his jump, breathing deep, slow, and relaxed.

The final jump's summer (action): As he starts to run up to the bar, everything happens in slow motion. He is present, relaxed, and engaged from his heart and soul, full of passion. The jump is executed effortlessly to perfection, just as it has been in his mind over a thousand times. His muscle memory does not know the difference between performing it in the mind versus the body.

The final jump's fall (completion): As he realizes that he won the gold and set the world record, he has to pinch himself to make sure that he is not dreaming or visualizing. As the slow motion sensation ends, he erupts in celebration that continues for hours after he receives his gold medal.

The final jump's winter (recovery): After receiving the gold, the high jumper is in a state of gratitude and appreciation, as he is ready for well-deserved rest.

Remember the completion of any cycle of any duration of time is a full four seasons cycle. The Four Seasons System can be applied to a short cycle of completing one task. Thinking about a longer duration, the high jumper's entire career, even entire life, could be described in terms of the four season cycle.

In your life right now you are in different seasons in your career, relationships, projects, health, fitness, etc. Each one of your cycles could be broken down into smaller cycles and be a part of a larger cycle. Take, for example, your marriage or commitment to your significant other. It could be described in terms of the entire duration of the marriage (or till death of either partner brings it to an end), or broken down to smaller cycles of day-by-day, week-by-week, month-by- month, or year-by-year.

Spring (fertilize and plant): Each morning you begin by forgiving yourself and your partner for causing tension or drama from the previous day. You decide how to change your approach, how you are, what you do, and how you react, based on how your approach worked yesterday. You ask yourself: Am I still committed to my partner? Do I still love him or her? You are honest with yourself about what you want, and your intention in the relationship. You get clear on how you want to be as a partner and what you need from your partner, doing so without judgment or blame. You can even re-state your wedding vows in your mind. If you wake up one morning and you cannot make yourself forgive or re-commit, then you need to be honest with yourself and your mate. Continuing without forgiving and committing, plants poisonous seeds in an unfertile soil and the harvest will not be to your liking.

Summer (water and weed): Throughout your day, keep thinking about all the good things you like about your mate. Anticipate with excitement seeing him or her; visualize his or her face smiling. Communicate authentically from your heart your love and your needs.

Fall (harvest): Receive and accept your mate the way he/she is. Receive his or her love. Request what you need. Ask for clarification when you do not understand or feel hurt by what your mate says or does, rather than jumping to conclusions assuming what he or she meant.

Winter (store and preserve): Show appreciation towards your mate. Listen sincerely to what is said. Spend quality time together.

In the same way can you break down your current job into a larger cycle for the entire lifespan of that job, or into smaller daily, weekly, or monthly cycles. In a daily cycle for your work:

Spring (fertilize and plant): Each morning is the spring and a new beginning. Use yesterday's experiences, good or bad, to get clear on what you want to accomplish and how you need to change your approach. Get clear on your purpose and intent. Write a to-do list and prioritize the importance of the things you want to get accomplished. Once you are clear on what you want to accomplish today and why you want to accomplish it, make a commitment to get it done.

Summer (water and weed): Get engaged in what you do. Keep focusing on the good and what you want from your work. Smile, have fun, be authentic and optimistic, focusing on the solutions instead of the problems. Be inspiring and part of the solution instead of negative, gossiping, and part of the problem.

Fall (harvest): On your way home from work think through all the things you accomplished and what you learned today. No matter how your day went, you can always learn from the experiences.

Winter (store and preserve): As you are retiring for the day, appreciate your job and the payment it brings. Remember what you learned. Make sure you get enough rest to recover for another workday.

As you can see, the four seasons cycle can expand and contract to almost any duration of time, depending on your situation. Any imbalance in any season of any cycle can perpetuate further imbalances in later cycles. This is how problems grow exponentially—remember, whatever you sow, you reap.

What if You're Out of Balance?

Being out of balance in any one season affects the whole cycle. In spring, if the farmer did not dispose of accumulated waste products by fertilizing his soil, his barn would become toxic and his soil unfertile. If on the other hand he failed to plant, he would have no harvest to reap. If he did not research what crop was best for his soil and climate, he would not get the most from his efforts.

If the businesswoman did not free herself of destructive habits and change her approach from lessons learned, it would cause her to repeat fruitless business ventures. If she procrastinated investigating potential markets, doing her due diligence, and planning sound business strategies, success would be unlikely. If she was not clear on what she was "sowing" and rushed her decisions, she might not approve of her subsequent harvest. On the other hand, if she procrastinated and failed to take advantage of opportunities—if she failed to sow at all—inflation and taxes would eventually devour her capitol and resources, and the opportunity would pass by.

If I had not cleansed my own mind through self-realization and inquiry, counseling, books, and seminars, I would not have been able to change my behavior. I would have kept my destructive beliefs, bad habits, and lack of trust from my previous marriages; I would have entered any new relationship with suitcases full of old garbage. If I had not gotten clear on what I wanted in a relationship, I would have found myself alone or in another relationship as dysfunctional as my previous one.

In summer, if the farmer did not anticipate a harvest, why would he bother tilling the soil? If he did not water, his anticipated harvest would dry out and bear no fruit. If he did not focus on weeding when necessary, the weeds would eventually take over and strangle his crop. If the athlete did not enjoy what he was doing, if he couldn't envision himself succeeding at making the jump as he approached the bar, he would fall flat, wasting his time, energy, and money. He would be a phony if he continued to train without believing he could succeed. If his positive expectation and focus were not stronger than the impending obstacles, the obstacles would emerge the declared winner despite his best efforts.

In fall, if the farmer did not go into his field to gather his righteous and well-deserved harvest, it could not come in by itself. Eventually he would face starvation. If I had been unable to receive Sue's love, thinking I did not deserve it or not believing she was true, I would never have realized the relationship. If the businesswoman had not cashed in when the business venture was ripe, then she would not have realized the harvest.

And in winter, what would happen if the farmer did not exercise caution by storing away the excess of his harvest? It would waste or rot. What if the farmer impatiently attempted to plant during the winter, with snow and ice on the ground? Nothing would grow. If he failed to maintain his equipment, it would fail to perform when he needed it. If he failed to preserve his harvest, he might not survive the rigors of winter. If the businesswoman failed to save and instead spent her financial gain as soon as she received it, she would have to start over again, assuming of course that she could obtain seed money to re-invest when the right opportunity came along. And if I became too involved in my work and career, if I took Sue for granted and failed to show her the appreciation she deserved, if we did not spend ample time together enjoying each other, our relationship would slowly die. I could potentially lose not only love, but my health as well.

Anytime we get out of balance in any of the seasons, we will experience stress and tension which ultimately affects our health. If we stay out of balance, get stuck in one season, or keep repeating the same mistake in the same season every go-round, the tension and stress will accumulate to the point that it will cause us injury or disease. Every action has a reaction. Every effect has a cause. Living in balance with your cycles of life will accumulate (multiply) greater health, peace of mind, peak performance, and success. Living out of balance with the four seasons will accumulate (multiply) greater pain, suffering, and failure. As you sow, so will you reap. Each time we successfully complete a cycle, the harvest will increase for a greater life. Each time we repeat an imbalanced behavior the consequences will get greater and our suffering will increase.

All things you have ever completed, all things you are about to complete, and all things you will ever complete must pass through the various phases of the Four Seasons. By discovering where you are, you realize what you need to do. Health, peace of mind, peak performance, and success in any area of life all depend upon doing the right thing at the right time, in harmony with the cycles of the Four Seasons.

Way to Do . . .

夏
SUMMER

SPRING
春

FALL
秋

WINTER
冬

The Metaphor of Spring 春

the Wood Element

In the spring the farmer spreads manure, collected over the year from his livestock, onto his fields. He turns the soil over, and then takes his best seeds and plants them.

In the Four Seasons metaphor, spring is associated with birth, new beginnings, fertilization, and planting. When you look to the natural world, the earliest signs of spring might be daffodils emerging from the defrosting earth, green buds appearing on otherwise bare tree branches, and birds nesting, preparing for a new beginning. Gardeners till their soil and plant their seeds. The sun gets stronger, giving more energy. After a long, quiet winter, things start to happen.

In the Four Seasons System, spring stands for planting a seed, getting things going, starting something. And it's an important phase because it involves identifying our needs that must be met and making plans for doing so. We plant these needs in the spring phase, and if we're not clear on our needs, then we cannot plant them or expect them to be met. When we don't plant the seeds of our needs, nothing grows and there is nothing to harvest in fall.

Everything in your life has a spring phase. For example, every morning is like spring - an opportunity to give your day direction and focus so that you are successful. Think about your current morning habits. What do you do when you wake up? Do you just get out of bed like a zombie and drag yourself to work? Or do you get up and think about everything you need to do that day? What is most important? Why do you want to get that accomplished? Are you completely clear on what you need to do, what your priority is, and your purpose for doing it? Some people think through these questions at the start of every day. Others have no idea, and at the end of the day they often find themselves somewhere they don't want to be. If this sounds familiar, then you can improve your results by better aligning yourself and your actions with the spring season.

Spring is also about respect, responsibility, integrity, and honesty - making sure those needs and plans that you plant as seeds are fertilized in the soil (your mind) and prepared to grow successfully. If you are balanced in spring, you are honest with yourself and others. You are clear on your direction - on what you're going to do, and why you're going to do it. You don't speak without thinking. You think about what you're saying and what the consequences could be; you respect other people without judging them, and you have integrity by setting up boundaries and making clear what's okay with you and what's not.

Nadia came to my office because she had hit dead ends with everything she tried to relieve her pain. She complained of pain in her right upper trapezius that was shooting into the back portion of her head and temple. She was forty-seven years old at the time, and she'd been experiencing the symptoms which began three years prior to her visit. Over that time, the pain in her trapezius gradually got worse, leading to the headaches that she had been experiencing for at least a year. Any activity where she moved her arms and shoulders made her pain worse. She claimed that she had a hard time falling asleep both due to the pain and inability to shut down her mind. She tried acupuncture as well as conventional medicine before she came to my practice. Her doctor had given up on finding a therapy that would work and finally diagnosed her with fibromyalgia.

When I started asking her questions about other possible symptoms, I suspected she was blocked in spring. She said she experienced right hip pain that had lately started getting worse. She claimed that greasy and oily food made her nauseous and bloated. She claimed that she disliked wind and that her neck and shoulder problems got worse when she was exposed to wind. Nadia had a big dog - over 100 pounds - that pulled on his leash when she walked him. She held the leash with her right hand and often became frustrated with the dog when he pulled. She thought that the strain from walking her dog could be causing her neck and shoulder pain, but she also recognized that her symptoms were worse when she was under stress - a big clue that these physical problems were actually manifestations of her behavior and interactions with other people in her life.

Upon questioning, she admitted that she had been under a lot of stress over the last three years. She was holding in a lot of anger and resentment towards her husband (passive- aggressive). She claimed he was selfish and stubborn, and as we continued to talk I found out that she does not speak up, was unable to set boundaries, and actually enabled her dysfunctional marriage. She was tip-toeing around her husband, avoiding being honest and speaking up for herself, to avoid his outbursts of anger. She constantly found herself going along with things she really did not want to, and subsequently did not like the outcome of her life. She said they should never have gotten married, and she told me that she was carrying the divorce papers in her purse but was unable to make up her mind about whether she should file them or not. This inability to make a decision was frustrating her.

As I released gall bladder acupuncture points and trigger points (muscle knots) in her chest, shoulder, and neck, I suggested making some changes in the way she dealt with others. I told her that she needed to be calm, assertive, clear, and honest with her husband. She needed to state her boundaries or she would always find herself in life situations she didn't like. She needed to own up to her reality because she trained or allowed others to push her around by not speaking up in the first place. She was not walking her dog; he was walking her because she was not present, calm, and assertive in her body language and communication. Likewise, she had allowed her husband to overstep her boundaries for years.

She came back two weeks later and was happy to report that her life had improved. The headaches were gone and her neck pain and tension greatly decreased. She was present, calm, and assertive when walking her dog and she did not allow him to pull his leash. Therefore, her dog recognized that she was in charge and stopped pulling. She had also filed her divorce papers and continued to calmly and assertively state her boundaries with her husband. She recognized that whenever she did not speak up clearly in a matter, she could feel the muscle tension in her neck and shoulders coming on. By changing her behaviors and regaining her balance in spring, Nadia got clear on what she needed, stood up for herself, asserted her boundaries, and dramatically decreased the pain and suffering she had been experiencing for so many years.

A balanced spring gives you clear direction on your intention and purpose for where you are going, what you are doing, and why you are doing it. People who never stop to think about where their lives are headed and why, are very often people who find themselves being resentful or frustrated or passively aggressive about the fact they're not happy with their lives. Why is it so important to be balanced in spring? Being balanced in spring allows you to change your future for the better, by taking responsibility for everything you think, say, and do. Everything you think, say, and do is a new beginning; it's a seed that is planted. All seeds grow into something, whether good or bad. By being present and aware and assertive, and by taking responsibility for this, you can actually direct your life to what you want instead of just being a victim of circumstances or blaming others.

Balance in Spring

Every beginning is a new spring, and to be successful in the future, you must be clear in the present, on what you're going to plant, what kind of mind frame you need to be in, what's important to do, and why it's important. And you must be assertive in communicating your needs so the message you give others clearly reflects your intention. What you plant, so shall you reap.

People who are balanced in spring are self-directed and self-starters. They are determined, assertive, and clear about their directions, motives, and decisions. They know what they need and why they need it, and they have specific goals in their lives. If they are not clear on a direction, they stay present and patient until they are. They neither procrastinate nor force action when the time is not right. Balanced spring people like coming up with concepts and new ideas; things that no one else has done. They are visionary, forward thinking, and very quick. They have great vision, as well as a strategy or plan on how to get started.

The balanced spring set clear boundaries in their interaction with others, they do not hold grudges, and typically forgive others easily. They realize that life experiences from their past that they perceived as bad, are fertilizers that serve them well in their future growth. Everything happens for a reason. It might stink at first, but it will ultimately serve a purpose. When things don't work out the first time, they get clearer on what they want and how to get it done. They will change their approach each time they don't get the results they want so that by process of elimination their chance of getting it right increases each spring.

These people think about what to say or do because they are aware they are responsible for the consequences. People who are balanced in spring have no problem confronting others when it is appropriate; they are bluntly honest in their communication and often make dynamic leaders. They know what they want and they say what they want. You never have to wonder what they think about anything, they will tell you. The balanced springs take responsibility for their life situations, actions, and decisions, and they don't whine, complain, or make excuses.

Every word that you speak and every thought that you think is a seed. So it's very important to keep your spoken words impeccable and clean because your spoken word is the seed that you plant, and whatever you plant is what you will reap. If your spoken word is not impeccable and you speak negative words, then you will harvest more negative. The principle of the seed is to multiply. When you plant a seed, you do not get one seed back, but rather ten times as many. Remember the old saying: "If you don't have anything good to say, don't say anything at all." If you're speaking words of gossip or words of anger, blame, jealousy, or any other negative source, then you're spreading poison. You want your seed to be an impeccable seed, a good seed; so say something good, say something encouraging, say something constructive.

This is not only true when you speak to others, but also when you speak to yourself—the thoughts in your own head. If we constantly have negative thoughts and we put ourselves down, then we're not using our words in impeccable ways. We're not planting good seeds; we're planting bad seeds. So you could speak a language that is constructive and plant good seeds, or you could speak destructive language where you blame, gossip, speak of jealousy, criticize, or put things down. Every word you speak and every thought you think is a new beginning—in this split second a new beginning starts. And the only thing you have any control over is this moment right now. The words you speak right now and the thoughts you have right now are what shape your future. That's why it's important to be present and clear in your communication, to take responsibility for what you think, and to treat yourself well by thinking constructive thoughts, thinking good seeds, speaking good seeds.

A few years ago, after my separation and two years into a long divorce process, I went on vacation to Mexico for Christmas. It was a stressful time, and I was looking forward to a week away. However, the problems from my past marriage and my divorce followed me.

In this failed marriage, I had avoided conflict and suppressed my own needs and feelings to avoid drama and keep peace at any price. I believed I had to keep the marriage together for my kids no matter how bad it got. Not being assertive, not setting boundaries, and not speaking up had made me an enabler in a dysfunctional relationship. Even though we had been separated for almost two years, sixteen years of behavior were still deeply rooted. In the process of the divorce, I still allowed myself to be manipulated and to feel guilty; therefore, I was not setting boundaries or putting my foot down. There were so many conflicts and so much drama going on that it seemed easier to let some things slide. This, of course, only perpetuated the dysfunction.

After a few days in Zihuatanejo, I started to have abdominal pain in my right upper abdomen, with nausea whenever (and whatever) I ate. The condition got worse each day. I called my family doctor and friend at home in northern California and went to a local pharmacy to find any medication that could help me feel better. We suspected food poisoning or a parasite, and finally I had to cut my vacation short by two days. As soon as I got home, I saw my doctor. Stool tests, blood tests, ultrasounds of gall bladder and pancreas, as well as an endoscopy all came back clear, while my abdominal pain and nausea continued. It became clear that my body was trying to tell me something. I asked myself what could be the cause of my suffering. What was I doing or not doing to have this pain? Then it dawned on me: I was stuck in spring. I had symptoms of gall bladder meridian dysfunction even though all of western medicine's medical tests showed my gall bladder to be normal. I had to change my approach, or I would continue to suffer and possibly get even worse. I needed to change my old behavioral patterns with my ex-wife. I was trying to start a new life, but I was still repeating the same behaviors I had while I was married. My problems would not go away unless I changed my approach. I needed to get clear and assertive, set firm boundaries so I wouldn't get walked all over, and say no. I could not let myself enable or be manipulated by guilt. I got clear on what I was doing and the consequences it had on my health. I committed to setting firm boundaries and not being a pushover anymore. Once

I did this, my abdominal pain and nausea disappeared within a few days. In this example, I did not get any trigger point or acupressure point therapy; I didn't need it. Just realizing the effect my behaviors had on my health and changing my approach healed me.

Spring is a metaphorical start, and when things aren't started at the right time and under the right conditions, that in itself can lead to problems. Rory, a fifty-year-old man and owner of a glass company, came to see me for pain in his neck, shoulders, and between his shoulder blades (upper trapezius and rhomboids). I asked him when his pain started; Rory told me it was on Monday morning when he had a bad start to his workweek. I asked him what happened. He told me that he had a huge glass job starting that day and he'd made sure to have enough workers and his supplier had assured him that all the sheets of glass would be delivered early that Monday morning. When Rory came to work Monday morning, he discovered that the supplier had failed to deliver the glass as promised. Because of this, the job had to be delayed. That was when Rory started to experience his pain.

I told Rory that the symptoms were related to an imbalance in the spring and gall bladder, and I asked him if he got angry and how he handled it. Rory said that in the past he would have been exploding, yelling, screaming, cursing, and kicking. As he got older, he had learned to temper his anger so he wouldn't make himself look like a fool. So I asked him if he got angry when the supplier did not deliver as promised. He said inside he felt like he was blowing a gasket, but instead of getting outwardly angry, he became passive-aggressive and resorted to sarcastic remarks. I told him the tension that comes from anger often settles in the muscles of the neck, shoulders, and upper back. Keeping his cool and avoiding outward rage was an improvement, but holding his anger inside could cause not only tension and pain but high blood pressure as well, which could be dangerous to his heart. Rory admitted that he had high blood pressure and high cholesterol.

I told Rory that spring stands for starting a job, keeping a commitment, and having integrity. But in life, spring does not always start when it is supposed to, and sometimes things happen that we have no control over. I said there is nothing you can do if you don't get a promised delivery. You can choose to hire another supplier in the future. Rory said he had been in business for over twenty years, and this was the only supplier that could handle this kind of order. I asked him how he knows that he's starting a job on time. He seemed confused. I replied that you're starting a job on time when you have everything you need to get started. This is the nature of business and life. Other people do not always deliver what they promise, so you have to go with the flow. "If the job is not meant to start," I said to him, "it is not meant to start." As I released painful gall bladder acupressure points in Rory's neck and shoulders, I was "planting a seed" in his mind by telling him that his behavior was the cause of his pain. I told Rory that if he did not learn to stay calm and assertive, to forgive others' shortcomings, and to change his plans when circumstances change, it could cost him his health or ultimately his life. Rory left free of tension and pain with a commitment to himself to change his behavior.

Here's another example of a spring imbalance leading to physical discomfort—only in this case, the underlying behavior started in the patient years before it became a debilitating problem. Vick, a fifty-two-year-old man who retired after thirty-four years as a truck driver, came to my office with chronic pain in his right buttock that radiated down his lateral thigh, lower leg, and ankle. He had seen a physical therapist, a pain management doctor, and taken prescription medication for pain and inflammation. The two epidural injections he'd been given to relieve his pain were no help. Vick claimed he had a bulging disc between his fourth and fifth lumbar vertebra, but his surgeon was unwilling to perform surgery. He had begged his neurosurgeon to do the surgery. The doctor did not think there was enough medical evidence to require surgery at the time. Vick's reflexes were normal, and he had full, pain-free range of motion in his lower back. He was irritated with his doctor for not wanting to do the surgery, and he was angry with all the doctors and therapists for not fixing his condition after so much time had passed. As I examined him, I found that he really did have normal range of motion without pain, so I asked him when he felt the pain. He said the pain in his right buttock was always there, but the leg pain came as soon as he sat down to drive ten minutes or more. His pain followed the gall bladder meridian, so I asked more questions to see if my suspicion was right. He craved greasy food, but it would cause him bloating. Following up on the tone of anger I heard in his voice when he expressed his frustration with not getting any relief from his symptoms and that his pain was aggravated when driving, I asked him if he was frustrated or angry behind the wheel.

His wife, who had accompanied him to the visit, started to chuckle. She said, "I told him he needs anger management because he is always mad when driving."

I asked him why he was angry when driving. He said, "I get mad at all the idiots that get in front of me. They do not know how to drive and drive too slow."

"But you are retired. What's the hurry?"

Anger, irritation, judgment, and impatience are typical gall bladder and liver meridian symptoms, as well as a classic spring imbalance. Vick, being an unhappy truck driver for thirty- four years, had created a pattern of anger and irritation about not getting there fast enough as well as judging or cursing everyone in his way. He had adopted the belief that other drivers deliberately went out of their way to make his life miserable. I believed his pain was caused by muscle spasms due to a stressful behavioral pattern repeated over and over. What convinced me further was when Vick told me he could play eighteen holes of golf without any pain in his back, buttock, or leg. He was a jovial man who loved to hang out with the guys, have fun, talk sports, and play golf. When he got behind the wheel, he'd grow angry and tense and could not possibly get where he was going fast enough. I asked Vick how he'd feel if the doctor performed the surgery, but after months of rehabilitation he still had the same pain. He growled, "Doc would be on my list if that happened."

I released trigger and acu-points in his right lateral low back, lateral hip, lateral thigh, and lower leg. Vick felt some relief but said he would not know if he was better until he had been driving for a while. I only saw Vick one more time. He said his stress level was down when he was driving, and he had felt better but still had some pain. I told him to focus on his breathing to help him stay calm while driving. It's hard for people with a spring imbalance to take responsibility for their own condition and pain. They often judge other people or they blame others or circumstances. I hoped Vick would see that his own anger caused his pain and that taking responsibility would make him change his behavior. Otherwise, all the surgery and pain therapy in the world wouldn't take his pain away, and he'd never be able to enjoy the retirement he'd worked so hard to start.

Balanced emotions for the spring season are calmness and feeling present and assertive. Anytime a person is not balanced in spring he or she will experience negative emotions and feelings. They will either experience feelings of a hypo-active nature, such as depression, passivity, unassertiveness. Or they will experience feelings of a hyper-active nature, such as anxiety, irritation, frustration, or anger. Unbalanced Spring is characterized by anger either expressed or suppressed (passive aggressive resentful.) In either case, the anger causes a build-up of tension in our body. The individual is often not aware he or she is angry.

Your emotions and feelings can be your most important clues to the season in which an imbalance exists in your life. A person with an imbalance in the spring will tend to have too little spring or too much spring. Remember in Chinese philosophy: too little and too much are both harmful.

Too little spring is often characterized by the following patterns.

- Not asserting one's own needs. Not knowing or being clear on those needs.
- Not speaking up, or speaking with a quiet, meek voice.
- Having a hard time making decisions.

- Not knowing how to say no.
- Procrastinating.
- Being a "pushover," letting others tell them what to do, avoiding confrontation at any price.
- "Beating around the bush," not getting to the point when communicating.
- Having a hard time getting angry, or having a slow burning fuse.
- Holding anger inside, resentment, holding grudges, not forgiving or taking responsibility for one's situation.
- Being passive-aggressive, holding all anger in until it finally erupts out of control, getting physically ill, or experiencing physical pain.
- Avoid stating one's own viewpoint, not wanting to upset others, and therefore communicating the viewpoint they think others want to hear.

Too much spring is often characterized by the following patterns.

- Feeling irritated, frustrated or angry.
- Continuing to do everything over the same way even though it did not (bring a harvest) work in the past.
- Passing judgments or blame on others for not having one's own needs met.
- Speaking with a firm, hard, and sometimes angry voice.
- Trying to force things to happen.
- Saying yes or no and jumping to conclusions or judgments too fast.
- Making decisions too hastily without proper clarity or motive.
- Being overly judgmental and hence closed to new experiences.
- Being overly confrontational, sometimes picking fights or bullying others to get one's own way.
- Being bossy, thinking one always knows best and telling everyone what to do, while disliking being told by others.

- Getting frustrated or irritated when others don't get to the point, or when people are slow to getting it.
- Being ruled by constant eruptions of anger and being unable to control one's temper.
- Always knowing what's best.

In addition to these emotional and behavioral patterns, an imbalance in spring may also cause physical symptoms. The following descriptions come from the ancient Chinese wisdom and the writings Huang Di Nei Ching, the Yellow Emperor, (with a few of my own additions) on the organs, meridians, human functions, and associations that relate to balance or imbalance of the spring and wood element.

The Liver Meridian and Organ System:

The liver controls all release of Chi (energy) in physical as well as emotional activities. This is true in an explosive muscle contraction for speed or strength as well as the release of a shout. Anything that requires a quick burst of energy is related to the liver and the spring. The liver is responsible for cleansing our body and mind from toxins on a physical, chemical, and emotional energy level.

> *"The liver is an important organ which stores and transforms the blood."*
> *–Ling Shu*

The liver regulates the blood's return to the heart via the veins.

LIVER MERIDIAN

The Leg Jue Yin Liver Meridian

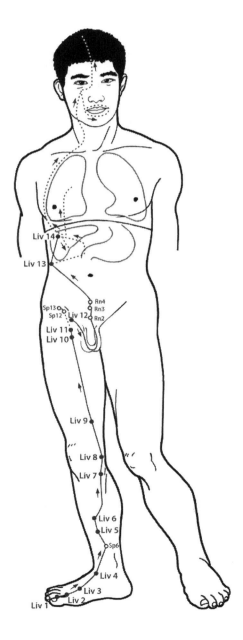

In an ancient Chinese statement explaining the spirit and character of the organ, Nei Ching says the liver is like a military leader who has great capacity in strength and planning. A clear and clean liver Chi will help you envision a plan and see your direction in life. A clear liver will change approach and plans if something did not work out in the past. The liver will cleanse us from stinking thinking and help us forgive others and ourselves.

Inability to show restraint under stress, outbursts of anger or frustration, as well as an inability to take a firm stand and speak up can cause blockage of energy and an imbalance in the liver. On the other hand, keeping your spoken word and your intentions impeccable and clean keeps the energy flowing and the liver Chi balanced.

A patient of mine, John, is a perfect example of how an imbalance in spring can cause problems in the liver and gall bladder meridians. John, a very bright forty-six-year-old, was hired as a CEO for a fast growing, up-and-coming corporation. He had the great ability to grasp complex concepts, to understand and get things right away, and he was hired to lead the company to the next level. But about a year into the job he found himself stuck. He was impatient with other executives for not getting his goals and concepts as fast as he could and often said things in a harsh tone. He needed to get them to see his vision and commit to his strategies, but his impatience, frustration, and blunt and honest communication caused friction with other executives, who felt attacked or threatened by his approach, actions, wording, and tone of voice. Those co-executives responded by being defensive and resisting any change of direction for the company. When things did not move ahead, John grew more and more frustrated and angry, because he felt that his integrity and ability to do what he was hired for was compromised. John also felt resentful and questioned himself. He never intended to hurt anyone, but he was internalizing his frustration and anger, while always appearing cool on the surface. This stress deteriorated his health to the point where he needed heart surgery.

When I saw John, he had fully recovered from the heart surgery and returned to work, but the cause of the heart condition - the stressful situation - was not resolved. He came to me with a lower back injury that he suffered while gardening in his backyard over the weekend. He was lifting and moving things around for hours. After talking to him for a while, I began to suspect the reason the injury occurred in the first place was because he was not present in his gardening activity but rather thinking of something else. He confirmed that while he was working, his mind kept thinking about returning to work the next morning and facing the same stressful situation again. Thinking about this suppressed stress while performing physical labor caused tension in his back to build up so much that his lower back, lateral torso, and hips went into a spasm. He was unable to sleep at night due to the pain, and had a hard time turning around in the bed or getting up from a seated position. As I released gall bladder and liver acu- and trigger points in spastic muscles in his buttock, hip, lateral abdomen, and lateral torso (Iliacus, gluteus medius, oblique abdominals, and quadratus lumborum), I suggested that if he kept repeating the same pattern he would drain his Chi energy, experience more failure, more tension, and more suffering. This would lead to more injuries, disease, and pain. Learning from what did not work and changing his approach was critical to his recovery. As I released the tension in one muscle at a time, I asked him if his way of communicating with key co-executives was working for him. He said it was not. I asked what he had learned from that and if he'd ever tried different approaches. He said he had not. The way he communicated was him; it was his style. I suggested that he try calmly communicating what he needed and what he thought the company needed to grow successfully. If he communicated the frustration he had felt when his needs were not met, and how internalizing this frustration had made him sick to the point where he needed heart surgery and blew his back out, he would be able to get them to understand and be more eager to help. Trying a different approach by making a clear request to co-executives about what he needed, and what he thought the company needed to grow, would offer a better chance for keeping feelings or egos from being hurt and mobilizing everyone to work together to solve problems. Learning from bad experiences (stinking manure) and changing the approach (fertilizing) before attempting to start over (planting), instead of repeating the same ineffectual behaviors, is the only way we can grow and move forward. The patient got the concept quickly and again got excited about the future of the company and his work. He started to think of his quick, visionary, and creative mind as his greatest asset again, instead of a curse. He jumped off the table and had full range of motion without any pain. This new way of approaching his work problems would help keep his liver and gall bladder meridians clear and ensure his health, well-being, and peace of mind.

The Gall Bladder Meridian and Organ System:

> *"The gall bladder is appended to the Liver and they*
> *mutually assist one another to perform their functions."*
> *–Zhangshi Leijing*

If the liver is the military leader, the gall bladder is an important and true officer who shows his capacity for decision-making by using good judgment. It makes sure that the liver's strategy will be followed. Indecisiveness, procrastination, as well as the tendency to make decisions in haste without clarity or planning things through cause an imbalance in the gall bladder meridian. When a person has a balanced spring and gall bladder he/she is taking responsibility for the outcome of his/her life without blaming others or making excuses.

GALL BLADDER MERIDIAN

The Leg Shao Yang Gall Bladder Meridian

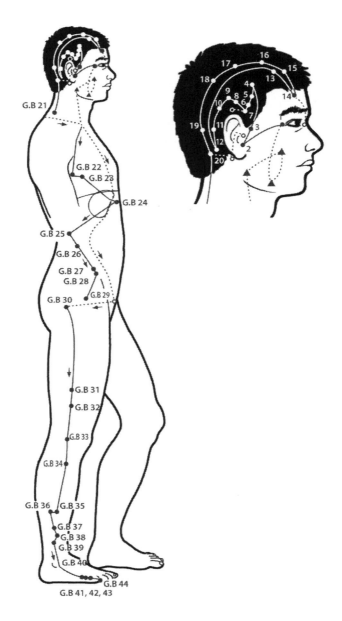

Any symptom of pain, dysfunction, or disease of the gall bladder and liver meridians is related to an accumulation of tension and a blockage of Chi circulation. Here are some common symptoms when the spring is out of balance and a blockage exists in the liver or gall bladder meridian:

- Eye problems, conjunctivitis, and other more severe problems.
- Dryness or tearing of the eyes.
- Twitching of muscles around the eyes.
- Tension headaches from the lateral neck into the base of the head (occipital) and temples.
- Migraine headaches often affecting the sight (lights, black spots, etc.).
- Disorders affecting equilibrium (balance).
- Dizziness and vertigo.
- Nausea.
- Pain in the lateral (sides of) neck and top of shoulders.
- Pain between the shoulder blades (right side more common).
- Tenderness in the pectoral region (anterior chest wall, especially the right side).
- Intolerance or craving of greasy food.
- Intolerance and/or addiction to alcohol, often causing anger or rage.
- Fullness and gas after eating fatty food.
- Pain in the right lower ribcage.
- High cholesterol.
- Abdominal pain,Toxic conditions.
- Jaundice.
- Allergies affecting the eyes.
- Lateral (sides of) lower back pain.
- Lateral (sides of) hip pain.
- Pain along the lateral thigh, lower leg, and ankle.
- Medial knee pain at the site of the medial meniscus or medial collateral ligament.

- Twitching, numbness, and pain along the outside (lateral side) of the torso, legs, and feet.

Other Spring Imbalance Clues

Geographical Direction:
East. The direction associated with spring is east. The sun rises in the east and the new day (spring) begins. Some people with an imbalance in spring might feel either better or worse when they travel east.

Color:
Green. Imbalances in an element or season can cause the color associated with it to show in the hue of their skin, most commonly noticed in the face. This hue of color was used in ancient Chinese medicine to diagnose disease or imbalance. In nature's spring, green is the predominant color we see. A person's preference or disliking for the color green is also a clue to a possible imbalance in the element of wood and season of spring. An individual might surround himself with or dress in this color, or completely avoid or detest it.

Climate Relationship:
Wind. The Chinese says that excess wind could cause a hundred diseases. People with an imbalance in spring tend to have a sensitivity, aversion, or fondness of windy weather. Discomfort with stiffness in the neck and soreness of the throat, as well as dry or teary eyes, are commonly attributed as wind symptoms. Tingling, numbness, and twitching sensation in the muscles could also be symptoms of over exposure to wind.

Sound Relationship:
Shouting. This person may have a stern, loud voice that might be intimidating or interpreted as being aggressive or angry by others. On the other hand, they may be extremely timid in speech, so quiet you

seldom hear them. Those too unassertive often fail to gain respect. Too loud or too quiet a voice points to a spring imbalance.

Sense Relationship:
Eyesight/Vision. The eyes are vessels for vision. The balanced spring has clear eyesight, as well as a balanced mind capable of envisioning success and observing his needs without judgment and blame of others. They keep their eyes set on their goals, exercising clear judgment in their decision-making. Problems with the ability to visualize where we are going in life as well as problems with the physical eyesight, indicates a spring imbalance.

Human Tissue Relationship:
Muscles, tendons, and ligaments. The spring connection to muscles, specifically the anaerobic muscles, is one of strength and related to sudden explosive contractions. These are the thick muscles with great explosive strength but less endurance - like what you'd see on a sprinter, rather than a marathon runner. Anaerobic muscles use glucose as a fuel, which is stored in the muscles and released by the liver. Balanced spring people tend to have firm, developed muscles, while a person with an imbalance in spring might have poor muscle development and lack strength.

Body Orifice Relationship:
Eyes. The ability to see clearly and visualize goals being met is related to the spring. When you have a spring imbalance, you might experience the common allergic reaction in the spring (hay fever), which is often amplified by windy weather. Swollen, red, watery eyes, and even conjunctivitis can result from a spring imbalance.

External Physical Manifestation:
Nails. The fingernails and especially the toenails indicate balance in spring. The ancient Chinese likened the toenails to the roots of a tree, and their condition can reveal if a person is well rooted,

sets boundaries, and takes a firm stand or is a pushover. Being well rooted also relates to a healthy relationship with one's family, culture, and roots. An imbalanced spring can be indicated by striations, discoloring, peeling, cracking, ridging, and even fungus of the nails.

Body Secretion:
Tears. Tears clean the surface of the eyes from debris to enable clear vision, so problems with your tears (too little or too much) may signify an imbalance in spring. You may feel like your eyes are dry all the time, or maybe your eyes are watery. The purpose of the tears is to moisturize the eyes so they're clean and allow you to see clearly.

Flavor:
Sour. People who love or crave tart tasting foods, or dislike sour tastes, are feeding or starving a spring imbalance.

How to Achieve Balance with Spring

The cycle of seasons persists whether we're ready for it or not. Every morning leads to an afternoon. Every beginning shifts into the next phase, and if you haven't fertilized and planted your seeds, you won't be ready when the next season comes.

The Four Seasons System teaches you that your past experiences - good, bad, and ugly - are not failures, but rather cleansing experiences that can make you more clear on what you need and do not need in life. Realize that all your past experiences have made you who you are today and have prepared you for this moment. With each go around, each life experience, we can get clearer. We should not repeat the same actions unless the approach and strategy brought us a harvest last time around. Holding grudges and repeating the same approach over and over will give us a toxic soil and an angry mind that will not allow for a future harvest. When things do not work out we need to forgive ourselves and others, as well as change our approach and limiting belief systems. It is our responsibility not to blame others or stay angry. As the saying goes, "once shame on them, twice shame on me." The way we fertilize is to use waste of the past to grow in the future. Forgiving means getting rid of anger, hate, and resentment ("stinking thinking"), that can make you toxic. You forgive others, not for their sake but for your own sake, health, and future growth.

To plant seeds for a better life, most importantly, you must take time to understand your needs and where they are, or aren't, being met. Those unfulfilled needs are the seeds you need to plant. The fact is that most people do not really know what they need in life or why they need it. They aren't clear on their needs, which can only lead to problems. "Be careful what you ask for you might get it"—the old saying is so true. Looking back on your life, how often did you not realize that what you asked for was not at all what you wanted or needed? Failing in past relationships; making career mistakes; moving to an area you ended up not liking at all; befriending people you later discovered weren't good people or good friends; acquiring a busy, stressful, materialistic lifestyle; etc.—repeating situations like these can be prevented when balance in spring is achieved.

Everything we think, say, or do, every action we take, every decision we make or choose to let someone else make for us has a consequence. Every seed brings a harvest. This is why being calm, present, assertive, and clear at all times is the responsible way to be. With every decision you face, you have three options: yes, no, or I don't know. You and only you are responsible for understanding your needs and making a decision in your best interest. Don't say yes if you mean no. Don't say no if you mean yes. And don't say yes or no if you don't know. Don't be impatient or feel rushed and pressured by others to make decisions. If you do, you may find yourself filled with remorse when it comes time to accept the outcome (harvest). You need to speak up, assert your needs, set clear boundaries, and get comfortable saying no. Being present, calm, clear, and assertive and responsibly owning your decisions (planted seeds), is the first step in growing and harvesting the life you want.

Anger and your Health

A person is either openly angry and tense—verbalizing their anger with angry voice and foul language, or passive aggressive—just quietly or resentfully stewing.

Anger occurs when we do not learn from past life experiences and hence repeat the same patterns over again. If something does not work for someone, why would he keep doing it over and over? No wonder he keeps getting angrier. If someone does something to you that makes you upset or angry once shame on them. If they do it twice (and all other times after that), shame on you. You can say a firm calm and assertive "NO"—set boundaries or remove yourself if necessary.

Anger arises when you don't take responsibility for your current life situation but rather blame and judge others or circumstances for your situation and feelings.

Roger, a 48-year old male, came limping into my office with his back bent over to the right. He described pain that became worse when sitting, and since his business required a lot of driving, the pain had been really bad for three weeks. It was also painful for him to turn over in bed; he had to roll over onto his belly and get on all four to get out of the bed in the mornings. Even though he was limping when he walked, he said he actually felt less pain while walking.

When I asked how this started, he said he had been working more hours lately that required more lifting and driving. As I probed further, he told me he was starting up his own company and was working ten plus hours a day repairing race cars. He was exhausted when he got home after work, and all he could do was go straight to bed, only to get up and do the same thing the next day again. He custom built his shop into a van, so he drove to his customers instead of them coming to him.

The pain had started on the outside of his left thigh and knee. He thought he might have favored his left side by leaning more to the right and using his right side more. When he came to me, his pain was all in his right hip and outside thigh all the way down to his knee. When he got out of bed or tried to lean his torso to the left, he also felt a deep pain in the small of his low back, which radiated into his right hip.

I started to release tension in muscles and acu-points along his gall bladder meridian on his outside thigh, hip and lateral low back (vastus lateralis, tensor fascia latae, gluteus minimus and quadratus lumborum). While I was working on him, I continued to inquire as to what might have been the cause for those muscles to hold so much tension and go into spasm. I asked him if he had a hard time saying no to his customers, or if he held anger, frustration or irritation - both symptoms of an imbalance in the gall bladder meridian. He said he did. He had a hard time saying no to some jobs due to persistent or manipulative customers. I told him if he did not know how to state his boundaries, say no to jobs that did not want to do because they were insignificant or not worth his time, he would never have any time for himself. Suspecting he was passive aggressive, I cautioned him that continuing to do jobs he did not want to do would cause him tension and pain, making him resentful, irritable and exhausted.

Roger got quiet for a minute, and then he said, "You are more right than you know. I love what I do repairing race cars. I am good at it and it is my passion. What I did not tell you is that I was doing this business once before, 8 years ago. One of my customers asked me to do something with his car that I said would not work. He continued to persuade me and even though I did not think it would work I did what he asked me to. When it turned out that it did not work he turned around and sued me. I got so angry that I gave up the business and practice I loved. For eight years I worked in another field and did alright, but I missed my passion and love for working on race cars. I just started the business up again."

I told him, "And here you are again suffering for not saying no and doing jobs you do not want to do, if you do not learn how to say no you can lose your love and passion again."

Roger walked out of my office free of pain with a straight back and without a limp.

Dr. Marshall Rosenberg, a world renounced psychologist, believes all anger stems from needs that we have that are not being met. Most people are not clear on what their needs are and are not in touch with them or accustomed to verbalize them in a successful way.

Dr. Rosenberg states it is not what happened or what someone says or does that truly makes us angry, but rather what we think about this action. Anger is a reaction triggered by what happened or what someone said or did. The cause of this trigger, the real cause for anger, is a need we have that has not been met. The longer this need continues to be unmet, the stronger the need gets, the more powerful the trigger gets and the angrier we get. We either let this anger explode to the outside, as a person with a temper or short fuse, or we stuff it inside, as a passive aggressive person does. Both of those behaviors are hazardous to our health and well-being.

If we don't take responsibility for our current life situation (feelings) by getting aware and clear about our needs and communicating them appropriately, they may never be met. This anger over having unmet needs causes us to blame or judge others for their actions, making them wrong and at fault. This, in turn, causes opposition and defensiveness in others and make it less likely that our need will be met.

In his work; *Non Violent Communication (NVC), a Language of Love*, Dr. Rosenberg stresses the need to communicate what we need without anger, blame or judgment.

We feel anger when we repeat something over and over without getting what we need (harvest). The anger grow when we are unable to see how unwanted experiences that we perceive as bad can serve us and help us grow (help our spiritual growth). The wastes of your past are the fertilizers for your future growth. When something happens in the past, and you never come to closure with it, get over it, or learn from it, you are unable to see how this can serve you in your growth. You are not able to get clear on the fact that any outcome of the past, even the real stinkers, can help you see what works and what does not work—that it helps you get clear on what you need and what you do not need. Holding on to what you **do not** want (stinking thinking) makes you toxic and angry. If not dealt with, this anger will consume you and prevent you from growing. Not seeing how the waste of your past can serve you, will cause the anger to take over your life as you keep repeating a pattern that does not work. When you are able to fertilize—see how any waste of the past serves your growth and helps you get more clear on what you **do** want—then you are able to forgive and forget with ease.

The liver is the body's poison control and detoxification organ, and its purpose according to ancient Chinese medicine, is to purify our body physically as well as emotionally.

The liver can become overloaded and toxic by unhealthy diet (fats and sugar), drugs, and anger.

One of the many functions of the liver is to store and metabolize fat. An excess of anger can cause an overload of the liver and thus inhibit its functions to regulate blood fat (cholesterol) levels in our blood stream. Excessive cholesterol of the bad kind will clog up arteries which lead to high blood pressure. At this point the anger that you can't forgive and forget can strain your heart, and if you don't change your ways, it can eventually kill you.

The liver also converts cholesterol to bile salts that are used to digest fat in our daily diet. The expression that someone is full of bile is often used to describe someone full of anger. An overload to the liver can affect the quality and quantity of bile released and thus causes a failure in breakdown of the fats you digest in your daily food intake. This often causes indigestion with nausea, diarrhea or bloating. An excess of bile salts in the large intestine can be the cause of colon cancer. In ancient Chinese medicine it was believed that holding onto anger and resentment or any other negative emotion causes a form of emotional constipation, an inability to let go and move on, that causes dis-ease in the large intestine system.

Your New Beginning

Whatever you think, say, or do is a seed you plant. The seed's principle purpose is to multiply. So, what goes around comes around; or as you sow, so shall you reap. If you are present, assertive, impeccable, and clear on what you think, say, and do, there are no limits to what you can harvest. And knowing how to harvest and meet the needs you have in your life by design on a regular basis is essential. Everyone could sometimes stumble into something great. Through life, if you want to consistently be able to harvest and grow, have peace of mind, radiant health and success, you must take responsibility for your own thoughts, spoken words, and actions. Realize that every moment and every word and every thought and everything you do has consequences. By being present and keeping your actions, words, and thoughts impeccable by planting your best seed, you will enhance your life and the lives of others.

Spring represents a new beginning, and being clear on boundaries and setting ground rules right from the start are paramount. Entering new relationships, having children, or getting a puppy are all situations that benefit from this. Entering new contracts and agreements are best done in writing to make sure both parties are clear on purpose, obligations, and direction.

Every present moment can be a new beginning and a new spring. It could be the beginning of something great based on your present thoughts, your present action, and the present words you speak. And that's why it's so important to be present and assertive and think about what you do, what you think, and what you say. People with a spring imbalance should focus on aligning their behavior with the spring characteristics that will make them most successful. Every moment can also be a missed opportunity to a better life.

The Metaphor of Summer

the Fire Element

*In the summer the farmer waters and weeds his
fields. He labors in love as he inspects his fields daily
with joy, because he anticipates a rich harvest.*

IN THE FOUR SEASONS OF nature, summer is associated with
watering, weeding, blooming, and flourishing. Summer is a time
of blooming flowers and lush landscapes. It's a time full of life and
buzzing energy. Gardeners tend the seeds they've planted and enjoy
watching them grow and bloom into something beautiful. The days
are long and warm, and all the preparations and work done in spring
start to pay off.

In the Four Seasons metaphor, summer stands for being engaged,
being passionate, loving life, being connected with your heart, being
enthusiastic, being inspired, having fun, having joy, and playing.
All this is important because it allows the needs you established in
spring to grow and strengthen and eventually yield fruit. Obviously,
if you don't plant the right seeds in spring, you won't feel the joy that's
possible in summer. And if you don't do the weeding and watering
throughout the summer, you won't have a positive harvest in the fall.

Everything in life has a summer. It's like the middle of the day,
the time from when you decided to start working on something
to when you finish working on it. And during this time it's very

important to be able to see what's good and what's bad to weed out obstacles, to stay authentic, to be true to your heart, to be engaged, and to be passionate and believe in what you do. So when you're at work, completing the tasks of your day, how do you feel? Do you feel engaged and energized? Or do you feel bored? Or anxious? Some people are so engaged in, and enjoying what they do that the hours pass in a flash, while others feel like time drags on when they're working and laboring in something they do not enjoy - when we are all living the seeds we planted. If you don't have passion and love for what you're doing and you're not engaged in it, then your summer is out of balance. It would be like marrying someone you don't really love, like, or enjoy, and you have no passion. Yes, you can try to fake it and act like everything is fine, but it's not going to work out. You'll never harvest happiness. It's like planting seeds and not enjoying the watering and weeding. You can't anticipate a harvest, because it's hard to be happy when you're married to the wrong person. Just like a high jumper - if you're running up towards the bar and you don't believe you can make the jump, why do you even waste your time and energy trying? Any task, labor, or relationship where one does not anticipate or believe in a harvest is fruitless. If you're disengaged and melancholic and life feels like a chore, or you are faking being in to it and forcing yourself to do something, then you can improve your life by aligning your thoughts and activities with the summer season.

Summer is about communication and action that match each other, being able to express how we feel and what is alive in us. The characteristics of a person with a balanced summer include having a positive anticipation and attitude, being fully engaged in what he does, and being persistent, persuasive, and inspirational. Summer is also related to the ability to have authentic relationships. This includes romantic, family, and friend relationships.

Individuals with a summer imbalance act or pretend to be into it, making them hypocritical, fake, or phony. They pretend to be engaged and pretend that they enjoy their work or relationships. In fact they are living a lie. They do not know the meaning of labor in love and they do not understand what a true, authentic relationship is. Imbalanced summer have been conditioned to seek love and approval from others. This person will say and do what they think the other person wants them to in order to gain their love or approval. Likewise, they will feel unloved if their lover, friend, or family member is not doing or saying what they want and expect of them. When a person has been living like this for some time, they no longer know who they truly are. They are not connected to their heart or what's alive in them. Their friends and loved ones love or approve of a façade because they do not know the true person. This creates a phony and fake love, friend, or family relationship.

A person with a summer imbalance often has a distorted view of love – often believing: "If you love me or approve of me, you do what I want and agree with me." In a true authentic relationship either person can say and do what he/she believes and feels. Any romantic relationship needs true love and affection to flourish. If someone is trying too hard to gain your love or approval, it is a turn off, like an obnoxious salesperson or desperate first date. If a person is not authentic, but rather manipulative in actions and words, true love or friendship (harvest) cannot exist. A person can only fake it for so long. A relationship that is not authentic and true to the heart damages the spirit, soul, and body. Anytime we are insincere and pretend to be engaged in a relationship or work, we are hypocrites.

For example, Ann, a fifty-year-old woman with pain and numbness in her chest and wrist, had been married for twenty-seven years and had adult children and a grandchild. She enjoyed her status, home, and family, but she had to pretend that she loved and respected her husband. She had not been true to her heart, authentic, or genuine in her relationship with him for over twenty years. She had pretended for so long that she was not in touch with her own heart, and her behavior had affected both her and her husband's health. This realization hit her like a ton of bricks as I released the tension in her tight muscles.

Perhaps you've heard this joke: One neighbor talking to another said, "Why don't you come and join us for church on Sunday morning?"

His neighbor answered, "Church is nothing but a bunch of hypocrites."

The neighbor replied, "Don't worry about it; there is always room for one more."

The truth is: we have all been hypocrites at one time or another. With awareness we can recognize when we are not authentic and true to our heart, so we can make changes in our life. We will never realize a full harvest if we do not get passionately engaged in our labor, relationships, and activities. We need to look for something good (water) and anticipate a harvest in whatever we do, or we will labor in vain, wasting our time.

Balance in Summer

Spring is always followed by summer. And being successful in this season means being engaged, present, and passionate about what you're doing. It means tending the seeds you've planted, enjoying that process, and looking forward to a bountiful harvest in fall. When you picture a balanced summer, imagine a flower blossoming and flourishing, a person that is enthusiastic about their life and what they do. The balanced summers look at the bright side of life, and always see the glass as half full. They are active and engaged at work, in their relationships, and whatever they do. They are authentic, energetic, active, positive, and inspirational. These people are warm; full of fire, energy, and vitality; lively; and colorful.

People who are balanced in their summer enjoy their work and feel energized. They focus on the solution (what they want - watering), instead of the problem (what they don't want - weeds). They sort out (weeding) disturbing thoughts and negative attitudes, staying focused on what they are doing without being disturbed or distracted by other people's attitudes, activities, or sound surrounding them.

They give their full attention to the task at hand while maintaining their joyful positive attitude. They always expect a successful outcome in whatever they get involved with or they would not get involved.

Those who are balanced summer do not take what others say and do personally. They are not jealous, but rather excited and happy for the success of others. They inspire and support others through their positive attitude. They are experts at communicating and verbalizing their needs, opinions, thoughts, and feelings. People who are balanced in summer communicate authentically, and their actions match their words. They say what they do and they do what they say. They can express how they feel and what is alive in them, speaking from the heart. They are great believers in freedom of speech and do not hesitate to tell others what they are passionate about. A balanced summer individual is the same person all the time, not a phony or fake, changing when in different circumstances or with different people.

Unbalanced summers are those who act or pretend to be what they think others want them to be; they pretend to know what they are talking about and act as if everything in their life is fine and their crop is growing even when it is not. What they see is a mirage or delusion. In some cases, they could be so good at deceiving that they believe themselves.

This behavior is very much like the fairy tale "The Emperor's New Clothes" by Hans Christian Anderson. In this story, the Emperor paraded before the townsfolk in what he believed was a fine and splendid suit of clothes, but he was in fact naked. This form of summer imbalance is often hard to correct, since it is hard to help someone who will put on a happy face for themselves and others, but does not realize they have a problem.

Michelle, a fifty-five-year-old woman, came to me for a second visit to relieve post- surgery pain in her right shoulder. She had a rotator cuff repair eight months before. Her condition had greatly improved since the surgery, but she still experienced pain in the back portion of her shoulder, especially when she reached with her arm straight up over her head. She explained that she had felt great when she left the last visit and she had done all her exercises faithfully to stretch the shortened muscles and strengthen weakened muscles. Yet her condition gradually came back and was still lingering. She said her shoulder clicked when she reached over her head and there was discomfort and light pain. She was unable to do a single push-up without pain. She also informed me that her shoulder and neck felt stiff.

Michelle owned and coached at a gymnastic school and frequently had to lift and spot young gymnasts and children in their gymnastic activities. Michelle was a happy, optimistic, full-of-life woman who I had known through her different activities and phases over the last twenty years - including power lifting, water skiing, belly dancing, and yoga. Michelle had always been passionate and fully engaged in her relationships, her life, her hobbies, and her work. When I examined her range of motion and tested her muscles to determine where she held her tension, I discovered that the condition was exactly the same as when I saw her four months prior. The same muscles were contracted and they were all along the small intestine and heart meridians. I asked her if her neck ever got so tight that it was hard to move it. She said that some days she could hardly turn her head. I asked if she had any ringing in her ear or jaw pain, and she said that lately she experienced intermittent ringing in her ear. When I told her that the blockage was in the small intestine meridian (the system responsible for separating the pure from the impure in our bodies), the heart meridian, and in the summer season, she said she never had anything wrong with her heart, that her blood pressure and cholesterol were fine. She thought her intestines were fine as well because she did not have any problems with her appetite, digestion, or elimination. I told her the heart was related to communication and being true to your heart. If a person did not separate pure from impure, discern authentic from phony, and truth from lies and be true to their heart it could cause tension and blockages in those meridians.

That's when she told me that she was the president on the board of a nonprofit organization that focused on raising spiritual awareness worldwide. On the surface, the position seemed to align with Michelle's passions and desire to make the world a better place by increasing spiritual awareness. Six months before, her organization joined forces with a similar organization, but she'd not been aware that the board was fraught with hypocritical games of egos. Michelle was very upset over the fact that the words of the other organization's president didn't match his actions. She found his actions to be hypocritical and she felt they were wasting their time. Because of this, she had lost her passion and excitement and did not think the organization would get things accomplished. She wanted to tell everyone involved exactly what she felt, but at the same time she did not want to hurt the other members and her friends on her board or take away their excitement. She had lost her passion was depressed and felt stuck.

As I worked on her and released the tension in one reflex point at a time Michelle came to the realization that she had to be true to her heart and herself. If she did not feel the people she had to deal with were authentic, if she did not believe them, if their actions did not match what they said, she could not put her heart and energy into this cause. She left the visit with full pain- free range of motion and strength in her shoulder, without any clicking, and the realization that she could only be engaged in this organization if she believed in the people she worked with and believed they could accomplish their mission. She e-mailed me a couple of weeks later to tell me she'd addressed all her issues with her board, as well as the board and president of the other organization. And she told me she was able to do ten push-ups for the first time in a year without pain. I could tell from her e-mail that her passion and engagement in her cause were back.

Balanced emotions for the summer season are calmness, joyfulness and pleasure; a feeling of being present, authentic and true to one's heart. Anytime a person is not balanced in summer, he or she will experience negative emotions of either a hypoactive or hyperactive nature. If a person is hypoactive in summer, there may be patterns of depression, despair, gloom, melancholy, or joylessness (living in a dull, lifeless, and colorless state). This person is essentially missing their fire. A person with a hyperactive summer nature may experience anxiety, delusion, over-excitement, or frenzy (in a hypocritical, fake, or phony way). This person "burns too brightly" and may have over-the-top laughter at inappropriate moments.

A person with an imbalance in the summer will tend to be too little summer or too much summer. Remember in Chinese philosophy too little or too much are both harmful. You can kill a plant both by watering it too much or by not watering it enough.

The too little summer behavior is often characterized by the following patterns:

- Having an inability to express feelings, needs or what is alive in one's self. Lacking passion and disconnection with the heart (spirit).
- Difficulty concentrating at one thing, frequently failing to follow through.
- Not staying focused for any length of time and getting distracted easily (under-focused, depressive).
- Lacking enthusiasm and action, depression, joylessness, melancholy, or gloominess about life (often reflected in how a person dresses.)
- Talking very little, and if they do talk, it comes out slow and reluctantly.
- Experiencing a hard time getting needs, thoughts, messages and feelings across.
- Seldom laughing.
- Not staying present in the here and now, becoming fatigued, melancholic or depressed and often spacing out or day dreaming.
- Often craving nicotine, caffeine or chocolate as artificial energy to make it through the day.
- Disliking what they are doing, often showing in appearance.

- Believing that dreams are for dreamers, that storybook myths never come true.
- Disliking work and lack of energy cause their crop to be strangled by weeds, overcome by negative obstacles. The crop dies from not being "watered," lacking positive expectations.

Too much summer is often characterized by the following patterns:

- Talking too much without connecting with the heart.
- Trying to do everything at once, jumping from one thing to another; consequently wasting energy and time.
- Never staying still long enough to focus.
- Being over-enthusiastic, bordering on manic or frenzied, often too colorful and flashy in appearance and manner of dress (look at me).
- Not having the ability to stop talking, talking too fast and still not getting needs, message, thoughts or feelings across.
- Taking action that does not match one's words.
- Not having the ability to discern or filter what one is saying, hence putting "foot in mouth" frequently.
- Not listening, but rather thinking of what to say next.
- Talking and laughing a lot, but little or nothing actually gets done.
- Acting frenzied or anxious.
- Often getting too hyper on coffee, cigarettes or chocolate.
- Being phony, fake and pretending to like what one is doing, pretending to know what one is talking about, and that one's dreams are coming true.
- Being unrealistic and believing in one's own illusions.
- Killing the crop by over watering it (over doing, over selling or over talking).

In addition to these emotional and behavioral symptoms, an imbalance in summer may also cause physical symptoms. The following descriptions come from the ancient Chinese wisdom and the writings Huang Di Nei Ching, the Yellow Emperor, (with a few of my own additions) on the organs, meridians, human functions, and associations that relate to balance or imbalance of the summer and fire element.

The Heart Meridian and Organ System:

> *"The heart is the root of life; it is reflected in the blood vessels and its Chi communicates with the tongue."*
> *–Ling Shu*

According to Nei Ching, the heart is the emperor of life, the superior monarch who rules with intuition and understanding. The heart is the home of the spirit, the authentic self and unconditional love. In the physical realm, it distributes the blood by moving it through the blood vessels. Not being true to your heart will cause imbalance in the season, element, and meridian. Speaking untruths (double tongued), talking too much, gossiping, using words that don't match your actions, and not being authentic or real will cause stress to your heart and spirit.

HEART MERIDIAN

The Arm Shao Yin Heart Meridian

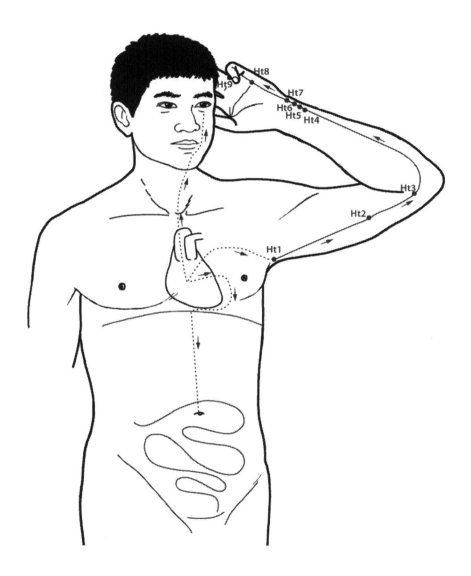

Douglas, a fifty-three-year-old man, came to me with several seemingly unrelated complaints of pain that turned out to be symptoms of an imbalance in the heart and small intestine meridians. He had sharp pain in his left inner forearm and little finger, which he said came from over-doing it when playing his piano. He said that he was practicing and trying to master a hard classical piece and had to spread his fingers wide and push with force on the keys. He had played for hours every day for over a week. In that time, the pain in his little finger and forearm flexor muscle got so intense that he had to stop playing the piano. He had taken a week-long break, but still experienced pain when he attempted to play the piano. He also experienced a burning pain in his shoulder blade area. This pain was aggravated when he was sitting in front of his computer or piano. This pain alleviated if he stood up. His final complaints were ringing in his ears and pain in his jaw that he believed came on after having four molar teeth removed at one time about three years ago.

When I tested the strength of the little finger flexor muscle (a muscle that curls the little finger into a fist), he was clearly weak. This test also elicited the same pain that he experienced when playing the piano. The middle and lower trapezius (muscles that hold the shoulder blades back and keep the upper body from slouching forward) also tested weak. I released the tension in trigger points and muscles on the heart and small intestine meridians in his forearm, shoulder blade area, neck, and jaw. After the treatment the patient was strong on the previous weak tests and did not experience any pain in his little finger, forearm, shoulder blade, or jaw area. However, this didn't solve Douglas's true problem.

When he came back two weeks later, Douglas had improved, but was still experiencing some symptoms. He expressed that his shoulder blade and jaw pain were gone as was the ringing in his ears. He avoided playing the piano for five days after the treatment then started to play easy pieces, not playing the complex classical piece he was practicing when he first got injured. He felt only a slight pain that then subsided. This encouraged him. The following day he started to practice the hard classical piece again and after about thirty minutes his sharp pain in the little finger and forearm returned. I told him that when the pain of an injury was removed with therapy followed by rest, he should get better—a scab will heal unless you keep picking it. The fact that his pain returned made me believe something else was going on in Douglas's life that was causing the problem.

The hardest thing about helping patients is figuring out what the person is doing, thinking, or believing that caused the injury to return. It could be just a physical stressor, such as over-use or trauma, it could be an emotional or mental stressor, or it could be some combination of both factors. In this case, only the patient's left little finger and forearm were injured even though he used both hands equally. So I started to inquire about what happened when he first got injured. Why was he playing this difficult piece for so many hours and for so many days straight? He said he had committed to a date for recording the piece, but mastering it was harder than he expected. He wasn't improving fast enough to meet his commitment. I asked him how he felt when the music did not come out the way he wanted, and he said he felt anxious, frustrated, and disappointed. Then we started talking about why he plays the piano in the first place.

His face broke into a smile and he said, "Because I love the way it sounds and I love how it feels."

I said, "Did you love how it sounded and how you felt when you were practicing that advanced classical piece for hours every day?"

He got quiet for a minute; then he said, "No, it did not sound good, and I did not feel good." He kept playing though, in order to meet his deadline for recording, and in doing so lost touch with the reason he loved playing the piano. As I kept talking to him, I found out that he got stuck on the same place every time he practiced this classical piece. It was a difficult passage where he had to reach to the far left and spread his fingers wide when hitting the key hard with his little finger. As he was playing along fine, he started thinking about that tricky part of the difficult passage—he stopped being present and started worrying about screwing up. He got more and more frenzied trying to force his performance to work, and as he kept repeating the same mistake over and over he started to get a sharp pain in his left little finger and forearm. I told him that the injury was along his heart meridian, and by forcing his performance, he was not having fun and he was not playing from his heart. An activity that he passionately loved had turned into forced, frustrating, painful labor.

I released the trigger points and tight muscles along the heart meridian one more time, until all tension and pain were removed. Then I told him to go home and practice his piano piece again, but this time he had to stop playing immediately, if it did not sound good or if he did not feel good playing.

"I'll never meet my deadline that way," he said.

"That is not what's important. What is important is that you play from your heart and love it," I explained. "The moment it does not sound good or feel good, you will stop playing (weeding). But do not leave the piano. Sit with your eyes closed, and visualize yourself playing the piece perfectly (watering). See yourself playing effortlessly, being present with passion from your heart. See how your fingers move effortlessly to hit the keys with perfect timing. Feel your fingers touching the keys. Hear how beautiful it sounds, and feel how good it feels to play the piece. Play the piece in your mind perfectly three times; then play it for real again. Every time it does not sound or feel good, stop immediately and practice the piece three times perfectly in your mind. You can play as much as you want to as long as you stop as soon as it does not sound or feel good."

The patient came back for his third visit two weeks later and told me that amazingly he had not had any pain playing the classical piece. He also stated that his fingers found the keys far out to the left without him even looking at them. His wife and her friend had entered the room when he was playing from his heart and they were moved to tears by his music. He brought me a CD with the classical piece recorded for me to enjoy. He told me that he now is a better piano player because of this injury. The injury, as they often can be, was his friend and teacher.

The Small Intestine Meridian and Organ System:

"The Small Intestine is the official who receives the
abundance from the stomach and is concerned with the
transforming of this matter."
–Su Wen

The small intestine is the creator of change in physical substances. It separates the pure from the impure, and an inability to do this efficiently will cause digestion problems, such as food poisoning, indigestion and diarrhea. The small intestine is like a filter that will discern constructive Chi from destructive Chi. This ability to separate pure from impure applies to beliefs and thoughts as well. The small intestine helps us separate (discern) truth from lies and authentic from phony. Keeping impure thoughts and belief systems can be damaging to an individual, poisoning his or her mind. "Weeding" the metaphorical action of summer is also related to one's ability to keep the good and throw away the bad, the ability to focus on the solution instead of dwelling on the problem.

SMALL INTESTINE MERIDIAN

The Arm Tai Yang Small Intestine Meridian

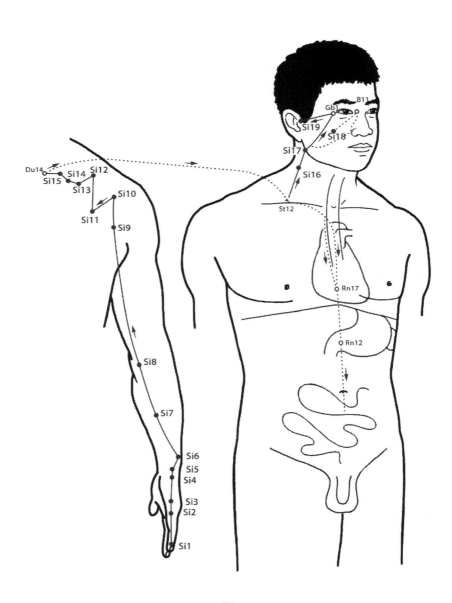

The Pericardium Meridian and Organ System:

"The pericardium is part of, and a protector of, the heart.
Together they help the brain to function."
–Ling Shu

In this way the pericardium Chi works as a protective buffer and connector between the heart (spirit) and the brain.

The Pericardium is a central officer that guides the body in happiness and satisfaction. It protects the heart Chi physically and emotionally so that the heart can function without ever ceasing, thereby giving the spirit peace. It is in charge of circulation and sexual secretion, and has a vital part in all forms of relations, in particular, unconditional love relations. The people that can hurt your feelings the most are the ones you love and care for the most. Avoid taking what others say or do personally to keep your pericardium strong and protect your heart. If you are being present, you can protect your heart by questioning your interpretation of what loved ones said or did before you take it to heart. Negative comments are only words, and in and of themselves they are powerless unless you give them meaning and take them to heart. If you never take anything personally, you cannot be hurt. Whatever others think, feel, say, or do to, or about you, are their perceptions. They interpret their own reality, and it is different from your interpretation of what is true to you. They have not lived in your body and mind to experience everything you have experienced, so how can they possibly know better than you what is true for you? Their opinion is based on their reality and not yours. You can take what others say as feedback and then evaluate if what they said will benefit you and help you grow or not. If what they said will not serve you then do not take it to heart.

When a person has endured emotional heartache or trauma, the pericardium can put up a wall around the heart. This is initially a protective mechanism that can get stuck permanently. This wall will then close the heart, affecting the person's ability to fully express or experience love. Individual self-work is needed to heal the wounds and open the heart.

If you are not authentic in your relationships, you can cause injury to yourself and your partner. Remember Ann, the woman who was not authentic in her marriage? She had chest, wrist, and forearm pain and numbness along her pericardium meridian.

PERICARDIUM MERIDIAN

The Arm Jue Yin Pericardium Meridian

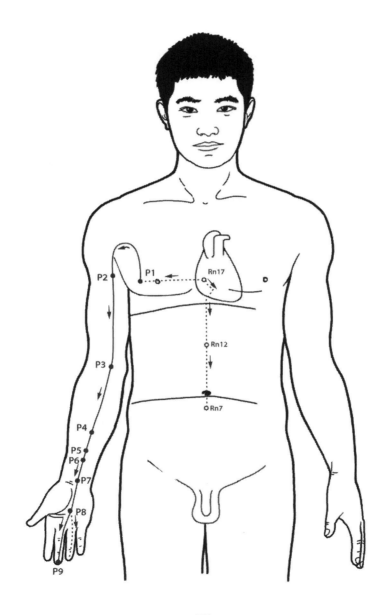

The Triple Warmer Meridian and Organ System:

*"The triple warmer is the protector of the solid and hollow
organs."*
– Zangshi Leijing

The Chi of the triple warmer regulates, integrates, and protects the other organs, keeping the body in balance by controlling body temperature and metabolism. There are some theories that the triple warmer is part of what in Western medicine is referred to as the endocrine or hormonal system, the thyroid gland in particular. If the fire is too strong or too weak, either represents an imbalance. Fire gives us passion. A lack of fire leads to a dull, melancholic life or burn out, just as too much fire causes a hyper state of frenzy. The Triple Warmer is divided into three regions: the upper region being involved with respiration and circulation, the middle region with digestion, and the lower region with elimination. All three regions must be in balance with each other for the body to maintain these functions.

TRIPLE WARMER MERIDIAN

The Arm Shao Yang Triple Warmer Meridian

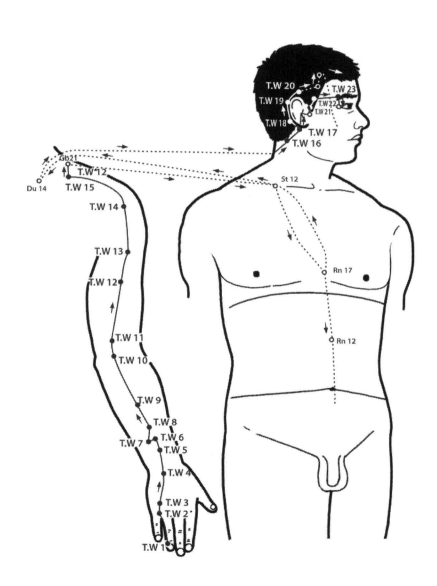

Jimmy, a thirty-eight-year-old motorcycle police officer, came to me with severe neck pain and restricted motion in his neck, a problem he'd had for two or three years. He knew he had lived and played tough his whole life. Besides riding motorcycles, he used to ride in the rodeo, and he had practiced wrestling and jiu-jitsu for years. He said that as the neck pain and stiffness got worse toward the end of the day, he developed tension headaches at the base of the head below his ears. The neck pain radiated from the posteriolateral neck into the shoulder blade and was worse on the left side. When I tested him I found that all the tension was located in the levator scapulae, a muscle that is commonly associated with a "locked neck" (torticollis), and the posterior scalenes. Both of those muscles often harbor active reflex points that radiate pain in the neck and shoulder blade, all of which follow the small intestine and Triple Warmer Meridians.

He had other symptoms that followed those meridians as well. I asked him if he had any problem with loose stool or digestion or ringing in his ear. He said he had loose bowels for some time and he did have ringing in his ears, but he thought it was due to the motorcycle riding. I continued to explain to him, as I released tension in reflex points in his neck and shoulder blade, that the summer is related to being passionate, having a fire burning, and being authentic and engaged in what you do. I told him that the summer represents pulling the weeds and watering the crop for a desired harvest. The small intestine is supposed to separate pure from impure so that we can realize a harvest - not only in our digestion, but in everything we do. I asked him if he had any problem with those things in his life, relationships, or work.

Then Jimmy told me he was burned out on his work. He works in a city where the crime rate is extremely high, budget cuts had reduced the police force, and the lack of resources and politics in the legal system prevented him from making positive change as an officer. Because of this, he had lost his excitement and his hope to help people in the community. He was discouraged by people's lack of respect for life and property. He liked to give people the benefit of the doubt, but felt there were very few good apples among many bad apples. Jimmy had taken the job in the police department with passion and a desire to protect the innocent and weak, and to make life better in the community in which he worked. He no longer believed that was possible in the department he was working, so he'd applied for a transfer to a city where the crime rate was significantly lower and he believed he could still make positive change.

I told Jimmy that if he continued to work in an environment where he did not believe he could be successful, it would wear him down and cause greater problems with his digestion, as well as tension and pain in his neck and shoulder. Until he was able to transfer to another city, he had to look for the good in his work and believe he could make a difference. If nine out of ten apples were bad, he needed to find the good one and do whatever he could to help. When I finished the treatment, Jimmy was pain-free and told me he had not been able to turn his head like this for ten years.

Any symptom of pain, dysfunction, or disease of the Heart, Small Intestine, Pericardium, or Triple Warmer meridians is related to an accumulation of tension and a blockage of circulation. Here are some common symptoms when the summer is out of balance and a blockage exists in one or more of these meridians:

- High or low blood pressure.
- Decreased circulation in hands or feet.
- Dysfunction of arteries or veins.
- Metabolic disorders (hyper- or hypo- metabolism).
- Hyper- or hypo-thermia.
- Hot flashes.
- Hyper- or hypo-libido.
- Chest pain.
- Inability to open up in love relationships.
- Indigestion.
- Diarrhea.
- Hemorrhoids.

- Spasms of the neck.
- Pain in the shoulder area.
- Pain in the shoulder blade and armpit.
- Frozen shoulder
- Ringing in the ears (tinnitus).
- TMJ (temporo-mandibular joint syndrome), clicking or locking jaw.
- Wrist and forearm pain.
- Pain or numbness in the 3rd, 4th or 5th fingers.

Other Summer Imbalance Clues

Geographical Direction:
South. The direction associated with summer is south. A person with a summer imbalance may feel better or worse when they travel in this direction.

Color:
Red. The color associated with the fire element and summer season is red. Red stands for warmth or heat. An imbalance in summer can be reflected as an excessive red hue of the face or the absence of red, as in a pale or ashen color. A person with high or low blood pressure will be bright red or pale in their face complexion. An obsession or aversion for the color red is also a clue for a summer imbalance.

Climate Relationship:
Heat. A person who hates warm weather, or loves it and cannot thrive without it, is likely expressing an imbalance of summer. Extreme heat is known to be injurious to the heart.

Sound Relationship:
Laughing. A person who is constantly laughing, or maybe even has a laughing quality to the voice, is showing evidence of a summer

imbalance. Often a complete absence of laughter can accompany a summer imbalance as well. A never-ending jokester is the polar opposite of the serious, humorless, joyless person. Either extreme can be significant.

Sense Relationship:
Tongue and Speech. The appearance of the tongue provides information about the summer season, especially about the heart and the circulation. As the Chinese state: "The heart rules over the tongue." The Holy Scriptures imply the same thing with: "Out of the abundance of the heart the mouth speaketh." A person who talks all the time, or goes to the other extreme by seldom speaking, is expressing a summer imbalance. A person who is unable to verbalize his or her needs, thoughts, and feelings to the world also suggests a summer imbalance. Speaking from the heart and expressing what is alive in us with passion and inspiration will bring balance to summer and joy to our spirit.

Human Tissue Relationship:
Blood Vessels. The blood vessels are connected to the heart, directly or indirectly. The blood fills the pulse with the force of life. Symptoms that may occur with an imbalanced summer include hardening of the arteries, varicose veins, cold hands and feet, thrombosis, phlebitis, etc. These are all symptoms that can arise from poor diet, lack of exercise, as well as from living a life without authentic passion and laboring without expecting a positive outcome or desired harvest.

Body Orifice Relationship:
Ears. Remember the hallmarks of summer: watering and weeding. The purpose of the small intestine is to separate the pure from the impure. The ear's ability to separate pure from impure sounds is also a function of summer. Dysfunction can often bring about symptoms of ringing in the ears (tinnitus).

External Physical Manifestation:
Skin and Complexion. Evidence of an imbalanced summer might be reflected in the skin or complexion as a red hue, especially of the face, as in the case of high blood pressure. On the other hand, an absence of red - a sort of ashen color - can also indicate an imbalance.

Body Secretion:
Sweat. Perspiration is a natural phenomenon that seldom receives the credit it deserves. An important function of perspiration is to help cool the body when it is too hot. The ancient Chinese were aware of the consequences resulting from a lack of, or excess of, perspiration - both of which indicate an imbalance in summer.

Flavor related to the Fire Element:
Bitter. An imbalance of summer is often accompanied by a craving for bitter or burnt flavors, such as coffee, tea, dark chocolate, etc. A dislike of all foods and drinks with a bitter flavor also points to a summer imbalance.

How to Achieve Balance in Summer

Summer is the time between the start (spring) and the finish (fall). It is a time to labor in joy, anticipating a harvest. It is work, but it is supposed to be enjoyable and fun. We are supposed to be engaged and captured in our "summer activities." When we were kids, the summer activity was called play. When a particular game wasn't fun anymore we stopped playing. Then we grow up and the summer activity is now called work. Most people believe work is not supposed to be fun, when in fact the happiest, most radiant and successful people find a way to have fun in whatever work they do. "If you catch fire, people will come from miles to see you burn," is a phrase I once heard, illustrating how someone with passion for what they do will be very successful. A balanced summer person is authentic, engaged, and having fun and playing in whatever they do to truly labor in love.

Now, what if you did not pay attention to what you planted in spring, or if you were not clear, rushed to plant something, and now you realize you do not like your summer? If this is the case, then you are probably acting frenzied, faking that everything is fine and that you are going to harvest. Or, you are in despair, feeling gloomy, melancholic and lifeless in what you do; you're not connected to your heart or believing in a harvest. When this happens, if you do not like what you are doing, you can change your attitude (weed). Start looking for something good, exciting, or positive in whatever you are doing. Whatever you focus on (water) will grow. This way you can find more joy and anticipate a harvest (more good).

If you cannot see anything to be excited or passionate about, you need to remove yourself. You can only fake it for so long, and not being authentic will cause stress, tension, and pain to yourself and others involved in your summer. At some point, you have to stop wasting your life. Remember at any present moment you can start a new cycle, planting new needs, goals, and dreams. Find joy and purpose in whatever you do or start something else you do want to do. This does not mean you quit your work immediately. You take the present moment (new beginning, spring) and start to come up with ideas on what to do. Get clear about what you need to feel engaged and passionate in a job or a career. Your body and mind will start to feel better as soon as you start to make plans for a new beginning. Then you keep your old work, being as authentic and engaged as you can until you have planned, committed, and are ready to start your new job. Our ego would like to tell us that the only way we can be successful is if we gain fame, fortune, and power with our job and career. The truth, however, is that fame, fortune, and power have nothing whatsoever to do with authentic passion, being engaged, and staying true to your heart. Remember the saying: "What good is it to gain the whole world if you have to sell your soul."

The same thing is true about exercise. Very often my patients tell me that they exercise and diet, but don't achieve results. I always ask them if they enjoy exercise, and they always tell me they hate it. If you cannot get passionately engaged in exercise and love your workout, then you will have little or no results. Often they hire a trainer or work out with a friend. But this can become more about socializing and less about being engaged and focused on the exercise. To get results and harvest fitness, it is absolutely essential that they find an exercise they love. I tell my patients that I do not believe in quick fix diets. A diet that is restricted and you resent might work short term but as soon as you go back to how you used to eat you will gain all weight back. The first three letters in diet is "die", which is the opposite of "live". For a meal plan to work it must become a lifestyle that one can enjoy.

People who do not enjoy their work spend an excessive amount of time taking breaks, drinking coffee, smoking, and/or gossiping. If people do not find things to be authentically engaged and excited about in their jobs, they will eventually get fired from that job or get injured or sick so they no longer can do that work. I commonly see patients who were injured while employed in jobs they did not authentically enjoy; often these are chronic injuries that do not heal. Think about it: do they really want to go back to work if they do not enjoy what they do? Subconsciously they'd rather be injured than regain their health and return to a job they don't enjoy.

All work affects your summer Chi, and if you don't like what you do, you need to realize this yourself. You need to either find or focus on something you like with it or remove yourself and go work (bloom) somewhere else.

When people have been working in jobs for many years, and have benefits and retirement and security, they often think, "I'm too old to change jobs. I need my retirement. I have to keep working." When they get hurt at work, they still get paid from their worker's compensation. No wonder they don't heal. Why would they want to?

Likewise, if you are committed in a relationship with a significant other and are not passionate or engaged, you need to focus on everything you like and enjoy about your partner. Whatever you water will grow. If you still cannot find enough to be authentically engaged in the relationship, there will never be a harvest. If this is the case, you may be wasting both your own and your partner's opportunities to flourish in a relationship with someone else.

Engaging in Your Summer

If you were a gold miner deep in a mineshaft digging for gold, most certainly you would encounter a lot more dirt, mud, and rocks than gold. The fact is that if the world had more gold than rocks, then the rocks would have been more valuable. Rare things have great value. In your daily life, you will most likely have more rocks, dirt, and mud than you have gold. Just like the miner, you must keep your eye on the gold. The miner is deep down in a wet, cold, and muddy shaft. If he did not keep his eye and focus on the gold, believing he will make a great find, how would he otherwise keep going?

See the beauty in nature and all around you, focus on solutions instead of problems, exterminate the weeds, and water the crop. Overcome negative obstacles (weeding) by focusing on the positive, the solution (watering). Be present and aware of your thoughts and attitude. If they are negative (weeds), exterminate them and replace them with a positive affirmation (water). Otherwise you're wasting your life. You're wasting your opportunity for happiness. Being authentic and true to your heart and watering, focusing on the positive—letting the positive occupy your mind—will let all the negativity and stress and misery in your life wither away.

The Metaphor of Fall

the Metal Element

*In the fall the farmer is rewarded for his work as he
accepts and receives his harvest. As nature teaches
him each year he learns from his success as well
as his failure to improve as a farmer and grow as
a man. He accepts the harvest he is dealt and the
change of the seasons to move on with ease.*

IN THE FOUR SEASONS METAPHOR, fall represents reaping the
harvest you've planted and tended over the spring and summer.
This is the time farmers are rewarded for their labor and reap their
crop. In the natural world, the trees draw their nutrients inside and
drop their fruits holding the seeds of new life, to the ground. Leaves
that have grown strong all summer change colors in a final show
before tumbling to the earth to nurture the soil for next spring.
Animals feast one final time before hibernation. Everything prepares
to rest in a state of dormancy for the winter.

When you embrace the Four Seasons system of living, fall is
a time for harvesting your life experiences. Harvest stands for
receiving, closure, and completing, as well as the ability to ask or
request (bringing it in). It is the season for accepting the passage of
time and that you are maturing; accepting and approving of yourself,
your own body, and your accomplishments; and understanding and

learning from your life experiences with empathy. Balance in fall is important because it allows you to grow and have accomplishments in your life, which are very important to your self-esteem and the way you feel about your life.

I believe that anyone who doesn't accomplish things, or who feels that he/she hasn't accomplished anything, won't feel good about him or herself. There are three ways this might happen. First, there are people who just don't recognize their accomplishments, or never feel they've done well enough. Perfectionists, for example, may do amazing things, but feel that nothing is quite good enough and therefore never feel accomplished at all. The second type of people may never give much thought to the needs they want to meet, and so they just go along through life never really watering anything, not having much to get excited about or expecting any harvest. And the third type of people don't feel worthy of a harvest. In any of these three scenarios, the people find themselves in the fall of life, as it happens when each day or each year is coming to an end, and as we get older, feeling like something is missing - like they haven't accomplished enough. Their self-esteem is affected, and they feel poorly about themselves. Typically, we don't feel great about everything we do in life. Everyone is likely to experience one or more of these cases at some point in life. Nothing can change what happens, but we can learn from the past. Every life experience is a harvest; a person with a balanced fall will learn lessons from these experiences to realize a harvest.

Each year, as the seasons turn from summer to fall, people often experience an acute awareness of time passing and of growing older. For those who perceive they have not reaped their harvests in life, fall is the time of sadness or desperation because they don't want to accept that time is passing by and life is happening in ways they may not have chosen. They bemoan that another year has passed with nothing to show for it. Anyone who has lived life a little has probably already found out that things do not always work out the way we expected them to. The difference between what is (reality) and what we expected is called "the gap." This gap is where we get stuck.

Not being able to accept reality is the greatest cause of tension, pain, and suffering. Let's say you got stuck in the mud. It's not what you expected or desired, but sometimes it happens. How you react to the situation is what determines if you will suffer or not. You could have any number of different reactions to getting stuck. One reaction is denial, thinking, "I'm not stuck in the mud." This reaction and denial of what is a reality will not get you anywhere, but will prolong the suffering. Another reaction is the victim, thinking, "My mother/boss/husband/teacher/newspaper/government/etc. told me to go this way, it's their fault they gave me wrong directions." The victims will not take responsibility for their situations but rather blame others, circumstances, or the world at large, hence never learning from their own mistakes. Opposite to the victim is the martyr, who chastises him or herself with thoughts like, "I'm so stupid; how could I do this again; I should have known better." The martyr keeps beating him/herself up over what he or she believes are unforgivable mistakes, thereby perpetuating the suffering and never learning or moving on. Not one of those three approaches will get you out of the mud. However, the final reaction will. Surrendering to the fact that you got stuck in the mud and accepting the reality of your situation (accepting what is) is the only way to move forward and learn from your past actions.

The moment something happens, it is in the past. The past is our teacher. This of course does not mean that you have to resign yourself to being stuck in the mud forever. Once you accept and learn, you can stay calm and present, and you can ask yourself what you can do right now to get yourself out of the mud. You can evaluate the situation and take action. Let's say you start moving your arms and legs to get out of the mud, when you realize that this action makes you sink deeper into the mud. You accept this fact and calmly consider other actions. Maybe you start screaming for help, but you realize that you are starting to lose your voice and no one seems to hear you or comes to your rescue. So you calmly stop yelling to preserve your voice so you will be able to yell if you see someone in the distance that could hear your calling. Now you stay calm and still until you come up with another solution or someone comes to your rescue. If you believe that everything that happens in your life has a purpose, then it is your job to learn the purpose and accept what happens to you.

This applies to other people in your life, too. A common misconception exists that if you love or care for someone, you need to feel bad for them and with them. When a loved one suffers, do you suffer with them? And if so, does it help your loved one? Probably not. Think about it - have you ever seen a toddler fall off a bike? There are two ways the child's parents might react. One way is to say, "You are okay; you are tough; I know you can do it." When parents react like this, the child stands up and looks startled for a moment, then realizes the fall wasn't that bad, is back on the bike a minute later, and the whole event is forgotten. The other reaction is when the parent comes rushing, nervous and upset, saying, "Ooh, poor baby, are you okay? Are you hurting? I am so sorry you fell." The child may be a little startled at first, but upon seeing this reaction from his or her parents, the child starts bawling and sobbing uncontrollably. This makes the parent even more emotional, which perpetuates the crying of the child. Of course, depending on the severity of the accident or injury, you may not tell a child with a broken leg to stand up and walk it off, but suffering with your child only makes things worse. You should always remain calm, present, empathetic, and accommodating.

The first Christmas after I moved to the United States, my girlfriend and I had just broken up, and I was all by myself in a new country, though not unhappily so. I was looking forward to a few days off. I was planning to go out and have a good meal, watch some movies on TV, and sleep in to catch up on my rest. I felt perfectly fine about my holiday plan until a patient asked what I was doing for Christmas. When I told her, she said, "Oh that's horrible! You are in a new country and have no friends or family to spend Christmas with." Upon hearing this I almost got tears in my eyes. I started to feel bad and sorry for myself, but only because she drew attention to the loneliness of my situation.

Another patient told me that in a class he was taking through his church on counseling married couples, he was instructed not to offer a tissue to the person he was counseling when they were crying, unless they asked for it, because the simple act could perpetuate the client's crying. Instead, staying calm and present, sincerely listening with empathy, and letting the person ask for what they needed would instill confidence that the client will be okay. Feeling sympathy or pity for someone cripples them and sends a message that they are not okay or able to take care of themselves. Feeling empathy for a fellow human, on the other hand, empowers them to learn, grow, and move on.

Mike, a fifty-four-year-old man, came to me with severe neck pain that radiated into his chest, down his upper back, into his right arm, outside the elbow, and into the thumb and index finger. The pain was severe and made it difficult for him to sleep - he woke up screaming in pain when he moved his neck the wrong way in his sleep. If he tried to turn his head to the right or extend his neck he felt a sharp stabbing pain, and the muscles in his lateral triceps had started to atrophy. An MRI had revealed a bulging disc in his neck that was putting pressure on his nerves and spinal cord. He had seen a neurosurgeon who recommended that he have surgery to fuse two vertebrae in his neck. At the time, Mike's wife was battling terminal cancer and his attention and all of his energy were directed towards finding a cure and spending quality time with her. Mike was considering going ahead with the surgery, but the timing was not good, so he came to me to see if I could help give him relief and address the injury holistically.

After examining him I found his tension was located in the scalene (neck muscles that bring the head forward and assist in shallow breathing) and the pectoralis minor (a deep upper chest muscle), which indicate a blockage in fall. I told him fall was related to the ability to accept life as it happens. Life does not always happen the way we want or expect, and accepting his wife's cancer did not mean that they had to resign to the cancer. Holding on to the past or not accepting what has happened will affect the breathing, cause grief and a form of mental or emotional constipation, as well as create tension in his neck and chest muscles. I mentioned that it was quite possible that his pain came from guilt (an emotion often accompanying a fall imbalance) and believing he had to suffer with her. Mike admitted that he felt guilty and regretted treating his wife poorly in the past. She was a very loving woman and Mike, who had done a lot of work on himself over the years, told me that throughout his life he had a hard time receiving love and kindness. Since his childhood he had adopted the belief system that he was not good enough or worthy of receiving love. Early in his marriage, he had fought and resisted his wife's love and giving, by treating her poorly and thus causing her pain. They had overcome these challenges together, but now that she had cancer, he felt horrible about his past actions and felt he was at fault.

I told him he needed to stop beating himself up and let go of the guilt. I asked him if he ever deliberately tried to cause his wife hurt or pain. Never, he said. And I asked if he could honestly look back on their past and say that he'd done the best he could with the time, energy, resources, state of mind, and belief systems he had at the time. Yes, he said he had. I said loving somebody does not mean you have to suffer with them. If two people suffer, then two people are stuck in the past and that does not help either one. I said it was important that he continued to seek treatments and cures for his wife, but he shouldn't pity her or feel sorry for her or himself. By showing her empathy, asking what he could do for her, listening to her, and accepting and receiving her as she was, he would be showing her love and empowering her. It was important that they both took this unwanted experience as an opportunity to love and support each other and to learn about life and themselves.

As I was talking to Mike, I released tension on the lung and large intestine meridians in his arm, chest, upper back, and neck. As Mike accepted the new belief system - that supporting his wife did not include suffering with her or feeling guilty - the tension and pain in his neck was released. When he left he was almost pain-free and able to turn his head. I told him I was happy to give him relief, but that it wouldn't last unless he stopped suffering and feeling guilty about his wife's condition and learned to accept what life brought them.

Balance in Fall

Whether it's what you want or not, fall will bring a harvest. There are no mistakes, only learning opportunities. Everything in life happens for a reason. Learning, understanding, and accepting what life brings, with empathy for others and ourselves, is what makes us mature, grow, and move on. To be successful during this season, you must accept your circumstances without blame or guilt. Beating yourself up, or having a pity party will not change the reality of what is.

The balanced fall is full of empathy. These people nurture and support others without pity. They care for others and themselves with love and empathy and without taking on the suffering of others. These people provide substance, strength, and endurance, pulling together all of their resources for harvesting. They are hard-working, unselfish, supportive people who finish the job. They are calm, accepting, understanding, and empathetic with themselves and others, even when things do not work out the way they expected. When everything works out the way the balanced fall expected or anticipated, they are humble in their success and victory. They give unconditionally, but are still good at receiving without feeling they have to reciprocate. They know how to ask for or request what they need from an individual without demanding or making the person feel guilty. They are sensitive and empathetic to other's feelings and needs and often very intuitive. Other people feel comfortable with the balanced fall and seek them up for counsel, confession, or support.

People who are balanced in fall know how to make peace in confrontations because they can empathize with both sides and understand that every story has multiple sides. When the balanced fall finds a word they don't understand, they look it up in the dictionary. They do not assume anything, but rather come to conclusions by gathering information and asking questions to get a full understanding. They accept what life brings them, are good at learning from their past mistakes, and can let go of past expectations without regrets. They accept and surrender to reality (what is). They can handle unexpected changes of circumstances with ease - they learn, move on, and go with the flow. Change is inevitable; that is a fact. Nothing will ever be the way it was. Not accepting the truth of life will cause us to get "stuck" in fall.

Balanced emotions for the season are feeling calm, present, and empathetic. Anytime a person is not balanced in fall, he or she will experience negative emotions of either a hypoactive nature, such as depression, apathy, indifference, or rejection, or emotions of a hyperactive nature, such as anxiety, sadness, regret, guilt, or grief. These can be your most important clues to where an imbalance exists in your life. A person with an imbalance in the fall will tend to have too little fall or too much fall. Remember in Chinese philosophy: too little and too much are both harmful.

Too little fall is often characterized by the following patterns:

- Often beating themselves up and blaming themselves for everything.
- Often regretting their actions, chastising themselves by constantly saying or thinking, "I should have…."
- Not feeling worthy enough to receive.
- Never feeling good enough, rejecting themselves, lacking self-approval and acceptance.
- Having a hard time asking for or requesting help.
- Trying to please everyone and feeling guilty if they did not.
- Often feeling they have to take care of and share others' pain and suffering.
- Never having any time for themselves.

- Feeling unlovable or unaccepted, thus separating themselves from family, friends and co- workers, not feeling worthy of being included. In an extreme, acting antisocial.
- Never learning hence continuing to do the same mistakes over and over.
- Having a difficult time accepting gifts or compliments without having to reciprocate immediately (which makes it a trade rather than receiving a gift).
- When exhausted being full of self-rejection, indifference, and apathy. Hence ceasing to care and let go of everything.
- Often suffering from irregular bowel movement, mostly tending to have loose stool and excessive bowel movements.

Too much fall is often characterized by the following patterns:

- Inability to accept what life brings, taking no responsibility but rather blaming others and circumstances.
- Being selfish takers that attempt to gain at the expense of others.
- Coming across as lacking empathy, acceptance, or understanding for others.
- Being in a state of self-pity, and not caring about the tribulations, unfairness, or injustices suffered by others.
- Demanding that their requests are met and manipulating to get their way using guilt.
- Often believing they are entitled.
- Often needy to the point that it drains others, frequently hungering for and asking for compliments, as if they can never get enough of them.
- Never learning, hence continuing to make the same mistakes over and over.
- Tending to be extremely possessive with loved ones, family members, co-workers, and friends, often using guilt trips and manipulation to get what they want.

- Assuming others should know what they want and expecingt they should give it to them.
- Being overly emotional, sad, and often weeping for themselves.
- Saying life is not fair and not accepting what is.
- Typically holding on to and grieving the past. Grieving and holding on to expectations that did not come true, instead of accepting what is.
- Tending to have irregular bowel movement, mostly constipated.

In addition to these emotional and behavioral symptoms, an imbalance in fall may also cause physical symptoms. The following descriptions come from the ancient Chinese wisdom and the writings in *Huang Di Nei Ching*, the Yellow Emperor, (with a few of my own additions) on the organs, meridians, human functions, and associations that relate to balance or imbalance of the fall and metal element.

The Large Intestine Meridian and Organ System

"The Large Intestine transmits and drains the wastes."
–Su Wen

The large intestine Chi creates development and change (growth). Movement and moving on are necessary for growth. The large intestine also stores and eliminates the waste. As mentioned earlier, the Chinese did not separate the physical body and functions from the mind and the emotions. Just as a man could be physically constipated, he could be emotionally and mentally constipated by holding onto old crap, literally being stuck in the past. Any person who has a hard time letting go or accepting change, constantly regrets his actions, wallows in his own suffering, and holds onto how life should have been, is mentally and emotionally constipated. Or on the other extreme, any person who rejects (the equivalent of mental and emotional diarrhea), shows apathy, does not care about what happened, or fails to acknowledge the need to learn from the situation also shows sign of a large intestine imbalance. A person with a fall imbalance may have difficulties harvesting their own energy. This may show up as digestion problems, irregular bowel syndrome, constipation, and/or diarrhea.

LARGE INTESTINE MERIDIAN

The Arm Yang Large Intestine Meridian

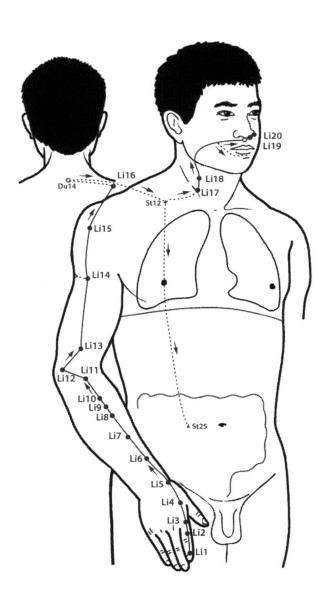

When Kevin, a forty-nine-year-old man, came to my office with a tweaked lower back, I found a blockage in his large intestine meridian to be the underlying cause. He told me he woke up in the mornings with a stiff back and after bending over his back pain got worse. When I looked at him, I could see his spine was leaning to the left due to spasm in lower back muscles. He had seen his family doctor and took a day off from work, and at first he felt a little better. But the injury flared up again and lingered and was especially bad in the mornings, making it hard for Kevin to get out of bed or go to work. The pain was located in his left lower back at the large intestine reflex points just above the sacrum and hip bones, and he had a tender spot on the left large intestine alarm point located two inches lateral to his belly button. I told Kevin that the large intestine often experiences problems when we're upset about something in our life, when we hold onto things, or when we have a hard time accepting circumstances.

Kevin was a firefighter and liked his job, but his true passion was being the pole vaulting coach to a local high school. He himself had been a pole vaulter in high school and college. His department had recently changed the shifts from twenty-four to forty-eight hours, making it harder for Kevin to be there for the high school kids as much as he wanted and believed he should. Prior to the shift change, he already was having a hard time accepting how his team had performed at the state championship the previous season. He regretted the way he prepared the team and kept beating himself up for not producing better results and not being there for the kids at all times. With the shift change, he would need to be away from the kids for more than forty-eight hours at a time, and he no longer believed he could be successful coaching. As the new season was about to start, he said this would probably be the last year he coached. I told him that when you get stuck, you only have three choices: accept the situation just as it is, change, or remove yourself. Kevin said he had already accepted the shift change and there was nothing he could do about it. He would not remove himself and change careers. He liked his job, the income, and benefits, and he was close to retirement.

As I started to release trigger and large intestine acupuncture points in the spastic muscles of his lower back and abdomen, I talked to him about the cause of his pain. I asked, "What about changing the way you think and what you believe?"

Kevin looked at me like he had no idea what I was talking about. So I explained, "Is it not true that you did the best you could with the time and resources you had at the time?"

He said, "Yes, I love to coach."

"Is it not true that you did what you believed best at the time you coached last season?" Kevin nodded in agreement.

"Does the high school have any other coaches that know pole vaulting as you do?" "No," he said. "No one else knows as much about pole vaulting as I do."

I continued, "If you stop coaching are you helping yourself or the kids?" "Neither."

When belief systems don't serve us, we have to change them. I told Kevin, "You have to stop believing you are not good enough. Stop believing you do not have enough time to do well enough. Start thinking and believing that any time you have is a blessing that allows you to teach and pass on to the kids your knowledge and passion for pole vaulting. Start thinking how to get the most out of the time you have." I told him to change his definition of success. Success is not state championship gold medals, but rather doing the best you can with the resources you have. Learning from what works and what does not work. Using past results, win or loss, to learn and improve. Success is doing something you love and enhancing the lives of others. When I finished releasing his tension, Kevin got off the table free of pain and tension and full of excitement for coaching.

The Lung Meridian and Organ System

"Man's breathing connects the Chi of heaven and earth in order to form the true Chi of the body."
–Zangshi Leijing

The lungs receive pure Chi from the atmosphere, acting as a prime minister that regulates the rhythm of the body. Respiration constantly fills us with energy, thereby supporting all the other organs. The lungs represent a balance between receiving/inhaling and giving/exhaling. This is a perfect illustration of the balance in nature. As we inhale we receive oxygen, as we exhale all the plant life receives carbon dioxide. The plants produce oxygen and need carbon dioxide. Humans need oxygen and produce carbon dioxide. This balance is a win-win. Any imbalance a person may have in giving and receiving is related to the lungs and the lung meridian.

Any respiratory problem or problem receiving on any level physically, mentally, or emotionally shows signs of a lung imbalance. Accepting is a form of receiving—accepting what is (inhaling), and letting go (exhaling) are functions of the lungs. Learning and understanding from life situations is another form of receiving and also a function of the lungs.

LUNG MERIDIAN

The Arm Tai Yin Lung Meridian

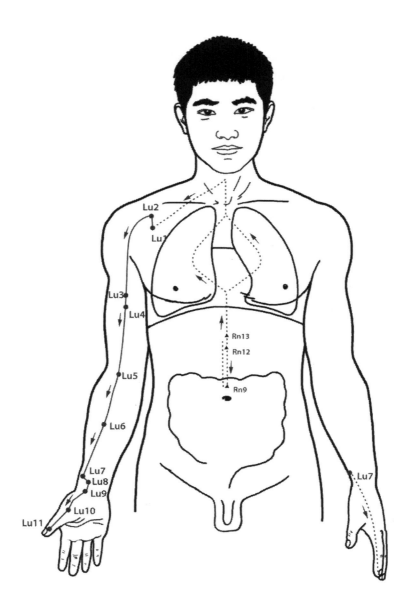

Debra, a fifty-three-year-old woman, came to my office with pain in her left front shoulder, upper arm, and biceps. Her ability to reach behind her with her arm was limited and moving her arm in this direction caused her sharp pain in her shoulder. I asked her what caused her injury, because everything always has a cause and an effect. She wasn't sure at first but thought it could be related to her and her husband moving two times in one year. She had to do most of the packing and lifting because her husband, who had Lou Gehrig's disease, was unable to help her. They had moved twice because as his disease progressed, they needed a space that was wheelchair accessible and could accommodate his care. Their old house had stairs, so they moved to a rental while they remodeled a one-story house they bought. She stated that she was working as well at taking care of her husband, who needed more help as time passed. She also took care of their son's two children because their mother was not around. All this was going on when she started to experience pain and restricted movement in her left shoulder.

I found all Debra's tension in her biceps, shoulder, and chest muscles (deltoid, coracobrachialis, and pectoralis minor)—all common areas for a blockage in the lung meridian. Even though she did not experience any respiratory or lung problems, an imbalance between giving and receiving is often a symptom of the lung meridian. I asked her what she was doing for herself, and she told me there was no time for her to do anything for herself. She was trying to do everything for everyone else, and they expected her to keep doing more and more. Debra was trying to please everyone and did not want to accept that she could not do it all. She told me that her husband was upset with her for taking care of their grandkids. She felt bad for her son's situation and felt guilty if she did not help him with the grandchildren. I said she could not take care of everyone and everything at the expense of her own needs. Her physical pain was her body telling her to stop. I told her there is a reason why flight attendants tell you to put the oxygen mask on yourself before you help someone else—or both of you could die. You have to take care of yourself first, and balance your giving with receiving. As I released all Debra's muscle tension and restored her shoulder range of motion, I said it is very important that she take time out for herself and take care of herself or her body will continue to break down and she could bring disease on herself. Debra understood the cause of her pain, accepted that she needed to take care of herself and that she could not please everyone else at all times. When she left, she could move her arm freely and her pain had almost completely vanished.

Any symptom of pain, dysfunction, or disease is related to an accumulation of tension and a blockage of circulation. The following symptoms are commonly related to a fall imbalance and a blockage of circulation in the large intestine or lung meridians:

- Coughing, asthma, and bronchitis.
- Spasm of the throat.
- Pneumonia.
- Allergies.
- Lymphatic congestion.
- Swelling or dryness of mucous membranes.
- Mucus drainage.
- Nasal congestion.
- Dry skin, eczema, psoriasis, and rashes.
- Constipation.
- Bloating.
- Diarrhea.
- Lower back pain or rigidity (lumbago).
- Chest and upper back pain.
- Shoulder and deltoid problems.
- Tennis elbow (lateral epicondylitis).
- Pain in thumb and or index finger.
- Neck pain.
- Tension headaches.

Other Fall Imbalance Clues

Geographical Direction:
West. The sun sets in the west as a day is over and it's a time to gather in. Some people with an imbalance in fall might feel either better or worse when they travel west. Seeing the sun go down and accepting another day went by can be stressful to individuals who do not think they accomplished enough.

Color:
White. The color associated with the metal element and the fall is white. An imbalance in the element is present when the hue of the patient's face is white or lifeless. An individual might have a preference for white, dress and surround themselves with this color, or have an aversion or strong disliking for it. The choice of interior design and color of a person's living or working space may reflect a seasonal imbalance.

Climate Relationship:
Dry. Excessive dryness can affect the balance of fall. If a person dislikes a dry climate, or on the other hand has an unusual fondness for a dry climate, it can indicate a fall imbalance. Symptoms might include a dryness of the skin or mucous membranes, especially of the nasal passages or large intestine. In today's environment of excessive positive ions, due to electrical machinery, heaters, air conditioners, etc., the air often becomes very dry, affecting the skin and mucous membranes and causing intestinal elimination dysfunctions, such as constipation.

People with an imbalanced fall tend to be more sensitive to an excess of dryness and prone to these symptoms.

Sound Relationship:
Weeping. Some people's voices have an unnatural, incessant weeping sound, not necessarily accompanied with real tears, but rather the

sound of tears. They sound like they're whining. This becomes more pronounced at times when this person feels insecure and suffers from a lack of confidence or self-pity, which commonly occurs when they are not capable of accepting a life situation. On the other hand, a person completely lacking an ability to weep, regardless of what is happening, and comes across as being cold and apathetic also has a fall imbalance. A person who can cry at the drop of a hat, cry watching movies, or is unable to weep is expressing a fall imbalance.

Sense Relationship:
Nose/Olfactory. The sense of smell is affected when fall is not properly balanced. An extremely keen sense of smell and the inability to smell both reflect a fall imbalance.

Human Tissue Relationship:
Nerves. In the human body, nerves are responsible for reacting to physical stimuli, linking the brain with the other parts of our bodies. In Chinese medicine, the nerves are also responsible for a person's sensitivity to the environment, situations, and other people—like intuition or a sixth sense. A balanced fall represents sensitivity, intuition, and the ability to adapt to others and the environment. A hyper-sensitivity with an inability to shield and protect themselves from other people's emotions and situations, or a hypo-sensitivity where the person is ignorant to others' needs and their environment, both represent a fall imbalance. You don't want to be so sensitive that you wind up in an institution because you pick up everything, and you don't want to be so insensitive that you lack empathy or don't even care about what's going on around you.

Body Orifice Relationship:
Nose. The nose and lungs are closely related - breathing (receiving oxygen) is normally done through the nose before the air arrives at the lungs. Many problems affecting the nose have a different bearing on the lungs and large intestine. The function of nasal apparatus is

to receive energy through breathing and eliminate the unwanted, a function in common with the lungs and large intestine.

External Physical Manifestation:
The external physical manifestation of the metal element is *skin and body hair*. The skin is an organ unto itself and is in fact considered the largest organ of the body. In a sense, the skin represents a third lung. The skin breathes, just as the lungs do. Many forms of skin problems, such as eczema, psoriasis, and rashes, reflect an imbalance in the body often coinciding with asthma. The body also uses the skin to eliminate waste products, and even more so when other mechanisms of elimination become either diminished or over- burdened. Toxic elements are typically eliminated from the body through: water vapor (lungs); urine (kidneys); bowels (large intestine), and mucous (nasal secretion). When these avenues of escape become over-taxed (because of excessive toxicity), or when they fail to function efficiently, the body resorts to using the skin as a port of elimination. Elimination of these by-products causes various eruptions and lesions of the skin in the form of boils, pimples, carbuncles, etc. The skin has traditionally been considered a primary indicator of body toxicity levels. Extremely dry skin can also be an indicator of overall body dehydration. Coincidentally, an excess of body hair or a lack thereof (in men) indicates a fall imbalance as well.

Body Secretion:
Mucous. All surfaces of the body that are exposed to the air are lined with mucous membranes, not just for the purpose of lubrication, but also for protection. Dryness of the throat and nose, coughing, difficulty in breathing, aching of the lungs, and constipation of the large intestine are all indicators of dysfunction of the mucous membranes. The presence of a constant nasal drip or suffering loose bowl movement can also be symptoms of a fall imbalance.

Flavor:

Spicy and Pungent. This flavor is commonly found in cheeses, curries, and peppers. A person who craves this food taste indicates a fall imbalance. In moderate amounts these ingredients can help open up the lungs, throat, and pores of the skin to help correct minor imbalances.

How to Achieve Balance in Fall

In the Four Seasons metaphor our harvest is synonymous with accepting, learning, asking, and receiving. The ability to do these four things is essential to balance in the fall season, but they aren't always easy.

Accepting what is, accepting reality, is easy when things happen just the way you expected or desired. It becomes much harder when the unexpected or unacceptable happens. Many people, in the face of unavoidable and unpreventable hardships, want to resist. They might say, "This is not right; this is not fair." But how can you argue that something shouldn't have happened when it did? How do you know something is supposed to happen? When it does! How do you know something is not supposed to happen? When it doesn't!

This means that I believe that everything that is supposed to happen will happen when it is meant to happen. I believe God's will is done. Not mine or yours or anyone else's. How could anyone know for a fact what's best for them? They can't! When it comes to accepting reality, you really have no choice. If you do not accept, learn, and move on, you will get stuck in the past and life will go on without you anyway. The longer you are stuck, the longer you suffer, and nothing can change what has already happened. Your only choice for health and harmony is to accept that you are exactly where you are supposed to be, doing exactly what you are supposed to do, and learning exactly what you are supposed to learn.

If you focus on what you can learn from every life experience, desired or undesired, then there are no mistakes. The only mistake is failure to learn. If we always do the best we can based on time, resources, and present belief systems, how could we possibly do anything more than that? If we always do our best and always learn, then we will continue to grow and mature. This is true success: the more we learn the greater sense of accomplishment and the greater sense of self-esteem.

It is essential that we ask and request from others to have our needs met. To have closure, understanding, and empathy in any relationship, asking - and not assuming - is essential. We cannot assume that our loved ones, friends, and co-workers should know what we need. Everyone lives in his or her own universe and has his/her own reality. There is no way we can fully know or understand why someone did or did not do something; it is simply our assumption. By asking and requesting from others without being demanding or inflicting guilt trips, we stand a much greater chance of harvesting our needs.

When the harvest is ripe, the farmer has to go out and bring it in. It doesn't get into the barn by itself, and if left out on the fields, the crops would rot.

I remember with fondness as a teenager in the 1970s, spending some time on a farm in the summers. When it was time to bring in the hay in the late summer, the farmer asked neighbors, friends, and relatives to help bring it into the barn. The great satisfaction came after the hard labor of bringing the dried hay into the barn before the summer rain came down. Lying on my back in the hay in the barn, while listening to the rain hit the tin roof and smelling hay and the scent of summer rain, was the real satisfaction. To successfully bring in a harvest one often needs to ask for assistance; everyone helping out will experience a harvest in the accomplishment.

With accomplishments (harvesting) comes self-esteem and a greater sense of worthiness. Take time to feel good about what you accomplish. Practice receiving; help, gifts, and compliments by accepting them and just saying thank you. Not receiving gifts could be a very selfish act, because in doing so you rob the giver of the joy of giving. Think about how you feel if someone rejects your gift. Like everything else, gifts come to us for a reason. You might have spent years working on a field without yielding a harvest, and then an unexpected gift comes from nowhere. The universal law of sowing and reaping does not have set rules on where the harvest will come from. It just says, "As you sow, so shall you reap."

There once was a man of strong faith who lived in a small town that was getting flooded. As all the townspeople started to evacuate, he just stood in front of his house and watched. A truck drove by the man and the driver yelled out, "Hop on, the flood is coming."

The man replied, "No, thank you, I am waiting for God to save me." Hours later the man was still standing with water up to his waist and a small boat came by. The boat driver yelled out, "Hop aboard, the flood is rising fast. You will drown."

The man answered, "No thank you, I am waiting for my God to rescue me." The flood kept rising and the man had moved up to his rooftop when a rescue helicopter flew by. The pilot threw down a rope and yelled, "Grab on or you will drown." The man yelled back, "No, thank you, I have faith my God will save me." The man did indeed drown, and upon entering the pearly gates of heaven he told God, "Oh Lord, how could you forsake me? I had faith and waited for you to rescue me."

God, slightly annoyed, answered, "I sent you a truck, a boat, and a helicopter, but you would not go."

When you block a gift, you block the universal blessings of sowing and reaping. How do you know you are worthy of a gift? You know when it is given to you! Do not stop another blessing.

The Metaphor of Winter 冬

the Water Element

In the winter the farmer stores and preserves the excess
from his harvest, so it will feed him and his family over
the cold, unproductive winter. It is a time for maintaining
equipment, rest, recuperation, and inward activity.

IN NATURE, WINTER IS ASSOCIATED with shutting down. Trees lose their leaves and suspend growth in a state of dormancy, conserving their energy. Hibernating animals retreat to their dens so they may also conserve their energy while temperatures are cold and fresh food is scarce. Humans, too, slow down a bit. We tend to be less active than in the joyful times of summer and the bustling times of the fall harvest. The harvested crop has been preserved and stored for the coming cold temperatures and long, dark nights.

In the Four Seasons System, winter is also associated with a shutting down of sorts; after taking in the harvest in the fall (reaping what you've sown), what you so carefully nurtured throughout the spring and summer must be retained. The knowledge you may have gained from this process is retained, or stored up, so you can better plant and nurture the following spring.

Everything in your life has a winter phase. The end of the day, like winter, is a time to rest and recover from a full day of work and retain what you learned. You must rest to take care of your body and recover your strength so you're ready to do it all over again the following day. Evaluating the outcome of your day—the harvest your seeds yielded allows you to make adjustments in your activities and behaviors so your results improve next time. Winter is also about remembering and processing the lessons you've learned, so you can pull from this knowledge in the spring.

Balance in Winter

Winter is the end of a cycle; some things will die, and some things will survive into the next spring. Within every ending are the seeds of a new beginning. To continue your growth in your next spring (beginning), you must have prior knowledge and wisdom to draw upon. You must have the resources (energy) to start anew, and without conservation in the tough times, without taking enough time to rest and recover, you will not have the strength to plant and nurture new seeds.

As we get older, our life progresses farther and farther into winter. As we age we need to be smarter and wiser, surrendering to our limits and age. Everything will come to an end, and one day our life will end. A person balanced winter is not reckless with his life, nor is he afraid of dying. Rather the balanced winter has faith, believing he cannot die a minute too early or a minute too late.

When Mike, the patient who I'd helped with various issues over the years, referred to in the previous chapter, came to see me again for a visit, he had recently experienced some very tough times. Mike's wife Margo had beat cancer twice when the cancer returned a third time. This last time it had spread throughout her whole body and she did not have long to live. Mike and Margo had sought all forms of healing. When they both accepted that the end was inevitable, they sought spiritual counseling and help for Margo to die in peace. Mike, Margo, and her parents were all receiving help to let go. Mike had accepted that Margo was going to die. They prayed, and talked, and spent the last hours together as Margo passed away in her sleep. Mike believed Margo was in a better place, without suffering and in complete peace. He believed that she taught him and everyone else everything she was supposed to teach. He believed she had learned everything she was supposed to learn. He realized that everything Margo taught him and gave to him was still there and could never be lost. She had graduated, and he was still here because he was not done yet. Mike's neck and arm pain mentioned in the previous chapter had improved an amazing 95 percent. He was regaining strength and muscle development in his right arm and surgery to his neck was no longer a consideration. This time Mike came to see me with a new pain along the spine in his mid-back and in his right calf, as well as right foot pain and numbness. All the tension was located along the bladder meridian and in the winter season.

Mike had come to the realization that his life as he knew it had come to an end (winter) and a new beginning (spring) was yet to come. This was a time to be still, to remember Margo with fondness, and to remember everything he had learned. But Mike seemed to be rushing things. Mike admitted that he did not like to come home to an empty house. He had some fear about living life alone, having recently lost his wife, and it was harder when he came home and she wasn't there. He did not like having no control, not knowing what was next, or not knowing when his new life would start. Impatiently, he had started several business activities and spread himself too thin. Mike felt anxious and an urgency to get on with his new life. He admitted that he'd struggled with this same pattern in the past: when cycles came to an end, he avoided being still and quiet. He used to immediately dive into new ventures, get overly busy and try to forget by drinking. This time he once again forced the start of a new spring before he was done with winter.

I told Mike that a winter imbalance could be related to reckless behavior or fear, and it could cause restlessness, impatience, and an inability to rest. Mike needed to be still, to recover, to remember everything he had learned, to appreciate Margo, and to reflect on the beauty of her life. He wanted to write a book about Margo's life, her fight with cancer, and her graceful death. But he told me he felt impatient and afraid he was running out of time.

I pointed out that if everything happened for a reason—a truth Mike had already learned about life—then how could he possibly run out of time? I said if he was supposed to write a book about Margo, nothing could stop him. The time of stillness, remembering, and reflecting on Margo and his life with her would cure his memories and help him write the book in due time. Mike's mid-back pain, right calf pain, and foot numbness disappeared as I released tension in spastic muscles. He realized that he needed to remain calm, still, and patient and avoid rushing into new projects before he was at peace.

People balanced in winter draw from their inner strength and are reserved and tactful. They are quiet, still listeners with good memories for details, such as names, numbers, dates, and places. They keep in contact with old friends and family. They are cautious in preserving their resources and seldom take on more than they can handle, and they do not make promises they cannot keep. They know their limits. Balanced winters are concerned, but not overly so, with security and high-quality performance. They are grateful for their accomplishments and show their appreciation and loyalty towards their spouses, mates, co-workers, or teammates. They are present, quiet, and sincere when listening, so that they can truly hear the needs of others. They are precise, organized, and detail-oriented. As great keepers, they take excellent care of their finances, personal belongings, car, and home.

They are grateful for their health and take good care of their own body with exercises, rest, and diet. People balanced in winter stay in shape and age gracefully and therefore look youthful. To protect themselves from the elements, winters dress practically in clothes that are both comfortable and suitable to the purpose and weather. The balanced winters can relax and rest and they value taking time off to recuperate and re-charge.

People balanced in winter exhibit common sense and an ability to appreciate and profit from their experiences. They remember lessons learned in the past, so they do not have to re-live and re-learn them. Wisdom is knowledge put to use. Therefore, in keeping with the wisdom of winter, they preserve (remember and appreciate) the knowledge they've acquired. They've learned tough times, like the hardships of winter, do not last, but tough people do. Remembering that things have worked out in the past helps winters trust in their ability to stay calm and still in the midst of difficulties and hardship. The balanced winters have an abundance of wisdom and patience. The word "patience" means to endure, to be still, to wait in quiet, not to hurry and rush.

When they face a tough life situation, balanced winter people assess the situation and ask themselves if they have any control over the situation. If they do, then they have the courage to take action. If not, then they remain still and cautious until there is something they can do about it. The balanced winters have amazing willpower and an ability to endure tough times by having faith. Experience has taught them to endure, because everything always worked out in the past. They stay calm, still, and patient, preserving their resources and carefully waiting until there is a new dawn or new spring.

The "Serenity Prayer" is a perfect description of a balanced fall and winter:

"God grant me the serenity
to accept (Fall) the things I cannot change;
the courage (Winter) to change the things I can;
and the wisdom (Winter) to know the difference."
–Reinhold Niebuhr

Trying to control things we cannot control drains our energy.

In contrast, the imbalanced winters are restless and impatient and lack satisfaction. An individual with a winter imbalance has an overactive fight and flight response. This is the reason they are jumpy, fidgety and hyper-vigilant, often having problems "turning off," relaxing, and sleeping. They rarely feel rested when waking up from a night's sleep. They are overly critical of themselves and others, often type-A personalities who are never satisfied. For this reason they are unable to be still or rest. They are often too serious in what they do, forgetting to live and have fun.

Julie, a sixteen-year-old ballet dancer and straight-A student, was a perfectionist who believed that she was never good enough. She loved ballet and desperately wanted to succeed. But she constantly beat herself up and was never satisfied or able to rest. When she entered my office, she was slouching with her shoulders rounded forward—the body language of defeat. Julie came in with pain in the back portion of her rib cage that was aggravated when she took a deep breath or raised her arms over her head, as she did frequently in her ballet dance. Her mood was very serious and she wasn't smiling. Winter is related to fear and Julie was scared of not being successful as a ballet dancer. Ballet was her life, but she was fearful of not being chosen in her auditions for the ballet schools and that she was running out of time, getting too old, and as a result got nervous at her auditions. I told her the pain in her back was caused by tension from fear of not being good enough and worry of failure, as well as not breathing in a deep, calm, and relaxed way.

"It sounds like you keep repeating the same pattern, every time you have an audition you freeze up, get fearful, nervous, and tense. Your dancing doesn't show that you are having fun or loving what you are doing." I asked her who her favorite ballet dancer was, and she named a famous Russian ballerina. I asked her why she favored this ballerina, and she replied that her dance was beautiful, effortless, and could bring tears to your eyes.

"What do you think will help you make it in your auditions?" I asked. "To practice more and harder," she answered.

I explained that more practice is not necessarily better. When you are tense and fearful of making mistakes, when you breathe shallow or hold your breath, dancing is exhausting, not beautiful or effortless.

More practice with fear of failure on your mind will only groom your bad habits and lead to more of the same results. When you are exhausted and keep practicing more and harder, it is like beating on a dead horse. I said that the underlying reason her injury would not heal and kept flaring up was because of the stress from being stuck in a pattern and belief system. I asked her how many girls showed up for the auditions. Twenty to thirty, she said.

"And how many make it?" I asked.

"One or two," she replied.

"I bet the ones they pick look like dancing is effortless," I said. Julie nodded her head in agreement. I told her that she could not control how the teachers favored her dancing or how the other girls danced. She could not change past dance moves or make her next dance move perfect. But the only failure is a failure to learn. If she did not make an audition, beating herself up and then doing it the same way next time would not make her succeed. The only way she could fail on another audition was if she did not have fun during her dance. She could only control the present dance move, her breathing, and her thoughts. If she stayed present in her breathing and got connected with her heart, her dance would become effortless and fun. I told her never to forget why she was dancing, to have fun, and appreciate and be grateful for every moment she got to dance. If she did this, her dance would be more beautiful than ever and everything else would take care of itself. Julie got up from my treatment table without any pain in her mid-back with deep breathing or lifting her arms over her head. She left my office walking tall and confident with a smile on her face.

Imbalanced winters do not believe they can rest until they are done. The problem is that we are never done. Think about it. Your inbox will never be empty. Just when you think you've got everything done, something else will drop in. If you clean your house or do your laundry, just as you finish, you will find another dirty sock or someone left a dirty dish in the sink. I was told they'd never finish painting the Golden Gate Bridge because as soon as they get done, they have to start over again. If you believe you cannot rest until you are all done, then you will not rest until you die. If you live like this, then your life will be like the cartoon of the donkey with a carrot dangling from a stick in front him. The donkey keeps walking to the carrot, but the carrot moves with him, always just out of reach. A life like this will never be satisfying, and this relentless pursuit without rest will cause injury, disease, and probably a premature death.

There once was a man praying out loud, "God, please, give me patience, and give it to me now." That was not very wise. Trust me. If patience is a lesson, understand that it will not be learned fast. If you learned it right away, then what did you learn? An imbalanced winter will attempt to control things they have no control over, trying to force things to happen before it is time. In doing this they will exhaust too much of their resources, hence jeopardizing their own health and well-being.

When people are balanced in the winter season they are feeling calm, present, safe, cautious, careful, still, patient, courageous, and secure. Any time a person is not balanced in winter, he or she will experience negative emotions or feelings of a hypo-active nature, such as depression, urgency, or recklessness. Or they will experience emotions or feeling of a hyper-active nature, such as anxiety, fear, or terror. The negative emotion of extreme fear has an obvious survival value, it is sudden and temporary. It alerts us to sudden danger. A balanced winter will find will-power to live and muster the energy to take necessary actions to survive.

They become calm and courageous to take action and escape from danger (flight) or they will stay put to combat it (fight). If a person remains excessively fearful he or she would be paralyzed and immobile, unable to overcome the danger. Most individuals with winter imbalance experience urgency or a fearful anxiety that is less extreme but chronic. This fear is often imagined or unrealistic. A Winter imbalance is characterized by fear with an inability to move forward or urgency with an inability to be still. This state of mind is mostly perceived, but never the less real to the person that experience it.

Your emotions and feelings can be your most important feedback to where an imbalance exists in your life. A person with an imbalance in the winter will tend to have symptoms of too little winter and / or too much winter. Remember in Chinese philosophy: too little and too much are both harmful.

Too little winter is often characterized by the following patterns:

- Being careless, reckless, or negligent with their own health, relationships, finances, and personal belongings.
- Taking too many risks.
- Always experiencing a state of urgency with inability to be still or rest.
- Experiencing sleep deprivation, too busy to get enough sleep.
- Taking one's own health for granted, eating a poor diet, and not getting enough rest.
- Not spending enough quality time with spouse, friends, or children and often taking them for granted.
- Not taking time to sincerely listen and hear the needs of their loved ones, friends, or associates.
- Are never satisfied, so they take on too much spreading themselves too thin, and the quality of their work ultimately suffers.
- Always having too much to do and claiming there's never enough time in the day.
- Making promises that can't be kept.
- Spending more than they can afford.
- Tending to overdo it when exercising (over training) and not taking time to recover.
- Experiencing pain or injury and continuing to exercising anyway.
- Being restless and unable to be still, pacing back and forth, tapping their fingers or feet.
- Having minds that are never still, always racing.
- Always checking voicemail, text messages, or e-mail 24/7.

- Having difficulty sleeping through the night, tossing and turning, their racing minds keeping them awake.

Wes was a thirty-seven-year-old high-power venture capitalist who came to see me for a multitude of problems. Wes was a type-A personality, driven and hard working. He was doing business with Asia and Europe and needed to make and take phone calls at all times from all time zones. He started working 5:00 in the morning and still checked e-mail, voice mail, and text messages until he passed out in bed at 11:00 p.m. With his cell phone on his night table, he slept restlessly, sweating, tossing, and turning all night. It's no wonder he was exhausted when the alarm went off.

He complained of exhaustion, cramps in his feet and calves, low back spasms with sharp pain, neck pain at base of head, and sinus headaches and pressure. Wes did not know how to relax. In fact he had a hard time even sitting still. His foot tapped the whole time he was telling me about his problems. He was in a constant fight-or-flight mode. He was sweating and restless in my office, often came late or missed his appointment, and always kept looking at his wristwatch during the treatment to see if it was time to leave. Most visits he jumped up, saying he had to leave even though there was five minutes left of his visit. As I worked on Wes's tight muscles I could literally feel how they tightened up and twitched every time his cell phone beeped. His body had adapted a fight-or-flight reflex to the sound of his cell phone. In any half hour visit the phone beeped up to ten times. I was able to give Wes relief but explained that he needed to make changes in his lifestyle or his health and life were in jeopardy. If he did not learn how to relax, recognize his limits, and find balance between work and rest, his symptoms would persist. Wes still has not changed his ways, and he is still coming to see me for relief of his symptoms.

Too much winter is often characterized by the following patterns:

- Being excessively fearful over their own and loved ones' health and life.

- Having excessive worry and fear about finances, life, and losing control.
- Often having phobias about heights, water, germs, new people, new things, sexual performance dysfunction, closed spaces, the dark, and death.
- Hovering over and being overprotective of their children.
- Lacking the necessary courage, being paralyzed and unable to take any action or move on.
- Seeming to have too much time on their hands.
- Being afraid to start new things.
- Appearing sluggish and feeling the need for frequent naps.
- Often having scary nightmares.
- Being afraid to spend money, always saving up for a rainy day that never comes.
- Feeling too tired to exercise and always having an excuse.
- Obsessing over details, and often trying to control things.

Asha, a forty-six-year-old woman, came to see me for an Achilles tendonitis; she had pain and numbness in her left heel and foot. I found her blockage to be in the kidney and bladder meridians and told her these problems were often related to fear and control. I continued to tell her the feet were often associated with fear of moving forward or recklessly moving ahead before it is time. Asha told me that she had been separated from her husband for four years and had been living in a separate household with their son. As far as she was concerned, the marriage was dead, but her husband was still in control of their finances and paying their bills. She was anxious and fearful every time he called because he was always critical about how she lived her life and spent money. She knew she lacked courage to start anew by getting a divorce and controlling her own life.

As Asha was telling me about her life, her fear, and her lack of control, I was releasing trigger points in her foot, ankle, and calf. After I finished the treatment she stood up and was able to walk and jump without pain or numbness in her heels, ankle, or foot. I told her that if the underlying cause of her pain was, as I suspected, due to her fear of moving forward with her life, the pain could come back. The true remedy would be to overcome her fear and regain control of her own life by making the decision to start a new spring.

In addition to these emotional and behavioral symptoms, an imbalance in winter may also cause physical symptoms. The following descriptions come from the ancient Chinese wisdom and the writings in *Huang Di Nei Ching*, the Yellow Emperor, (with a few of my own additions) on the organs, meridians, human functions, and associations that relate to balance or imbalance of the winter and water element.

The Bladder Meridian and Organ System:

The Kidneys unite at the Bladder where the fluid is stored.
Urine is the surplus fluid of the body."
– Chaoshi Bingyuan

The urinary bladder acts like an officer in a district that stores excess and controls fluid secretion. It is in charge of elimination of floating wastes. A balance of water and fluids is essential to prevent dehydration and preserve life. Imbalances in the bladder Chi show up as increased frequency of urination and/or a lack of control. Anything that has to do with storage, including energy reserves or memory, is related to the urinary bladder. Dehydration, exhaustion, and poor memory are symptoms of a bladder and winter imbalance. You might also be a very controlling sort of person, afraid of losing control or lacking control. An excess of fear and/or lack of control often cause an increased need to urinate. A person who spread himself too thin always has too much to do is unable to rest and relax and is always in constant state of stress or urgency. It is this urgency that causes a need to go and urinate even when the bladder is not full.

URINARY BLADDER MERIDIAN

The Leg Tai Yang Bladder Meridian

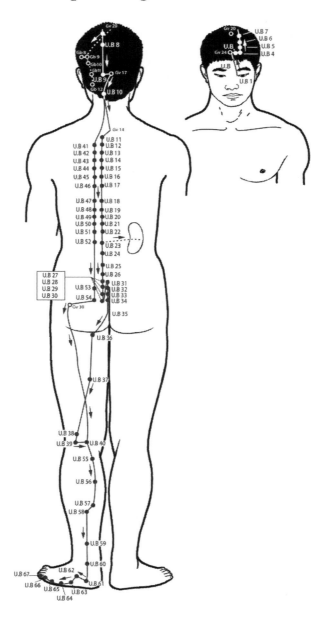

The Kidney Meridian and Organ System:

"The Kidneys control water. The Kidney Chi penetrates to
the ears."
– Ling Shu

The kidneys are officers that store and create emergency energy and rule through their wisdom. The kidneys are a storehouse for energy and stand for willpower. They are like a well you can draw from in need. The kidneys regulate the amount of water throughout the body. Each cell is comprised of water and fluids that bathe the entire cellular system. The flow of the fluid enables waste materials to be collected and excreted in the form of urine. The problem arises with people who do not know their own limits, constantly exhausting themselves and run on the reserve draining their well. The other extreme are people lacking willpower and are unable to muster extra effort and courage when needed. The kidneys also control the spinal column, vertebras, discs, and spinal fluid.

KIDNEY MERIDIAN

The Leg Shao Yin Kidney Meridian

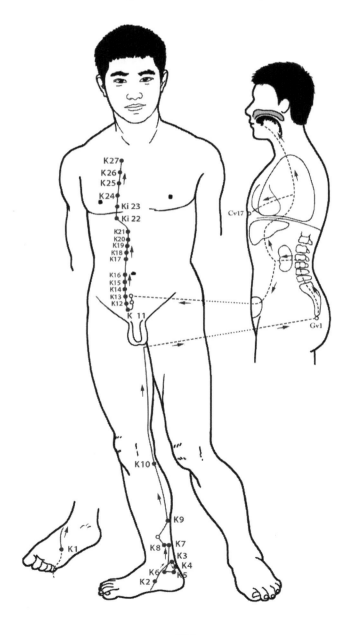

Jan is a fifty-four-year-old special education elementary school teacher who came to me with many characteristics of a blockage in the urinary bladder and kidney meridians. She had pain in her back along the last rib on the right side, and she felt the pain deep in her lower abdomen as well. The bottoms of her feet were cold, achy, and painful when she woke up in the mornings. She was tired all the time and her energy level was on empty. She had always felt that she had a purpose in her job. The summer break from school was over in a week, and usually at this time of year she would be full of energy and ready to jump into the new school year and the new students. But this year her excitement and passion were dead. Teaching English had always been her favorite, and she loved inspiring her students to read. Due to budget cuts, though, she had been assigned to teach math fulltime. Her school's test results were down and the school district was micro-managing all the teachers in their methods, and at the same time limiting the amount of homework they could assign to fifteen minutes per day. When I saw her, Jan was afraid of failing under the new restrictions and in her new position. She did not think she could fulfill her purpose of helping kids in need.

I told her the kidney meridian was a storehouse for energy that stood for perseverance and will power. Overwhelmed and emotionally paralyzed by the school district's decisions, she was unable to see the light, new life, and possibilities. This caused a fear that her life purpose wouldn't survive, and it was draining her energy and taxing her kidney meridian. I continued to explain that the bladder meridian is related to storage and control as well as fear of losing control. I asked if she had any bladder issues, and she admitted to recently having acute urges to urinate and almost losing control.

I told her about the serenity prayer: "To accept things you cannot 'control', have the courage to change the things you can and the wisdom to know the difference." I told her she needed to question her belief that she could not find a new way to inspire her students and successfully help them learn. I said, "Do not let this belief system, politics of the school board, bureaucracy, and things you have no control over kill your dream. Have faith in your purpose and courage to find new ways to make a difference." As I talked to her and released acu-points on the bottom of her feet and in her back along the kidney and bladder meridian, I could see how her energy and hope returned as her muscle tension and pain disappeared.

Any symptom of pain, dysfunction, or disease of the urinary bladder or kidney meridians is related to an accumulation of tension and a blockage of circulation (Chi). Here are some common symptoms that result when winter is out of balance and there is a blockage of circulation in the urinary bladder or kidney meridians.

- Dehydration.
- Disturbances in the regulation of blood, lymph, cerebrospinal fluid, joint lubrication, urine, sweat, and saliva.
- Swelling and edema.
- Sleeping disorders and fatigue.
- Lower back pain and sciatica.
- Bone pain or painful, dysfunctional joints.
- Arthritis
- Osteoporosis or osteopenia.
- Decaying or weak teeth.
- Problems with memory: poor memory, poor retention of new information, interruptions in the flow of thoughts.
- Alzheimer's and dementia.
- Ear infections or hearing problems.
- Pain or cramps in feet, ankles, and calf muscles.
- Cold feet.
- Achilles tendinitis or rupture.
- Hair loss or balding.
- Headaches or tension at the base of the skull or inner corners of the eyes.
- Sinus pressure and headaches.

Winter Imbalance Clues

Geographical Direction:
North. The direction associated with winter is north. It makes us think of cold weather and long, dark winters. The sun sets earlier and earlier. Many people with an imbalance have a desire to move south when winter comes storming with its darkness and cold. A winter imbalance might feel either better or worse when they travel north.

Color:
Dark blue or black. Dark blue or black are the colors associated with the element water and the season winter. When a person has a winter imbalance, a bluish black color could be seen with puffiness under the eyes or as a dark blue hue to the skin complexion in the face. A person with an imbalance will often choose black or dark blue as their favorite color and the choice of color in their clothing, car, and furniture. A strong disliking of black or dark blue does not seem to be as frequent but still reflects an imbalance.

Climate Relationship:
Cold. Cold storage has been used since ancient times and is still used today in our kitchens to preserve and store food. People with winter imbalances often experience a worsening of their symptoms in cold weather. In nature's winter, living things shut down and the crop is stored away. Humans too need to stay warm; enjoy quiet, restful, still times; and avoid overexerting themselves by expending too much energy. People that lack this ability must take extra caution as winter (literally or figuratively) storms in, otherwise they become chilled to the bone and experience stiffness of the joints, exhaustion, and fatigue. Other problems include suffering from pain in the back and kidney area, ear infections, sinus inflammations, and often bladder infections or the frequent need to urinate. It is important to stay warm and dry to avoid disease or injury. Winter (cold weather and tough times) requires preservation of one's resources and

economizing energy spending. Symptoms become more pronounced as cold weather settles deeper into the body. Sufficient hydration, good nutrition, and warmth, combined with appropriate amount of rest and recuperation are vital for self-preservation and a long and healthy life. People with a winter imbalance often have a greater urgency to urinate when their feet, pelvis, and lower back get cold.

Sound Relationship:

Sighing or groaning. A person who is unbalanced in winter might constantly sigh and groan. A person who constantly sighs and groans, without being aware of it, is showing a winter imbalance.

Sense Relationship:

Ear/hearing. Winter's association with ears and hearing has to do with the act of hearing itself, as compared to the summer relationship, which is about the ability to filter pure from impure sounds. Liquid (water) is vital to the hearing process. Hearing loss, inflammation of the ear, earache, the feeling of water in your ears, vertigo, and loss of equilibrium and balance are all symptoms of a winter imbalance. Another indication of an imbalance in winter is the inability to stay still, quiet, and really listen to and hear what another person is saying. If someone is important to you, and you wish to maintain and preserve your relationship, it is important that you stay still and present while you listen to what they have to say. True listening requires willpower. It takes effort to listen when you are tired.

Human Tissue Relationship

Bones, Marrow, and Teeth. The skeleton is our frame, which provides structure and protection, and is associated with winter. This encompasses all the bones of the body, including the skull, teeth, extremities, and spine. The cartilage and intervertebral discs of the spine are also related to the winter and water element. Any disease, dysfunction, or degeneration of bones or cartilage is considered a winter imbalance. Bone marrow is also related to winter, for within it new blood cells are formed. The ancient Chinese refer to the brain as "the sea of marrow," and it was seen as a storehouse of knowledge and information. The ability to remember, evaluate, and assess is related to winter, as is the flow of thoughts.

Body Orifice Relationship
Genitals, Urinary Tract, and Anus. Much of our sexual function depends on our relationship with winter and water. Reproductive health, ovarian and testicular function, and lubrication of the sperm and egg rely on a balanced winter. The genitals store within them the seeds of new life, waiting to be planted. Imbalances in winter often create sexual dysfunctions such as impotence, sterility, and frigidity. It is common to find those with extreme winter imbalances expressing extreme behaviors: workaholic, reckless health habits, not sleeping enough, bad diet, insufficient water intake, excessive partying and drug use, and not getting enough rest and recuperation after overexertion. This kind of behavior often leads to excessive or diminished sex drive. Excessive fear and worry can also be the cause of impotence, sterility, or frigidity. Infections and inflammation of the urinary tract (kidney, bladder, prostrate, uterus) are commonly found in those with a winter imbalance. Kidneys and bladder are associated with the emotions of urgency, fear and fright. The kidneys govern the lower orifices; if those emotions are extreme, then the kidney Chi may descend and the individual may temporarily lose control of urination and defecation.

External Physical Manifestations of the Water Element:
Head Hair. Extremes in the state of your scalp hair are an excellent indicator of winter imbalances. If your hair is oily or dry, fine and fragile, prone to breakage and split ends or if you have dandruff, you may have an imbalance in this season. Baldness or hair loss, partial or total, in men and women is due to tension in the scalp, often caused by stress, exhaustion, and fear— these are also related to a winter out of balance.

Body secretion:

Saliva. You may never have given this much thought, but a healthy person's teeth are bathed in saliva. The Chinese believe this is designed to protect and nourish the teeth. Too little saliva, which can cause dry mouth or teeth, or too much, which can cause drooling, can indicate a winter imbalance. Picture a teething baby, and you get the idea: as their teeth are growing in they need the nurturing of saliva.

Flavor Related to the Water Element:

Salty. Sodium chloride (NaCl), the main salt in the body, plays a large role in the regulation of water. Sometimes it's called the "electric salt" as it conducts electricity and helps circulate the current of life. Without it, we cannot survive, but too much can be dangerous. The average diet contains too much salt, and this creates water retention, which make the kidneys work harder to balance water levels. This can lead to hypertension (high blood pressure) and cardiac damage. A craving (or distaste) for salt often indicates a winter imbalance. In the ancient Far East, it was believed that salt, in the correct amounts and naturally derived from food, gave you power, strength, and energy: all things necessary to survive the rough times of winter. Salt has been used since ancient times to preserve food and prevent spoilage; it used to be considered a valuable commodity in trade.

How to Achieve Balance in Winter

Balance in winter is important because storing and preserving what you've worked so hard to harvest allows you to continue to grow and evolve as a person. If you worked to change your lifestyle and lose weight, you want to keep it off. And if you worked to save your money and buy a new car, you want to keep the car in good condition and take care of it so it will last. You worked so hard to gain your harvest, what good is it if you lose it right away? To master the winter qualities of storing and preserving what you have in your life, you must learn to appreciate what you have, remember what you've learned, know your limits, and be still.

If you appreciate what you have, you will get what you do not have. If you are unhappy with what you don't have, you will lose what you do have. Dissatisfaction, jealousy, restlessness, impatience, and always looking to move ahead will lead to chronic urgency, anxiety and lack of peace. A person who is never satisfied cannot be still in body or mind because they're constantly moving and racing, fearful of running out of time or getting behind. This behavior is reckless to our health because we will not get enough rest, causing constant exhaustion with decreased performance of body and mind. The stress from not getting enough rest will lead to muscle tension, causing oxygen deprivation with decreased circulation and inhibited immune system. It is important for us to listen to our own body, to know our limits. When our body is achy or tired it means we need to rest. There are times when it is necessary to push through, but an imbalanced winter always keep going. Not listening to your body is like continuing to drive your car while ignoring the warning light on your dash board that indicates you are low on gas.

Everyone has much to be grateful for and appreciate. Think about it, we have all at one time or another taken our health for granted. Then when we get a bad cold or flu and feel miserable, we realize how great we felt before becoming sick. Maybe you have an old car that you no longer care to wash. You park it like a bumper car, and you curse it any time you get a chance. Then when it suddenly breaks down and you have no car, you realize that your old car served you well. No matter how bad you might think your current situation is there is always someone who is worse off, and your situation could always be worse as well.

When we criticize what we have - our spouse, partner, car, home, or job —we stand to lose it. We need an attitude of gratitude, and on a daily basis we should show our appreciation for everything we've accomplished, received, achieved, and learned. We need to spend quality time with everyone who is important to us and those we want to keep in our life. We need to sincerely listen to them and appreciate them for who they are—that means stop reading the newspaper or watching TV when your spouse needs to be heard. When your children need you, get present and listen; do not let your mind be somewhere else or think about other things. No matter how old your car is, wash it and appreciate it. Take care of and preserve the neighborhood you live in by not littering. Do not waste the excess of your financial gain by spending it right away. A hundred years ago, nobody had any teeth left by the time they were fifty years old. Today dental hygiene, daily brushing, and flossing have helped us have strong, healthy, good-looking teeth that can serve us for life. As my dentist said jokingly, "Only brush the ones you want to keep."

A good habit that can help you balance winter is to make an inventory of everything which you are grateful for on a daily basis. This could be done by writing in a journal or in your thoughts. Remembering what you've learned is the second essential step to achieving balance in winter. Any life experience is a learning opportunity. To store what we learned from our experiences, we need a quiet, still time to reflect on and assess what we learned. When you pour concrete, you cannot remove the form until the concrete has hardened or cured. The word cure has many meanings. One is to preserve as by drying or salting - you've probably heard about curing beef or fish to prevent spoiling. The farmer cures his hay by drying it and salting it so that it can be preserved in his barn and last through the long and cold winter. Taking time to cure what you've learned is equally important so that you can retain it. If we do not retain what we learn, then we have to re-live that life experience to learn our lesson over and over again. When we learn something from a life experience that was unexpected or unwanted, this curing is even more important. The word cure also means to restore health or to affect a cure. In other words, taking the time to cure and retain what we learned is a cure for our well-being and spiritual growth.

Everyone has seen friends and acquaintances suffer from a heartbreaking relationship break up and then rush into drinking to forget or into a rebound relationship out of fear of being alone. Maybe you've even done this yourself. This reckless behavior never works and because the person either did not learn from their previous relationship or did not cure what they learned to heal from the broken relationship. They will repeat the same relationship and suffer the same outcome again. As tempting as it seems, we cannot skip the season of winter. Running around trying to force our seeds into a frozen ground is wasteful and fruitless.

In addition to remembering what you've learned, you must know your limits. Your body is not immortal. While a reckless, self-destructive lifestyle is common in young people, some never learn. Eat healthy, avoid excessive partying, alcohol or drugs, and exercise without abusing yourself or overdoing it. The most important factor in a balanced winter is getting enough sleep. Quality sleep, being still and having quiet time is essential for recovery to preserve your body and mind. A person who does not live by this wisdom will age and die prematurely. Realize you will not be "done" until the day you die. Preserve yourself by knowing your limits and giving yourself enough quiet time and rest to recover for another day.

Lack of exercising (being a coach potato) can lead to obesity, diabetes, heart disease, and many other diseases that can cause us to prematurely age or die. The other extreme is training and exercising too much. When it comes to exercise, more is not better. Exercise does not build up our muscles and get us stronger! It actually breaks our muscles down. Proper quantity and quality of rest and nutrition will, however, allow the body to repair the muscles and re-build them, bigger and stronger than before. Progressive training is based on a balance between breaking down (stress) and building up (rest, recovery, and nutrition). Stress, if applied gradually with proper time to recuperate, will help us grow both physically as well as mentally. One of my patients once told me, "If I would have known I was going to live this long, I would have taken better care of myself." Realize you will not be done until the day you die. Do not wait until it is too late to take care of your body. A person who does not live by this wisdom will age and die prematurely.

The final important step in achieving balance in winter is being still. In life we often find ourselves in tough times. When we are exhausted, scared, stressed out, and can't see the light, it is important not to run around like a chicken without a head. At this time we need to be still, draw from our inner faith, and preserve our energy and resources. Surrender to being still and patient. Have faith and beliefs that serve you. Reflect on your past and remember that everything in the past always worked out. Believe that you always have what you need when you need it. If you don't have it right now, you must trust in the fact that you do not really need it right now.

Balance in Your Future Winters

Winter needs stillness and quiet times in order for us to rest, relax and recover. Yoga, meditation and Tai-Chi are activities that can heal a winter imbalance by teaching relaxation, patience and stillness.

Balance in winter means preserving and storing what you've gained through the spring, summer, and fall. Without appreciating and remembering everything that has brought you to where you are today, you cannot continue forward successfully. When you take the time to appreciate what you have, remember what you've learned, respect your limits, and be still and recover before you start over, everything in your life will get better. You can evolve and build upon what you gained and you can better the seeds you plant in the upcoming spring.

Way to Be . . .

Earth

The Metaphor of Earth 土

the Earth Element

*The earth element is related to fruitfulness
and life ripening. It is about spiritual growth
and maturity. It is about being not doing.*

IN THE FOUR SEASONS METAPHOR, each of the four seasons is associated with an element and a geographical direction. Spring is associated with wood and east. Summer is associated with fire and south. Fall is metal and west, and winter, water and north. According to the ancient Chinese laws, this leaves one element unaccounted for: Earth. Earth is the geographic center and serves as a reference point for all the other directions. Earth therefore represents the here and now, or in other words, wherever you go, there you are. Because the earth is the center point for everything, nothing can exist without it. From Mother Earth we derive our nourishment, support, and life. The farmer plants his crop in her fertile soil, and we all depend on her for the food that feeds us and the atmosphere from which we draw our breath. Earth was considered special in ancient China because it represented the source of all other elements, the center from which all else arises. The four seasons and the other elements manifest in the earth element.

Earth also represents the transition that is always present and especially noticeable and dramatic at the time of seasonal change. As winter turns into spring, a struggle often ensues; warm days are followed by freezing temperatures. The winter does not always go away quietly. At the right time we need to plant and fertilize. As spring turns into summer, temperatures rise but could suddenly drop and turn colder again with late spring showers lingering before summer settles in. We labor in anticipation of our harvest as we water and weed our crop. Ready or not, summer transforms into fall, the leaves change color and fall to the earth, and we harvest our experiences. Winter often storms in with a cold blast that brings everyone inside to slow down and reflect. With sudden and drastic changes, we need to adapt to weather and temperature just as we adapt to changes in our circumstances, in every moment, to take proper action in each life situation.

With a change of season can come intense metamorphosis in nature and in our lives, as well. The earth element represents transition. We pass through many seasons in a lifetime, in a business, in relationships, even during a single day. Just as in nature, the seasons or circumstances in our personal life often change drastically or suddenly. Transitions can cause great tumult physically, mentally, and emotionally. Earth, then, is our center, and in a stable, balanced earth, we stand on a solid foundation of goodness, morals, and ethics. It is important to stay centered, present, and calm in the midst of the storm. From this concept, most likely, we get the sayings, "down to earth," and "keeping both feet on the ground."

Jack, a fifty-one-year-old male, was the owner of a commercial janitorial company that had major corporations and businesses as clients nationwide. Jack had seen me for different ailments in the past, and on this particular visit came in with pain on top of his left ankle and foot. He was not even sure how he injured it, but thought it might have been while running on a treadmill without wearing his custom made shoe inserts (orthotics). He also suffered a lesser pain on the bottom of his right foot inside the heel. The pain made him limp and unable to work out, which was an important part of Jack's life. He was a man of excellent fitness; in fact any twenty- five-year-old would have been envious of his physique.

I explained to Jack that his main symptom on top of the left ankle and foot was most likely related to his stomach and spleen meridian. I asked him if he'd recently had a hard time being present, if his mind was constantly going, if he was craving sweets, or if he had any sleeping problems. Jack then proceeded to tell me that lately he was obsessively, night and day, thinking about all the things he needed to do to take care of his business. He was exhausted because he kept waking up in the middle of the night and was unable to stop thinking about the business and go back to sleep. Jack, who always followed a very strict and healthy diet had lately been too busy to eat at regular times, skipped meals, and started craving sweets. I told Jack that the most common injuries occur when a person is not present. Thinking about work while working out is not a good idea. I asked Jack why his thoughts were obsessing about the company that he had owned for years. I told him there had to be a cause for him to have obsessive thoughts, as there had to be a cause for his pain.

Jack told me that his company had grown and transformed dramatically over a very short time. The company had gone from 600 to 1,200 employees in the last four months. Clearly the growth of his company was something Jack desired, but he was not ready for everything to change so fast. He had hired one vice president and two regional managers but was not letting them do their work. Instead he was trying to do their job, getting involved in everything, just as when the company had half the employees. He was trying to do everything, all over the country, all the time. His mind was never present or "at home," as he was jumping from one thing to another, anxious and nervous that he'd miss or forget something. His newly hired vice president even told him he had to let him do his job. Clearly Jack couldn't possibly micromanage and multi-task to be involved in all things as his company grew.

Everything was moving faster and faster and Jack was not grounded and at peace with his present reality. He was in counterbalance. His left foot showed symptoms of stomach and spleen with an earth imbalance. His right foot showed symptoms related to the kidney meridian and winter. The earth imbalance caused his anxiety, obsessive worrying, inability to be present or sleep, and cravings for sweets. The winter imbalance was indicated by fear of giving up control and of failure. Jack was trying to find his center and balance in his company's growth, but his mind was worrying about things that had not happened yet (the future). He had one foot stuck winter (fear of moving forward and giving up control) and the other foot failing to gain balance and stability (in the present) as his company was taking off.

After releasing acu-points points on Jack's stomach and spleen meridian on his left foot, ankle, and lower leg, he left pain-free without a limp. With some coaching, Jack realized he could only be in one place at one time, doing the job of one person at one time, and that there are only so many hours in a day. He needed to restore balance by sleeping through the night, being present with his wife and children, not skipping meals, and being present and engaged in his workouts. Jack needed to let the people he hired do their jobs. He needed to restore balance and harmony to his life.

The earth is our stable center. It rotates on its own axis, each time around giving us day and night. And it revolves around the sun, creating the four seasons. If you lack a stable center, there's nothing to grasp onto when everything around you starts to move and change. Earth is not a season, but ever present in and between all four seasons. This means that every time we are out of balance in any season (life situation), we are out of balance in earth.

Travis, a twenty-one-year-old male, came to see me for pain in his upper back that was aggravated when he took a deep breath. For five years he had pain on his right side of the neck, from the collarbone to below his ear, to the front of his head and around his eye. His headaches were constant. Four years ago he had an MRI and a cat scan of his brain, but the doctors did not find anything wrong.

He used to swim and play water polo competitively in high school, and after that he still swam for exercise and to relieve stress. When swimming he felt pain and restriction in his shoulders that affected his stroke, as well as pain in his neck when he was turning his head to breathe. His right and left arms fell asleep and got numb at night, and he had a hard time sleeping through the night. On top of all this he had a history of knee problems when swimming breast stroke or walking down stairs. He also complained of digestion problems with stomach pain and admitted to skipping meals.

I noticed how his shoulders were rounded forward, elevated, and tense. His upper back was also rounded forward. This is a common postural imbalance in swimmers that can develop from over-using and strengthening muscles in front of the chest and shoulders. But it can also be the body language of someone who is anxious, defensive, or under stress. I asked him if he ever found himself breathing shallow or holding his breath. Travis admitted that his breathing was never calm or deep.

Due to the location of his pain, I suspected the stomach meridian and earth element to be out of balance. His poor posture and difficulty breathing made me even more certain. I then proceeded to tell him that this imbalance often is related to stress, anxiety, a lack of peace, and not breathing properly. Travis then told me that he was one of twelve siblings in a Mormon family. He never felt at home or at peace embracing their religion, and at the end of high school he had rebelled and run away from home. He had travelled and lived in Colorado and Hawaii and resorted to using marijuana in an attempt to find peace and a place where he belonged. His search for peace had forced him to do a lot of work on himself. Through the tough school of life, his experiences, and reading self-help books, he had come to the realization that he could not run away from who he was and where he came from. So he went home to re-join his family. He wanted to belong and feel at home, but even after coming back to his family, he was still not embracing or fully accepting the Mormon religion. He wanted to be loved and accepted for who he was and what he believed. His family, in their belief and love for him, was trying to save him and confirm him to their religion. Travis and his family were each doing what they believed was right, but they were in conflict.

Travis had lived in a state of constant fight and flight, feeling anxious and lacking peace. He did not breathe properly and his posture was tense as if ready to defend any attack on what he believed or how he lived his life. As I was releasing trigger and acu-points on Travis's stomach meridian and neck flexor muscles (sternocleidomastoid and scalenes), I talked to him about the importance of being present, at peace, and able to breathe deep and relaxed. I told him that his poor posture was making it impossible to breathe correctly. That the anxiety and lack of peace from not feeling "at home" or having a sense that he belonged, along with constantly feeling like he had to defend what he believed, caused his bad posture to get worse and made calm deep breathing impossible. I told him that the people who loved him and, in their belief systems, thought he was taking the wrong path in life would most likely continue trying to persuade him to live life the way they believed was right. He needed to stay calm and present, without judging them, feeling the need to defend himself, or feeling anxious.

Releasing those trigger points in Travis's neck while we were talking about years of built-up emotional stress and tension was a painful process for him. As those tight knots released from my digital pressure, Travis experienced symptoms of pain and numbness into his arms, hands, upper back, and head, mimicking all the symptoms he had been suffering for years. Travis was crying from both physical and emotional relief. When he came back a week later, he did not have headaches anymore. His neck tension was gone and he was able to turn his head and breathe on both sides as he was swimming. His swim stroke was free and easy. He had not experienced any more numbness in his arms or hands. He was focusing on his breathing and his posture through exercises I had given him, and he did not feel anxious or defensive when he discussed religion, his faith, or what he believed. He did, however, still experience pain in his mid-back and his posture was still not ideal. I told Travis that at a young age, he had come a long way and grown as a man, and I believed he was on the right track. But he still had challenges to overcome. Travis has since transferred to a university and is now studying to get a degree in food science—something he always felt was his calling. He thanked me for making him aware of the importance of breathing and staying calm and present. It has helped him stay at peace as his life transforms from one season to another.

Stan, a fifty-four-year-old man in corporate management, is another example of an earth imbalance. Stan was a runner who ran three to four marathon races per year (he averaged fifty miles per week) and he came to see me for chronic knee pain that had plagued him for ten months. He had seen family doctors and orthopedic doctors, and he had x-rays and MRIs that showed nothing wrong. The doctors told him that his pain was caused by an inflammation under the kneecap from overuse as well as friction caused by uneven pulling and improper tracking of his kneecaps. He had extended physical therapy without any relief. Finally, a cortisone injection gave him relief for six weeks, until his pain came back as bad as ever. He was taking anti- inflammatory over-the-counter medication so he could continue his running. He felt pain and discomfort the first mile running, until the medication and endorphins kicked in. After the run, his knees would swell up and get stiff. Still, he continued his running routine.

In my office Stan was unable to squat or step up on a two-foot-high treatment table without experiencing sharp knee pain. I could immediately tell that Stan was obsessive about his running and that he stubbornly would keep running as long as he could walk, and I suspected that he was out of balance in the Earth element and that he had blockages in his stomach and spleen/pancreas meridians. I started to ask questions related to an Earth imbalance to see if my suspicions were correct. I asked, "When you run, what do you think about?"

"I think about everything except running," said Stan.

"That is part of the problem!" I said.

"What do you mean?"

"Do you have a hard time being present—in other words does your mind wander a lot?" Stan told me that he constantly multitasked and found his mind wandering at work. But he believed that was an asset that made him successful managing employees and tasks. He admitted his girlfriend often complained he wasn't "there" when they spent time together, but he quickly added but all women say that.

"Do you have a hard time falling asleep or staying asleep because you can't turn your mind off?" I asked.

"Yes I do. How did you know?" replied Stan.

"All your symptoms follow a pattern of an imbalance. Do you also have heartburn or acid reflex symptoms?" I said.

"Yes, I've had problems with acid this last year. I take Tums to keep it under control." Stan looked around my office for a moment and then pointed to a picture of a Harley Davidson motorcycle on the wall. "Do you ride?"

"I used to, sold it ten years ago. Do you have a bike?"

"Yes, I do," said Stan proudly. "I have a Harley Road King."

Seeing an opportunity, I asked, "What do you think about when you ride your Harley on the freeways?" I saw the lights go on in Stan's head.

"I think about nothing else than riding," he said.

"Exactly, and what would happen if you thought of something else?"

"I could die or be in a serious accident," he said.

"When you run, you need to think about nothing else than being the runner, paying attention to every part of your body and your breathing as well as the environment you are in. Being in the here and now, paying attention while running, will make your running experience and performance better than ever. There is a reason it is illegal to send text messages on your cell phone when you are driving your car. If you are not present while driving, you might be in an accident. You do not read a book or think about your work when you make love to your girlfriend. If you do, the experience will not be very good. Being present in whatever you are doing, at work or spending time with your girlfriend, will improve your performance and enhance the experience. If your mind is present when you are lying in bed to sleep it cannot be somewhere else, thinking about what you need to do tomorrow or what you should have done yesterday. If you get present and aware of breathing, deeply and relaxed from your diaphragm, you will most likely not experience the heartburn anymore."

As I kept talking to Stan, I found out that a couple of years ago he was divorced from a thirty-year-long marriage. He was never at peace while with his wife. His job required him to travel a lot, so he was hardly ever home. He started to run, and when he was home he went for long runs or kept himself busy by washing the family's three cars. He was running away from his unhappy marriage, constantly on the road running or traveling. Thirty years of habits are hard to break; no wonder his mind was always on the go. When his children left for college and his job changed and no longer required traveling, he realized he could not stay married.

I released stomach and spleen acu-points around Stan's knees and in his thigh muscles (rectus femoris and vastus lateralis). Then I stretched those muscles and showed Stan how to stretch them daily by himself. After the session, Stan was able to do a deep squat and step up on my treatment table without any pain whatsoever. He said, "I haven't been pain free like this in a long time. When can I go running?"

"You can go running right away, as long as you promise to stop running immediately the second your mind thinks of anything other than your running, breathing, and surroundings. Then you can start running again as soon as you are able to be present, in mind and body in your running again. This way you will train yourself to be present in your running at all times, since having to stop repeatedly will get very annoying. This running will become meditative and more fulfilling. It will also bring you peace and make you calmer. You will run with greater ease and with less or no pain."

Stan came back for his second visit three weeks later and reported that he was running with no pain in his knees. He was more present in his running, his everyday breathing, as well as in his work and his relationship with his girlfriend. He had not had any heartburn since his first visit. However, Stan claimed that he still experienced some stiffness and discomfort in his knees, but now he mostly felt it as he woke up in the mornings. I asked him if he immediately sprung out of bed as his alarm sounded, thinking about what he had to do that day. Stan said, "Yes, kind of."

I told him it was important to be present and aware of one's body when waking up. Stretching gently and being in a state of gratitude for what we have and for our life will help us transition into the new day. The transition from rest to action needs to be harmonious. Jumping out of bed in the same way a punched-out boxer stands up when the bell rings will cause an immediate fight-or-flight reaction. Such a reaction is stressful and causes increased muscle tension that will be experienced in our weak links, or in other words, our injured areas that have less tolerance for additional tension. From the second we wake up, to the second we fall asleep, we must be present and aware to maintain balance in earth, and all four seasons as well.

The shape of earth is a perfect circle that symbolizes our planet, a pregnant mother, fertile soil, as well as a seed. The earth follows a cyclic rhythm, like ebb and flow of the tide. Earth therefore represents the completion of an entire seasonal cycle. A well-rounded life and harmonious completion of the cycles of life signifies a balanced earth element. A person with earth not centered often experiences a disturbance in cyclic rhythms, such as breathing cycle (too shallow, too fast, or holding breath), sleeping cycle (cannot fall asleep or stay asleep), digestive cycle, metabolic cycle, blood sugar balance, and hormone cycles, etc.

Balance in Earth.......The Way To Be

In the Four Seasons System, each season is related to a specific action, or "doing." The earth element is about "being" present. As the ancient Chinese philosopher and spiritual father of the movement of Taoism, Lau-Tsu so simply put it, "The way to do, is to be."

Each season has its purpose. In spring, we fertilize and plant, meaning we get clarity about our intentions, change approaches that did not work and commit ourselves assertively to beginning a new cycle. In summer, we water and weed our tender crop, passionately and joyfully engaged. In fall we bring in the harvest, accepting with empathy what we've reaped. In winter, we store energy and preserve our harvest by remembering and appreciating what we've learned throughout the year, and the earth represents being present through all four phases of successful doing. Completion of a cycle leads to greater success in the next, and the next, and the next. This is how the seed principle works - to multiply, with each go around as we mature and learn to master the divine wisdom of the Four Season System. Being in harmony with the natural flow of the seasons is vital to a balanced earth and fulfilled, successful life. A balanced earth will assure maturity and spiritual growth.

Fullness, wholeness, success, harmony, and stability in all cycles of life are what being centered is all about. The fruits of the spirit: love, peace, faith, gentleness, patience, integrity, kindness, generosity, loyalty, tolerance, and self-control are qualities reflected in someone who has mastered balance in the earth element and is staying on the path of the Four Seasons System. The truly balanced person radiates love and peace; a kind of order and harmony emanates from within (their center). They aren't governed by chaotic, desperate, and frantic external energy.

Balanced earths live in the moment. They do not dwell on past failures or disappointments or obsess about future worries. Coming from a place of full awareness of their thoughts and belief systems, they deal with one thing at a time, staying calm and present while taking proper action in each season or life situation. The balanced earths are at home in their own flesh, at ease wherever they may be. The mark of a mature, balanced person is how well you can stay calm and present when all kinds of external energy swirls around you. It's not that a centered person experiences less trouble than others. We all experience stress and troubled times, especially in periods of change. The difference lies in how you interpret and manage the situation, how stressed you get, and how long you stay stressed out (not present.) If your earth element is in balance, you can remain present and calm while riding out the storms of life, because you know that resisting reality could result in emotional chaos and mental confusion, which can lead to more stress, tension, and disease.

Staying in the moment allows balanced earth to solve problems, envision solutions, and "think outside the box" using imagination and creativity. Your imagination can be your best friend or worst enemy; it could be used for good, or for your own destruction. A calm mind and balanced earth can find solutions in the most stressful and chaotic of situations, or on the other hand, your mind in an imbalanced earth can imagine chaos, stress, or negativity to the point of obsession. Whatever your mind thinks is what you will bring upon yourself through the law of attraction. Like attracts like. Every thought you have is a seed planted in your mind, and if dwelled upon that seed will manifest. A centered earth is reflected by present awareness of all thoughts and belief systems (not obsessing), dealing with one thing at a time, staying calm and present while taking the proper actions in each season or life situation. A balanced earth is aware of his or her thoughts and questions whether or not they are true before reacting to situations. Individuals who are not in balance with earth, dwell or obsess on the thoughts that don't serve them and therefore cause tension, pain, and suffering. This individual tends to think the worst of any ache or pain. Making a mountain out of a molehill, they think a headache is a brain tumor. The obsessive thinking or worrying about this headache only creates more tension and hence perpetuates or worsens the condition.

Your mind can be your own worst enemy. For example, Dorothy, a fifty-five-year-old recreational tennis player, came to see me for pain in her left lower back that radiated into her front left thigh and shin to the top of the foot. She had a surgical procedure two months prior to remove parts of a bulging disc to take pressure off the nerve that traveled down her leg. She was quite disappointed that she still had the same leg pain she had before the surgery and that she was not able to return to playing tennis. She gave me the exact date she had stopped playing tennis, to the day. Tennis was her life. I asked her how often she used to play and she said seven days a week. She had not played for eight months and had gained fifteen pounds from lack of exercise and eating too much sweets and carbohydrates.

When I assessed her, I found her left foot to be flat (pronated) and her left front thigh muscle (rectus femoris) was too tight, causing her left hip to rotate forward in the front and elevate in the back. She said that the leg pain came and went, but it got worse the longer she was on her feet, making it impossible for her to return to playing tennis. Her shin and thigh pain followed the stomach meridian. I started to tell her that pain along the stomach meridian often was related to anxiety, worrying, obsessive behavior, and an inability to be present. Dorothy told me that she always worried. She worried for her son who was a police officer; she knew his work schedule by heart so that she knew when to worry. Her daughter commuted to college and Dorothy worried about whether or not she'd reach her destination. She had her daughter call when she left and call a second time when she arrived. If the second call did not come within the time Dorothy expected it to, she started to worry. She worried about the family business. She told me that, years ago, she was diagnosed with cancer. It was a benign form and her prognosis was very favorable. However, she worried about that too. Her doctor told her she needed to find something to do that could be a distraction to her worrying. She had played tennis in high school and took it up again. She soon became obsessive, playing tennis every day of the week. She had replaced one obsessive behavior with another.

I told her I believed her excessive tennis play, pounding on a cement court with a flat foot seven days a week, and her constant obsessive worrying caused her back and leg pain. Not everyone is open to this kind of thinking. Dorothy did not want to play less and did not believe she could ever stop worrying. She did not want to believe her own behavior could be the cause of her pain. So Dorothy did not return to see me for a second visit, and if I had to guess, her earth imbalance and obsessive worrying are probably still causing her problems.

Balanced emotions for the earth element are calm, present, and in harmony. Unbalanced earth will experience negative emotions. They will either experience the negative emotion of a hypo-active nature: depression. Or they will experience the negative emotion of a hyper-active nature: anxiety. Because earth is not a season but ever present in all seasons at all times, anxiety and depression are the two most common negative emotions. Any time a person is out of balance in any season he or she will experience anxiety or depression coupled with the negative emotions for the season they are stuck in. All negative emotions are feedback on whether we are doing or not doing what we are supposed to do in the present season. When a person is aware they will be calm and experience the balanced emotion of whatever season they are present in. So many people struggle with a mild anxiety or depression that many believe it is part of life, when in fact it is a feedback telling us that we are not present or in harmony with our life situation. A more severe imbalance could manifest as an emotional roller coaster. A person who is always worrying about what is ahead or disappointed about what is in the past is never "home" or present. Anytime a person is not calm and present, they are not breathing correctly. If one breathes deeply and slowly from the diaphragm, they will become present in their breathing and experience calmness. If a person experiences anxiety or depression, their breathing is too shallow, too fast, or they are holding their breath. It is impossible to be present, breathe deep, slow diaphragmatic breaths, and experience anxiety or depression at the same time.

Six weeks before coming to see me, Emy, a twenty-one-year-old collegiate soccer player, injured her left hip flexor and groin during a workout with the college strength and conditioning coach. She was predominantly a right kicker. When she tried to kick the ball hard with her right leg and was forced to plant and balance on her extended left leg, she felt sharp pain and her left supportive leg collapsed. When I tested her muscles, her left iliacus (a hip flexor deep in the groin and lower abdomen) was weak and elicited sharp pain. When she was lying on her back with both legs straight and tried to lift her left leg, she felt sharp pain in her groin and lower abdomen.

Her painful area was related to a blockage in her spleen, stomach (the earth element), and kidney meridian (winter). So I asked her if she was excessive, obsessive, or stubborn in her soccer playing and training. She said that she never quit. She did not know when to stop; she trained every day and easily over-trained and felt run down. She was obsessive about her soccer and always worried she did not do enough. I then asked if she experience more than normal anxiety and nervousness or perhaps even fear of failure at game times. She said the butterflies made her feel sick to her stomach every time she played a game. I asked if she noticed if her breathing was shallow or if she held her breath when she was playing. Yes, she said. I explained that when she was anxious and holding her breath, she was not present but rather worrying about playing bad or fearful of making mistakes. She was projecting fear into her future based on old belief systems that she was never perfect and therefore never could be satisfied. I told her that her soccer would be perfect if she always did her best, stayed present, and had fun. The only way she could fail would be if she failed to remember what she learned from her old experiences.

We only have control over our present thoughts and present breathing. I told her that to play her best soccer, to play in the zone, she needed to be calm, present, and breathe deeply from her abdomen. The anxiousness or fear would only make her too amped up and tense. I found out that she was a much better player in practice, when she was loose and did not feel anxious, than she was in her games.

I told her to remember soccer was a game, and a game is supposed to be fun. I gave Emy home stretching exercises for the injured hip flexors, and I talked to her about breathing exercises to practice deep relaxed breathing and being present so she could play in the zone. Even more important than winning a game is the beauty of being in the zone and playing at your highest level with ease. Breathing was the key to easing Emy's anxiety.

In addition to anxiety and depression, an imbalance in the earth element may also cause physical symptoms. The following descriptions come from the ancient Chinese wisdom and the writings in *Huang Di Nei Ching*, the Yellow Emperor, (with a few of my own additions) on the organs, meridians, human functions, and associations that relate to balance or imbalance of the earth element.

The Stomach Meridian and Organ System:

"Liquid and solid enter the Stomach. The six solid yin organs and the five hollow yang organs are replenished with Chi from the Stomach."
– Ling Shu.

Once the digestive process has started with saliva and proper chewing, the stomach welcomes our food and breaks it down further, transforming it into nutrients that can be used for energy. The stomach stores and balances the five flavors of ancient Chinese philosophy: sweet, sour, bitter, pungent (spicy), and salty. It also nourishes our emotional and physical growth. How often have you heard someone say they felt something "in the pit of their stomach," or have "butterflies" in their stomach? Emotions are felt in this organ. If they are not balanced (stressed), you may experience food cravings and eating disorders that can lead to obesity or anorexia.

Joel, a thirty-six-year-old male patient, came to me with neck and chest pain. Joel also suffered from anxiety and heartburn, and he was constantly craving sweets, so much so that his sweet tooth led him to gain twenty pounds. Getting out of shape had made him depressed, and he asked what he could do to get back in shape. He and I were standing in the reception area of the office while we were talking, and I told him about breathing, being present, and the importance of eating healthy meals on regular times. Joel appeared to be listening and looking me in the eyes, but at the same time he reached his hand into the candy jar that was sitting on the front desk, grabbed a piece of candy, and proceeded to unwrap it. I tapped him on the hand just as he was going to put the piece of candy in his mouth and asked him, "What are you doing?"

"Oops; I wasn't thinking." Joel had such a hard time being present he was not even aware he was going to eat a piece of candy just as he asked me how to lose weight.

STOMACH MERIDIAN

The Leg Yang Ming Stomach Meridian

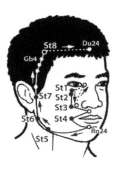

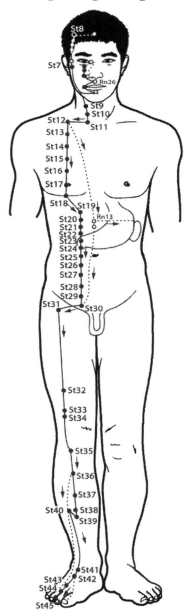

The Spleen/Pancreas Meridian and Organ System:

The spleen/pancreas is the source of life for all solid yin organs (liver, heart, spleen, lungs, kidneys, and pericardium) and all hollow yang organs (gall bladder, stomach, small intestine, large intestine, and bladder). Western medicine knows that the pancreas produces pancreatic enzymes and insulin, which are vital for successful digestion. Metaphorically in holistic medicine the pancreas is related to success or sweetness in life. Likewise, Western medicine teaches us that the spleen produces white blood cells, which are directed to neutralize infection and inflammation by destroying viruses and bacteria in our body. In ancient Chinese medicine, they believed that the spleen regulated and directed the blood. Our immune system is dependent on a healthy spleen. The spleen is also the master of digestion and distributes energy (Chi) derived from our food throughout our body. The ancient teachers believed the spleen was the master of digesting life experiences to help us mature and live in harmony with the seasons.

SPLEEN MERIDIAN

The Leg Tai Yin Spleen Meridian

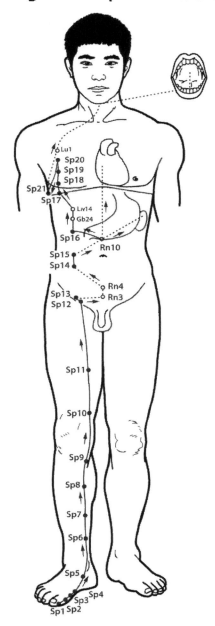

Any symptom of pain, dysfunction, or disease of the stomach or spleen/pancreas meridians is related to an accumulation of tension and a blockage of circulation (Chi).

Here are some common symptoms that result when the earth element is out of balance and there is a blockage of circulation in the stomach or spleen/pancreas meridians.

- Digestive problems.
- Obesity.
- Headaches and dizziness.
- Sinus problems, primarily pressure in sinuses under the eyes.
- Neck pain from the collarbone to below the jaw and behind the ear.
- Epigastric spasms (problem swallowing).
- Shallow breathing.
- Hiatal hernia.
- Heart burn.
- Acid reflux.
- Hyper- or hypo-acidity.
- Vomiting.
- Gagging.
- Burping and belching.
- Stomach pain.
- Gastritis.
- Abdominal pain.
- Hypo- or hyperglycemic.
- Emotional instability.
- Eating disorders, including anorexia or bulimia.
- Lethargy and depression.
- Obsessive and anxious.
- Stubborn or obstinate behavior.
- Female infertility.
- Autoimmune disorders.
- Blood disorders.

- Sleep disorders.
- Metabolic disorder.
- Hormonal disorders, particularly menstrual.
- Anterior hip and groin pain.
- Front thigh pain.
- Knee pain or joint dysfunction.
- Pain along the shinbone and shin splints.
- Pain on top of the ankle and foot.
- Bunions.

Carol, a forty-year-old working mother, came to me because she experienced pain in her mid-back and solar plexus area when she took a deep breath. She had heartburn and lived on Tums antacid medication. She worked from home so she could watch her children and their nanny at the same time, and upon questioning she revealed she was never present, always trying to do more than one thing at a time. She was skipping meals, not present enough to be aware that she was hungry. She often felt dizzy from low blood sugar. Carol even woke up in the middle of the night and could not fall asleep because her mind was working. She sat at a desk in front of a computer and phone all day long and admitted to slouching and working in bad posture.

I explained that one reason for her stomach acid problem could be that she did not use her diaphragm muscle to breathe properly. When under stress and not present and calm, we use muscles between our ribs and in our neck to breath in a less efficient way. As any muscle that is not used on a regular basis the diaphragm would become stretched out and flaccid, allowing the stomach and acid to be pushed up into the chest cavity. Treatment that relieved tension in trigger and acu-points in the lower ribcage on the back and abdomen gave her immediate relief. But I told her that if she did not change her behavior - improve her posture, become mindful, breathe deeply taking relaxed diaphragmatic breaths, stay present, do one thing at a time, and balance her blood sugar by eating something every three hours - her symptoms would most likely return.

Other Earth Element Imbalance Clues

Color:
Yellow. As with the previously discussed seasons/elements the profound liking or disliking of a color often reflects an imbalance. This could be illustrated in an individual's choice of color in the way he or she dresses, decorates or paints his/her home, or chooses a car. The choosing of a color could also be a subconscious self-treatment or attempt to restore our balance by altering how we feel. The ancient Chinese believed a lack of yellow color or too much yellow in the facial hue indicated an imbalance in the earth element.

Climate Relationship:
Damp (Humid). Weather has always had a profound influence on the lives of humans. We commonly become more aware of this influence when we're traveling, because we are often forced to experience unfamiliar climate conditions. An inability to adjust to these changes as the seasons change or when traveling could lead to colds, flu, infection, or other mental, emotional, or physical symptoms. A balanced person can easily adapt; however, someone lacking center or harmony can experience either negative or positive reactions to any climate changes, in general, or a humid climate in particular.

Sound Relationship:
Singing. Singing to yourself, or to an infant or young child, can produce a calming effect. Many parents sing to their young children when they become anxious or frightened. Some people sing to themselves to quiet a mind that will not stop running.

Sense Relationship:
Taste. Highly developed and sensitive taste buds could make for a skilled chef, sommelier, or food critic. But any extreme in your ability to taste - extreme sensitivity or an inability to taste certain flavors—can mean an imbalance in the earth element.

Human Tissue Relationship
Fascia (subcutaneous or connective tissues) and aerobic muscle fibers.
Fascia is connective tissue that surrounds muscles, groups of muscles, blood vessels, and nerves, binding those structures together in much the same manner as plastic wrap can be used to hold the contents of sandwiches together. Aerobic muscles are thin and stringy. Rather than explosive, raw strength, these muscles are responsible for endurance and use fat as fuel. Any extreme in the tone and texture of muscles can indicate an imbalance in the earth element. Firm, toned muscles with low body fat reflects a balanced metabolism, diet, and exercise routine and a balanced earth element.

Body Orifice Relationship
Mouth. Children in early development tend to focus on their mouths, because it is their center. We breathe, eat, and drink through the mouth. The components from this process give us our energy and are vital to our survival. You indeed are what you eat, as the saying goes; in fact, our physical bodies are the combined result of what we breathe, eat, and drink. To facilitate digestion and fat metabolism, which establishes a centered rhythm with the earth element, you need to eat a well-balanced diet, and eat at regular, fixed intervals. People with imbalances in the earth element often wait too long between meals, skip meals altogether, and eat a diet too high in sugar and fat.

Any eating disorder: bulimia, anorexia, or overeating when you're not hungry, is a sign of not being centered. Many people use food, and in particular sugar or carbohydrates, as a drug to feel good, to try to self-medicate when they are emotionally upset. They are often consumed with eating and obsess over their next opportunity to eat. To those people food is simply looked upon as pleasure, rather than fuel for the body. People out of balance in this way prefer to eat what tastes good to them, rather than what's good for them. This dysfunctional eating, and resulting weight gain, acts as a kind of compensation for not living a balanced, well-rounded life, and for not multiplying and bearing fruit in all areas of their lives. Instead, their bodies are becoming well rounded as their body fat and health problems multiply. They are caught in chaotic cycles of anxiety and depression as their blood sugar swings wildly. As Jesus taught, "Man shall not live by bread alone." We must not only feed our body, but our mind and spirit as well. If we are not mentally and spiritually fulfilled by growing, multiplying our seeds, and having our needs met, we will resort to food as a drug or an escape.

External Physical Manifestations of the Earth Element:
Lips. Misalignments with earth, stress, negative emotions, or a poor, unbalanced diet are frequently revealed in the texture and color of your lips. Cracked or dry lips, herpes simplex (cold sores), or other blisters can indicate a lack of harmony with the earth element.

Body secretion:
Saliva. You can't even begin the process of properly digesting your food without the presence of saliva. Not chewing your food thoroughly or producing too little saliva will negatively impact digestion. Too much or too little saliva points to an imbalance in the earth element.

Flavor Related to the Earth Element:
Sweet. It is often said that the taste of success (and life itself) is sweet. So is the "fruit of the spirit" and the honey of the earth. Falling out of balance with the earth, which manifests in lack of fulfillment, success, centering, harmony, or cyclic rhythms, can cause a craving for sweets. For instance, women with premenstrual syndrome (PMS) and those with high or low blood sugar symptoms, anxiety, or depression can have cravings for sweets. This craving indicates that the overall rhythmic cycles of the body are out of balance. An intense distaste for sweet flavors can also indicate an imbalance.

How to Achieve Balance with Earth

Being present means awareness and the easiest way to find awareness is through the breath. By developing an awareness of your breathing, you can control each individual breath to be fully present in this moment. Controlling the breath* you are taking right now is controlling the only thing you have any control over: this moment. You could take a deep, slow, relaxed, diaphragmatic breath and feel calm, present, and in harmony. The longer you maintain relaxed, deep breathing, the more present and peaceful you will be.

Breathing affects your emotions as well. If you breathe shallow, fast breaths or hold your breath, you will experience anxiety or depression. Anxiety is defined as nervousness about things that have not happened yet, not being present. If you worry about things ahead and feel anxious, your breathing will be shallow and fast. Depression is defined as being upset about something that already happened, another form of not being present. If you hold your breath you are holding on to the past and most likely harboring upset emotions about something that already happened. In both cases, the future and the past are something we do not have any control over. The only way we can have constructive thoughts, be creative, feel calm, and be at peace is when we are present. The only way to be present is to breathe deep, slow, relaxed, diaphragmatic breathing. Unfortunately, the most common behavior under stress is one that does not serve us is holding our breath or quick shallow breathing associated with stress and fight-or-flight response. If instead, we were present, calm, with relaxed breathing, our body and brain would be fully oxygenated and energized to perform under any circumstance at levels beyond what we could imagine. Poor breathing causes oxygen deprivation, negative emotions, and tension, which affect our ability to perform to our maximum capacity both in body and mind. If you've ever watched a tied basketball game go down to the last seconds, the team with the ball will often call a time- out. This allows everyone to take

---

* See breathing exercises in the appendix page 244-250

a deep breath, get present, and get clear on a play and a strategy. This is done so that the opportunity to win the game is not wasted by stressed-out players running up the floor like chickens without heads, not knowing what to do with the ball. Anytime you find yourself in a stressful situation, you can call a time-out in your own head. This awareness will allow you to take a couple of deep breaths, get calm and clear about what you can do, and have control over right here and right now.

Another form of awareness is posture awareness. Bad posture affects the breathing and breathing affects your posture. In fact, it is impossible to slouch and breathe deep, slow, relaxed, diaphragmatic breaths at the same time. Try it for yourself. Close your eyes and perform three or four deep, slow, relaxed breaths. Pay attention to how your posture changes automatically. To breathe correctly you relax your shoulders, let them move back and drop down. You bring your head back, straighten your neck, and open your chest up. When you are breathing incorrectly you are using muscles in your ribcage and neck to breathe, or not using any muscles by holding your breath. This inefficient breathing does not provide your muscles and brain with enough oxygen, causing your muscles to contract, your mind to tense, and your emotions to be stressful.

The final awareness to cultivate is emotional awareness. Your emotions affect your posture and your posture affects your emotions. Likewise, your emotions affect your breathing and your breathing affects your emotions. When you see someone who is depressed, unassertive, melancholic, apathetic, or careless, their posture looks defeated and slouched forward. When you see someone who is anxious, angry, frenzied, grieving, or fearful, they are carrying tension in their neck, and chest, shrugging their shoulders. When you are present, at peace, calm, assertive, in joy, engaged, passionate, empathetic, still, courageous and careful, your posture will be erect and your breathing will be deep and calm.

Try this for yourself. Whenever you feel anxiety, depression, or any other stressful emotion, straighten your posture by bringing your shoulders back and down, bring your head back, straightening your neck, and open up your chest. You will find that you cannot maintain a correct posture and your stressful emotion at the same time. Another thing you can try when you feel good, happy, and engaged in any life situation is to deliberately slouch and sit in a bad posture. You will find that you cannot maintain a poor posture and feel good at the same time. We have all seen the body language of someone who is depressed or defeated, as well as someone who is anxious, angry, fearful, or tense.

In ancient martial arts, masters in kung-fu and karate have long known that staying relaxed by breathing deep and slow in the most intense combat will allow the practitioner to reach a higher state of mind and body. In this state everything is effortless, as if everything around the individual is moving in slow motion and he has all the time in the world. His mind is quick and creative. His muscles are powerful, and his reflexes react with the speed of light. We have all experienced this effortlessness at one time or another: a time when our mind was limitless, a time when we stopped thinking and just became what we did, a time when out of nowhere, we got great ideas or created something beautiful, a time when our bodies performed with ease as if on autopilot. In sports this state of body and mind is referred to as being "in the zone." I call it being present, and mastery of the Four Seasons wisdom is striving to experience this state as often as possible and for durations as long as possible.

Your breathing, your posture, and your emotions all provide you with feedback to internally monitor if your body and mind are in balance or not. Once you have awareness of this, you can begin to use it to your advantage by correcting your breathing and posture. You can start to question why your emotions are negative. What are you doing or not doing? Are you stuck in a season repeating a pattern? You can start to question if your thoughts and belief systems are stressful and if they serve you or not. The only reason you experience stress is because you believe a stressful thought in your mind. You can be aware of what you think, say, or do and the consequences that follow.

You can question if what your mind perceives as stressful is true and real or not. When you manage to stay calm, peaceful, and present, you can stay grounded, no matter what external circumstances you are in. Practice being aware and present in each and every moment of your day. With a proper posture and relaxed deep breathing, your body and mind can perform beyond your greatest imaginations.

Corrienne, a 64-year old woman, came to me referred from an orthopedic spine surgeon with chronic pain in her mid-back, in the left lower ribcage and under her left shoulder blade area. She had suffered from this pain for seven years. Corrienne had seen a number of different doctors, had x-ray's and an MRI of her mid back that didn't show anything wrong. She had been taking medications for the pain, and tried extended visits of physical therapy on two occasions, with no relief of symptoms. All treatment was directed only to the area of her pain.

Her pain was only gone when she woke up in the mornings and then gradually got worse as the day went on. It hurt more when she was stooping and reaching forward such as cooking, doing dishes and quilting. Lying down, with a hot water bottle laid over the painful area, gave her relief. As I observed her posture, it was apparent that her shoulders and head were rounded forward. Since poor posture and improper breathing goes hand in hand, I asked her if she found herself breathing shallow or holding her breath. Corrienne said, "I'm not a good breather. I worry a lot, and when I do I find that my breathing is poor."

Worrying is a form of nervous energy or anxiety so I asked her if she also experience depression.

"I feel depressed when I can't do the things I love - cook and quilt - due to increased pain", she said.

With mid back pain and poor breathing I was suspecting her diaphragm to be weak, and since this often leads to acid reflux, I asked, "Do you have heartburn?"

"Yes I do all the time; I need to take medication for it." Since Corrienne exhibited so many symptoms of an earth imbalance, I asked to see if she had any additional imbalances. She confessed to eating a lot of sweets, had a hard time falling asleep due to worrying and inability to turn off her mind. She was unable to relax and feel peace. When she woke up in the mornings she often had headaches due to sinus problems. She had arthritis in her neck and tightness in her chest and neck. Corrienne also experienced pain down her left lower leg along the shin bone and on top of her foot along the distribution of the stomach meridian.

I treated Corrienne by releasing tension from blocked acupuncture points on the left stomach meridian; on top of her foot, left shin bone, organ points for the stomach and spleen on the front and side of her torso, as well as trigger points for the diaphragm on front and back of the torso and in the scalene muscles of her neck. I gave her breathing exercises to strengthen her diaphragm at night and in the mornings. I also told her to be aware of her breathing at all times and to take 1-3 deep breaths every time she felt pain, tension, worrying, or becoming aware that she was not breathing right.

As she left, Corrienne had no pain and asked, "Can I quilt?"

I said, "You can quilt right away as long as you only think about your quilting and your breathing, and the moment you start worrying, stop quilting." Corrienne responded extremely well to the treatment. On her follow up appointment, she let me know she was doing her breathing exercises religiously. After only one appointment, she had healed from the pain that she had for seven years in her shoulder blade and mid back area. She had made the breathing exercises a daily activity, and she had no acid reflex symptoms and was not taking medication for it anymore. She was able to fall asleep right away with help of the breathing exercises, and told me she was not worrying about things as much.

Then she proceeded to tell me about another benefit from her breathing. Corrienne said, "I am 64 years old, and I have been biting on my cuticles since I was 12 years old. I could never stop myself from doing it. Since we started the treatment and I started the breathing exercises and not worrying as much, I stopped biting my cuticles."

Being aware of her breathing helped Corrienne being more calm, present and peaceful. It had improved her posture, removed strain and tension to her mid back and torso, strengthened her diaphragm, and reduced the amount of stress hormones being released. Her symptoms of upper back pain, heartburn, anxiety, depression and insomnia had all been healed. Learning how to breathe right might seem simple, yet is more effective and lasting than any drug and costs absolutely nothing. Mastering your breath and being aware of it at all times is a major part of mastering life. Unfortunately, too many people think breathing right is too simple and could not possibly be the cause of their suffering.

Manage Your Mind - One Season at a Time, One Moment at a Time

YOUR MIND CAN BE YOUR greatest asset or your worst enemy. We have often been told that our minds have potential beyond what we can ever imagine. On the other hand, our minds can also be self-destructive. If your thoughts, beliefs, and interpretation of life are stressful, then your life is a living nightmare. Only when we are calm and present can we be connected with a limitless, creative ability that many (me included) know as God, our unlimited source and origin.

You control your own mind, even if you choose to be controlled by someone or something else. All your actions and simultaneous emotional feedback are the result of your thoughts. Your negative, stressful emotions are an alarm clock telling you to wake up, get present and clear, and manage your mind by questioning whether your thoughts are true and serve you or not. As Byron Katie wrote in her book, *A Thousand Names for Joy*, things are not as they appear. Imagine you're walking down a trail and see a snake just a foot in front of you. Terrified, your heart pounding, you can't move. Then the clouds clear, and the sun shines brighter. In a different light, you see it was not a snake at all, but just an old rope. Now, you are laughing and relaxed. You can stand over that rope for a hundred years, and you can't make yourself be terrified by it again. With a calm, present, open mind and some imagination, every stressful thought can be seen in a different light.

Now that you understand how the Four Season System works, the next step is making changes in your thinking and behavior so that you can live in balance with the seasons. The remainder of this book focuses on teaching you what to do and when to do it so that your life aligns with the seasons and your suffering eases. The only reason you suffer is because you believe in a stressful thought. But what if you found that the thought was not true? The balanced (earth) mind is ever present, ever calm, and has the ability to imagine and create. This mind does not get "stuck" believing stressful, limiting thoughts. This mind is free; it goes "outside the box." If you can be aware of each present thought in each life situation (season), then you can question if your thoughts are really true or not and then choose an action that will serve you.

Spring: Clarity of the mind, our needs, and our direction.

Every thought is a seed. Is it a good seed that will bring positive emotions and good fruit? Or is it a bad seed that will bring stressful feelings, negative emotions, and suffering? Only you can determine if your thought or perception of something is stressful or not. This requires a clear, honest, and present state of mind.

Seeing a stressful thought in a different light or questioning it from a different perspective can remove your stress and tension as well as change your emotions. What if you looked at every "snake" as a rope? What if you believed that all "crap" can bring something good? Think about your own life. How many times did you perceive that something bad had occurred only to later realize that this "bad" thing had to happen for something better to grow out of it? Certainly, stinking, toxic manure seems bad, but it can become the fertilizer that will bring a greater crop in the future. Everything that happened in the past brings something good; experience helps us gain clarity on what we really want and what is really important. It helps us see what did or did not work so we can keep or change our old approach for future growth. Taking time to mentally mull over what good came out of the past and how it helped you attain clarity on direction and needs is essential for a good future outcome (harvest).

If you can't see the good result in what initially appeared bad, you will be "toxic" and consumed with stressful thoughts. You will be full of resentment, frustration, irritation, and anger, unable to forgive and take responsibility for your situation or observe your present need without judgment or blame. On the other hand, if instead of remaining present you sleepwalk through life, you will be passive and unassertive. You won't question your stressful thoughts, or you may be out of touch with your needs, thoughts, and feelings. You will be easily led by others and constantly find yourself involved in things you do not wish to be involved in. You will be passive-aggressive and hold anger and resentment inside until the tension makes you unable to perform, physically sick, or injured.

We label our life experiences and judge them as bad when in fact the opposite, that they are good and could serve us, is equally true. Being able to fertilize, to see what good can come out of something that was initially perceived as bad, will keep you from suffering. If you rush to plant a new seed or start over without fertilizing, you will relive the same experience over and over.

To help you avoid negative "stinking" thinking, consider the following:

- Be present, calm, clear, honest, and assertive with yourself and others.
- State what you need and why.
- Be clear on and state your boundaries.
- Stay present, get clear on and make sure a decision makes you feel calm and assertive rather than stresses you out.
- Think about the consequences of your words and thoughts.

Summer: Watering and weeding of the mind.

If you were not present in spring and suffer tension and stressful emotions due to a negative seed (negative thoughts or beliefs) already planted in your mind, you now have a second chance. You can separate pure from impure by pulling the weed before it grows too big, nipping it in the bud.

To help with the weeding, consider taking the following course of action or ask yourself these questions:

- Question whether everything you hear is true and will benefit your growth and wellbeing or not.
- Question whether what you intend to speak is true and will benefit the recipients growth and wellbeing or not.
- Express your feelings and needs authentically from your heart.
- Make sure you are calm and authentically enjoying what you are doing, thinking, or feeling?

Focus on (water) what you want: thoughts, beliefs, and actions that make you feel good, happy, and calm, expressing that which is alive in you with passion. This will bring more good and allow positive emotions to flourish. Question (weed out) stressful thoughts, beliefs, actions, and people. This will bring you joy and peace. Be authentic, real, present, and joyous in your everyday labor of life while focusing on solutions (rather than problems) and expecting that everything will come to a harvest. This will require positive focus and present mind. Dwelling on the negative will "water" the weeds and cause them to grow. They can overtake your mind and bring you suffering, injury, and disease.

Fall: Mind realization.

If you planted stressful thoughts, watered them, and now have merely a garden full of weeds to harvest, it's still not too late to grow in a positive direction by accepting what is (reality), learning from it, letting go and moving on. Are you able to accept your life situation? Are you able to accept what is or what happened? Are you taking responsibility for your life, without blaming others, being a victim or beating yourself up? If your thoughts about the outcome are stressful, and you experience anxiety, depression, or any other negative emotions (feedback), then the answer is no.

Ask yourself:

- Is my perception of the outcome true?
- Did I do the best I could, based on the circumstances?
- What did I learn?

Learning from your experiences can turn failure into a harvest. If you do not accept the outcome of your life situation (what is), then you will be filled with disappointment, sadness, grief, resentment, regret, guilt, shame, or embarrassment. You will be stuck in the past and won't be able to move forward. This emotional/mental constipation will cause you much stress, tension, and suffering that, over time, will manifest in an inability to move on in life, physical injury, and/ or disease. Another way of not accepting a life outcome is when you feel defeated, rejected, and apathetic and stop caring. Emotional/ mental diarrhea or "not giving a ****!" might seem like a good idea at the time, but will cause you to be in denial and move on too fast, and hence doom you to experience the same result over and over. This, too, will lead to stress, tension, suffering, injury, and disease. In either case, you fail to see the good by not learning the lessons from the outcome (harvest).

Winter: Stillness and gratitude of the mind.

If you did not reap a "harvest" you expected or desired you may be fearful of losing what you have: your life, health, loved ones, money, and/or personal belongings. You may be frozen, paralyzed, unable to take any action, and suffering with tension and pain. You can't see the light at the end of the tunnel, the dawn of a new day, or the end of winter.

If you did not harvest, you may also face another imbalance. If you are unable to accept a life outcome and learn from it, how can you feel satisfaction? You may become reckless and impatient, in a rush to start over without any rest. You may try to control things you have no control over. You may fail to appreciate what you have, to take care of yourself, loved ones, or belongings. This controlling, impatient, or unappreciative behavior of not being still will drain your energy and hence cause you to suffer from fatigue, exhaustion, tension, and pain.

- Remember what you learn, appreciate what you have.
- Have the wisdom to assess what life situations you have control over and which ones you do not.
- Do not drain your energy by dealing with things you have no control over.
- When something comes to an end, rest and be still, cautious, and calm until the next life opportunity (spring) comes around.

Accepting what life brings you, remembering what you learn, appreciating what you have, and trying new approaches will spark passionate, authentic joy and growth. This is a true definition of success, and by process of elimination, you will eventually get what you are looking for. Each successful cycle will make life easier. This is when you own the truth that life is not a destination but a journey, and you realize you already have what you are looking for.

Take a Personal Inventory

JUST AS A SUCCESSFUL BUSINESSPERSON must take inventory of his or her business, individuals can likewise perform a personal inventory of their strengths and weaknesses. When we become aware of how our behavioral patterns influence the outcomes of our lives, we change course for a different outcome.

After reading the first half of this book, you may have some idea of where you're blocked in your life. The questions and exercises in this section will help you determine what behaviors and patterns are preventing you from living your life to its fullest. As you read through the lists, answer yes or no. Take time now, and every so often, to perform this inventory, not only to gain clarity of where you are, but also to appreciate how far you have come.

Spring Inventory

Change your approach.

- Do you find yourself repeating a behavior or approach the same way over and over, even though it did not work out in the past?
- Do you have a hard time forgiving others and yourself for past actions or outcomes?
- Are you unable to see how past experiences help get you clear on what you need and help you grow?

Give honest opinions.

- When asked for your opinion, do you tell others what you think they want to hear to avoid hurting their feelings, rather than giving them your honest opinion?

Treat others with respect rather than judging them.

- Do you judge others rather than respect them for who they are?

Set boundaries and stand up for yourself.

- Do other people walk all over you or show disrespect toward you?
- When someone says or does something that oversteps your boundaries or upsets you, do you hold your feelings and needs inside rather than speaking up?

Be clear and decisive on where you are going in life, what you need and why you need it.

- Are you unclear on your direction in life and the intent of your actions?
- Do you let other people tell you what to do or where to go?
- Do you have a hard time making decisions or try to delay or avoid making them?

Don't say "yes" if you mean "no." Don't say "no" if you mean "yes." Don't say "yes" or "no" if you don't know.

- Do you let yourself get rushed or pressured into making decisions?
- Do you have a hard time saying no?

Think and get clear about what you wish to say (and the outcome it will have) before you speak, so you can speak with integrity

- Do you speak without thinking about the consequences?
- Do you put yourself down with negative thoughts about your ability or appearance?

Be calm, assertive, and present when you need to make crucial decisions under pressure

- Do you get angry, frustrated, or irritated trying to rush decisions when the pressure is on?
- Do you have a hard time controlling your anger?

Number of spring questions answered yes: _____

Summer Inventory

Be authentic and passionate about your work and your life.

- Is it hard for you to enjoy, be authentic and passionate about your work?
- Do you have a hard time being authentic and passionate in your relationships?
- Are you doing exercises you do not enjoy?
- Do you try to be the way you think others want you to be?

Have positive expectations while you look for solutions.

- Are you mostly negative and feel overwhelmed by your problems?
- Do you constantly see and talk about your problems instead of focusing on a solution?

Develop the ability to discern (weed) between good and bad, true or false.

- Do you often speak negatively or gossip?
- Do you take what others say or do personally?
- Do you get stuck in negative thoughts that stop you from flourishing?

Be present and fully engaged.

- Do you have a hard time being present, authentic, and fully engaged in what you do?

Inspire others.

- Are you a poor, negative, or boring communicator?
- Do you have a hard time expressing your passion or what is alive in you?

Align Talk and action.

- Do your actions not match your words?
- Do you talk too much?
- Do you feel you have to say something when others get quiet?

Cultivate Joy and passion.

- Do you let others take away your joy, passion or excitement?

Number of summer questions answered yes: _____

Fall Inventory

Accept what life brings you.

- Do you wish things were the way they used to be?
- Do you feel grief, regret, resentment, or guilt about the way things happened?
- Do you have a hard time accepting and approving of your accomplishments?
- Is it difficult for you to approve of your physical appearance?
- Do you wish your partner was different, rather than accepting her/him for who they are?
- Do you struggle with why another individual did what they did?

Learn from situations that did not end up the way you expected.
- Do you have a hard time learning from life and your mistakes?
- Do you beat yourself up for making mistakes?

Let go, move on, go with the flow.
- Do you have a hard time letting go, dwelling on the outcome?
- Do you have a hard time handling unexpected changes and letting go of past expectations?

Ask questions to clarify.
- Do you assume you know what others think, intend, or plan to do?

Ask specific requests of co-workers, friends, and loved ones to have your needs met.
- Do you expect co-workers, friends, and loved ones to know what you need, instead of asking for it?
- Do you have a hard time asking for help?

Receive gifts, compliments, pay, and rewards
- Do you have a hard time receiving without immediately thinking of how to reciprocate?
- Do you often feel you are not worthy of receiving?

Have empathy for yourself and others.
- Do you have a hard time being calm, accepting, understanding, and empathetic with yourself and others when things do not work out the way you expected?

Number of fall questions answered yes: _____

Winter Inventory

Remember lessons learned.
- Do you have a hard time remembering what you learned and what was said, or do you forget names, places, and dates?

Appreciate what you have and what you have accomplished in life.
- Do you take your life partner or loved ones for granted?
- Do you take your job for granted?
- Do you take your health for granted?

Store and preserve.
- Do you neglect your health and fitness (diet, rest, and exercise)?
- Are you unfaithful in your relationships or have a hard time keeping friendships?
- Do you neglect taking time to sincerely listen and hear what loved ones have to say?
- Are you poor at saving/investing your money?
- Do you neglect taking care of personal belongings or your home?

Rest and recuperate.
- Are you constantly on the run, believing you never have enough time?
- Do you take on too much and spread yourself too thin?
- Do you get less than 8 hours of sleep per night?
- Do you still feel tired after waking up in the mornings?

Be cautious and still.
- Do you have a hard time resting and being still?
- Are you often fearful or reckless?
- Do you constantly live in a state of urgency?

Number of winter questions answered yes: _____

All-Around, Earth Inventory

Be present and calm.
- Are you often depressed and dwelling on the past?
- Are you often worried or anxious about the future?
- Is your mind constantly wandering?
- Is it hard for you to be calm, peaceful and present?
- Do you have a hard time falling asleep?

Have peaceful thoughts and belief systems.
- Are your thoughts and belief systems mostly stressful?
- Do you obsess over and think the worst about your health issues?

Use creative, open-minded, outside-the-box thinking.
- Is your mind often stuck (no way out), closed, limited, and self-destructive?

Practice relaxed breathing (slow, deep, present diaphragmatic breathing).
- Do you have shortness of breath, shallow breathing, or do you hold your breath?
- Do you have acid reflex, heart burn?
- Do you have frequent burping or hick-ups?

Maintain balanced blood sugar, balanced diet, and regular meals.
- Do you crave sugar and carbohydrates?
- Do you skip meals or forget to eat at regular times?
- Do you obsess about food?

Number of earth questions answered yes: _____

Add up your total score for each season:
Spring Season/Wood Element: _____
Summer Season/Fire Element: _____
Fall Season/Metal Element: _____
Winter Season/Water Element: _____
Earth Element: _____

A high score in the inventory of a season, indicates that area of your life is in need of change and awareness on your part. You may find that you have quite a few yes answers in more than one of the five areas. That's normal and fine. If you think you're far from perfect, don't worry; everyone is. In fact, I don't know a single person who has it all together. Since I myself haven't yet mastered living in harmony with the four seasons at all times, I had to wrestle with whether I was even worthy to write this book. As long as I remind myself that I am not a master but a student and remember how far I have come since I started, I feel good about sharing this information with my patients and you for your growth and journey. And no one will ever be perfect. We're human. What's important to remember is that this way of life is a process of constantly being aware of our emotions and physical symptoms, taking an inventory on how our life is going, learning, and then using that information to make changes to grow and improve our life.

Monitor Your Emotional Feedback

EMOTIONS OFTEN GET A BAD rap. You've probably heard people say things like, "I wish I weren't so emotional!" "I hate being so sensitive." And, "I wish I could control my anger!" And maybe you've said some of those things yourself. Although emotional outbursts can be problematic, emotions themselves are important indicators of how you're feeling and they should be expressed and monitored. Many people think they have little or no control over their emotions, but to deny or "bottle up" our emotions allows pressure and tension to build. This can lead to pain, injury, disease, and suffering. Without emotions, we can never grow to our full potential.

Practice and make it a habit to check how you feel. Noticing, for example, that you are feeling frustrated (spring), or disengaged (summer), or disappointed (fall) or fearful (winter), reveals what season is out of balance.

Our emotions and feelings represent an intrinsic biofeedback mechanism designed to monitor whether our behavior is in harmony with the law of the Four Seasons. In a sense, our emotions can be regarded as a guidance system, like GPS, to keep us on course. When you are present and on course, you will experience emotional ease and harmony. On the other hand, deviating from the balanced way of life can leave you in a state of emotional distress with anxiety or depression and other negative emotions. Negative emotions tell us when something is wrong. Experiencing a negative emotion means we have a need that has not been met. If being derailed and getting off-track becomes a pattern and you're constantly under emotional distress, you must look inside to learn from past experiences and change your approach to get back on track.

You are responsible for how you feel. In extreme cases, pharmaceutical drugs may be necessary to treat a symptom, but in no way will they offer a long-term cure. By taking responsibility and looking for the cause, accepting and learning from life experiences, and taking proper action in each season, we can use our negative emotions to guide us back on track. Here are some examples:

- If you feel anxiety or depression, you are not in the present. You are either anxiously projecting the future or depressed and stuck in the past. The only thing you have any control over is the present moment; simple breathing exercises can make us calm and present instantly.
- If you cannot stop feeling angry, you might be toxic from old "waste" that accumulates by not forgiving or by not changing your approach before starting over.
- If you feel passive or unassertive, you are not clear on your own needs or direction and not taking responsibility for your outcome.
- If you feel overexcited or frenzied, you are not being authentic or real, or you may be all talk but no action, faking it, or being hypocritical or a phony.
- If you feel gloom or despair and no longer believe in what you are doing. You need to find something positive to focus on to spark some life and belief into what you are doing, or you need to stop doing it in order to be true to your heart."
- If you feel melancholic, perhaps you have no passion or fire, or you're not engaged, being true to your heart.
- If you feel disappointed, sad or experience grief or guilt, you may be unable to accept what happened, learn from it, let go and move on.
- A feeling of apathy leads to withdrawal and separation from life or feeling distant and rejected. Moving on to fast will be a missed opportunity to learn and grow.

- Staying in denial allows you to continue avoiding reality, unable to move on or grow.
- If you are afraid, your fears project the worst thing that could happen (future) by lacking faith and not remembering that things always worked out in the past.
- If you feel reckless, constant urgency, or dissatisfied, you may be jeopardizing the safety and well-being of yourself and others.

When a pilot flies an airplane from Los Angeles to Miami, he must take certain navigational considerations into account: side winds, magnetic deviation (which can cause erroneous instrument readings), weight distribution within the plane, and even the potential for human errors (not being present). This means that during the flight, he must constantly monitor and re-adjust the course, second by second. If he approached the flight with the attitude that being off course by five degrees to the north was no big deal, then the accumulative effect of those five degrees would cause him to end up as far north as New York or somewhere else he did not intend. A pilot must adjust and readjust his course moment by moment to ensure he reaches his intended destination.

The same is true with navigating through our cycles of life. We must stay present and calm, doing one thing at a time, paying attention to our emotions and our physical states. For instance, how is your breathing? Do you take calm, deep breaths using your diaphragm? Or do you hold your breath or take shallow and/or rapid breaths, which cause excessive stress to muscles in your ribcage and neck? How is your energy level? Do you need to rest or eat? How is the quality of what you eat? Do you drink enough water? How is your posture? What are you thinking? Is it a peaceful or stressful thought? What are you feeling? Is it a happy or stressful feeling? Are your muscles tense and painful? Where is the tension? Just like the pilot, we need to read all our instruments to navigate through our cycles of life, constantly adjusting and readjusting our behavior and actions during our journey. To do that, we need to be present and pay attention to how we feel and why.

Each negative emotion is trying to tell you something about the season in which you are not in harmony. It is telling you about actions and patterns of behavior, what you are doing or not doing, that are causing you to be off course. By comparing the emotions you experience with the Four Seasons System described in this book, you can narrow down the area in your life that's out of balance. Keep in mind that this is never a one-time fix, but rather a means of checking your course. As negative emotions arise (and they will!), use them to adjust your course. Just as if you were trying to get in shape, you need to know that a diet is a lifestyle rather than something you follow for a short duration. If not, you will get out of shape again when you start eating like you did before the diet. Mastery of the Four Seasons is about perfecting a harmonious lifestyle through present awareness for a lifetime. You use your emotional feedback to work to regain balance in this season, in this present moment. Any time you fall out of balance, you can start over.

Use Affirmations to Change Your Thinking

IF YOU LOOK BACK AT your responses to the Personal Inventory, each of the questions to which you answered "yes" is based on your experience and behavior in your life up to this point. Your answers are based on habits and beliefs, or what you believe is true at the time you take the quiz. But is this really the truth? If so, then you're doomed to stay right where you are, happy or not. Thankfully, habits and beliefs can be changed.

I used to be skeptical about affirmations as something "New Age" and lacking substance, like wishful thinking. Then as I continued to live and study on my journey, I realized that all of us, me included, have this voice in our heads that constantly judges us. That voice can run amok and keep stating the same negative affirmation in our heads, over and over until we believe it to be true. The voice says things like: you are not good enough, you will never make it, you are so stupid, you are fat or ugly, nobody likes you, or you always cave under pressure. We have in fact been brainwashed by our own minds to believe in limiting thoughts and untrue beliefs.

We move toward what our minds dwell upon and those repetitive thoughts become a belief system that often does not serve us. Then those belief systems become self-fulfilling prophecies, so we keep repeating the same pattern to confirm that the voices in our heads were right all along. When we recognize and understand this dysfunction of our minds, we can determine which beliefs serve us and which do not. You probably discovered quite a few negative beliefs when you answered the personal inventory questions. Understanding what we're doing wrong, we can then start to use positive affirmations to change a behavior, belief, or habit to something that will serve us better.

Affirmations are statements asserting the existence or truth of something. Said over and over again habitually, they can change your interior dialogue from that defeated voice to an uplifting, empowered one. Affirmations should be stated as if they are already true. We need to repeat these affirmations until we start to believe them and act in a way that serves us. Look at each of your yes answers on the Personal Inventory, and then choose some example affirmations from the following list to start changing your behavior, beliefs, and habits right away.

Spring Affirmations

Change approach.
- I forgive myself and others. I use my past experiences to gain clarity about directions on where to go or what I need.
- I change my approach to improve and grow.

Express honest opinion.
- I respectfully give my honest opinion when asked.

Treat others with respect, rather than judging them.
- I respect others, without judgment.

Set boundaries and stand up for yourself.
- I stand up for myself. I take responsibility for my life, actions, and words.
- I assert my boundaries and speak up for myself.

Be clear and decisive about where you are going in life, what you need, and why you need it.
- I am clear on my direction in life; I know where I am going and why. I am clear on my intent and on my actions.

- I am my own person; I make my own decisions and take responsibility for them.
- I am clear and decisive.

Don't say "yes" if you mean "no." Don't say "no" if you mean "yes." Don't say "yes" or "no" if you don't know.
- I take all the time I need to get clear, calm, and assertive before I make my decisions.

Think and get clear about what you wish to say (and the outcome it will have) before you speak so you can speak with integrity.
- I speak only impeccable words. I speak only when I am clear on my intent and the consequences of my words.
- My word is my seed, and I only plant good seeds.
- I think only impeccable thoughts that serve my self-esteem and growth.

Be calm, assertive, and present when the pressure is on and you have to make crucial decisions.
- I am calm; I have all the time I need to get clear and make my decisions.
- I am calm and assertive.

Summer Affirmations

Be authentic and passionate about your work and your life.
- I am engaged and true to my heart in everything I choose to do.
- I am authentic, passionate, and engaged in all relationships I'd like to see flourish.

Hold positive expectancy, looking for solutions.
- I see the possibilities, I believe in what I do. I know everything will work out.

- I focus on the solutions, I see the answers.

Maintain the ability to discern (weed) between good and bad, true or false.
- I speak only positive words aimed to inspire.
- My happiness and joy come from within.
- Good things are happening; I see things working out.

Be present, authentic, and fully engaged.
- I am present, authentic, engaged, and enjoy what I do. I seek the positive in every moment.

Inspire others.
- I strive to include something good, positive, and encouraging in everything I say.
- I express from my heart with passion what I live for.

Balance talk and action.
- I say what I do and I do what I say.
- I know when to take action; I know when to be still. I know when to talk; I know when to listen or be quiet.

Emanate joy and passion.
- My joy, passion, and excitement come from within.

Fall Affirmations

Accept what life brings you.
- I accept what is. Everything happens for a reason; I learn from all life experiences.
- I always do the best I can under the circumstances and with the resources I have. I approve of my efforts and learn to improve.

- I approve of my body and the way I look.
- I accept and love my partner for who he/she is, or I release my partner to set us both free.

Learn from life situations that did not end up the way you expected.
- There are no mistakes, only learning opportunities.
- I always do my best; I always learn and grow.

Let go, move on, go with the flow.
- I am present and going with the flow.
- Change is good; everything happens for a season; there is always a reason.

Ask questions to clarify.
- I always ask questions to gain clarity and understanding.
- I ask and I receive.

Receive gifts, compliments, pay, and rewards.
- I receive all gifts and compliments that are given to me.
- I am worthy of and open to receiving all good things.

Have empathy for yourself and others.
- I have empathy for myself and others when things don't go as expected.

Winter Affirmations

Remember lessons learned.
- I remember all things that are important.

Appreciate what you have and what you have accomplished in life.
- I appreciate _____ for who she/he is and for all that she/he has given.

- I appreciate and I am grateful for all that my employment (work) gives me.

Store and preserve.

- I do everything I can to take care of and preserve my health and fitness.
- I am loyal and faithful in my relationships.
- I am considerate and appreciate my friends.
- I am still and quiet. I sincerely listen and hear what loved ones have to say.
- I invest wisely.
- I take pride in taking care of my belongings and home.

Rest and recuperate.

- I have all the time I need.
- I rest when I need to; I trust everything that is supposed to get done will get done when it is supposed to.

Be still.

- I am still and at peace.
- I am calm, still and patient.

All around, Earth Affirmations

Be present and calm.

- I am present, calm and at peace in the here and now.
- I always have what I need when I need it.
- I only have one thing to do at any given moment.

Have peaceful thoughts and belief systems.

- My mind and my belief systems serve me, help me grow, and bring me peace.

Use creative, open-minded, outside-the-box thinking.
- I am finding a way to make it work.
- I always find a way.
- I create what I need.

Practice relaxed breathing (deep, slow, present diaphragmatic breathing).
- I am present, calm, and aware in my deep, relaxed breathing.
- I am aware of how each breath fills me with life and makes me calm.

Strive for balanced blood sugar, balanced diet, and regular meals.
- I have a strong desire to function well and look good, so I eat food that is good for me. (or I crave food that makes me function well and look good).
- I eat healthy meals at regular, set times to keep my metabolism at peak performance.

It's quite possible that the affirmation you need the most will sound like a complete lie to you at first. This is because the negative programming has been repeated so many times for so long. Your mind may not accept the positive affirmation as truth, but with time and repetition, the new affirmation will ring truer and truer.

Choose one or two affirmations you think you need the most. Repeat it, or them, in your mind once every hour of the day. Also, every time you're in front of a mirror, look yourself in the eye and repeat the positive affirmation in your mind or out loud. Do this for twenty-one days to form new habits. After the twenty-one days, continue to repeat this positive affirmation (watering) every time the old, destructive belief pops up (weeding).

This might sound like a lot of work, but will get easier once it becomes a habit. Just like learning to drive a stick shift car might have seemed overwhelming at first, eventually it became second nature. Your habits and behavior will gradually change, and your mind will serve you instead of bringing you down.

Daily Work for a Balanced Spring

IF YOU ARE OUT OF balance in spring, it's important to get clear on what YOU need, what drives you, and what makes you tick. What make us do the things we do? What drives us? Why do we even bother to get out of bed in the morning? Even if we don't realize them on a conscious level, we are driven by basic human needs. Many of us have been conditioned to believe being needy, or even having needs, is a negative thing. Yet every action we take and every word we speak is motivated by a need that we want to have met. Unmet needs can lead to distress, tension, failure, pain, suffering, injury, and/or disease.

In addition to our needs, we have wants and desires. People often confuse needs with wants. For instance, you may need a car for transportation, but you don't need a Ferrari. Buying a Ferrari may not bring you peace and satisfaction. Unless you have enough wealth it could bring unintended consequences: going to deep into debt, worrying about maintenance, and being scared to drive it and have it scratched, nicked, damaged, or even stolen. This example could be the root of the famous proverb, "Be careful with what you ask for; you might get it." Think about it. How do you know that what you want is really what's best for you?

We also have goals and dreams. A goal is a plan of action for how we can achieve a need or want. A goal is something we believe we can accomplish. Many people are so bent on achieving their goals that they do not enjoy the journey. However, the journey (being in the moment), not the destination (reaching the goal), will bring you true peace and satisfaction. A dream has no limits, but there is a big difference between having dreams and being a dreamer. Dreams, creativity, and imagination set in motion have given the world some of its greatest discoveries, inventions, and other wonders. If you give up on a dream, a part of you will die.

Our needs, wants, desires, goals, and dreams are the fuel that keeps us going. This fuel is what makes us engage in life; it is what's alive in us. Our needs give us passion, fire, and motivation. Having needs that are not met, however, will cause us stress, frustration, resentment, anger (expressed or suppressed) with tension, pain, suffering, injury, and/or disease.

The Fuel that Drives Us: Basic Human Needs

The following list explains the basic human needs. Some people do not know what they need and have never spent time getting clear on what they need.

1. *Meaning or Purpose.* Each and every one of us has our own individual purpose, but the greatest purpose for all of us is to serve others, to learn and grow, do good deeds, to be whole and be a messenger of truth and love. Our purpose is to contribute to the enrichment and growth of our lives and those of others.
2. *Autonomy.* We need personal independence, the freedom to choose our own beliefs and actions. We need to develop our own individuality, find our own path and purpose.
3. *Love, Touch, Intimacy, and Sexual Expression.* Studies show that babies deprived of human touch do not thrive. Every human needs to experience love and to be touched, whether by a significant other, family, friends, or pets. As in all things, the best way to get something is to first give it. You need to be genuinely loving. It is important to remember that love is not a need that is filled externally; you already have an infinite source inside your heart.

4. ***Community/Belonging.*** In our early days as cave dwellers, being part of a community greatly aided our chances of survival in a harsh world. Modern man has still held on to this need to belong, to be part of a group, whether that's family, friends, teammates, co-workers, church, clubs, or interest groups. Feeling connected with others, united for a good cause, rather than feeling separated, is an essential need.

5. ***Air, Food, and Water.*** If nothing else, hunger or thirst eventually will drive you out of bed in the morning. Hunger and thirst are primal needs necessary for survival. To function and perform optimally we need healthy meals at regular times. We need to hydrate our bodies by drinking enough fluid (preferably water). We need to engage our diaphragms to breathe deeply, taking slow, relaxed breaths so we take in enough oxygen to maintain the healthy functioning of body and brain.

6. ***Shelter and Clothing.*** You need to be protected from the elements with housing and clothing appropriate for your climate.

7. ***Movement and Exercise.*** You need to use or exercise your muscles to maintain or improve your body's function and performance. As the saying goes, "Use it or lose it."

8. ***Peace, Harmony, Calm, Presence, and Creativity.*** Without calmness, harmony and peace with yourself and with the world, life can be chaotic and stressful. Stress and tension, as we've seen, lead to dysfunction and emotional or physical disease. Few possess true harmony and peace, and many may not know how important these needs are. Peace and calmness can only be experienced when you are fully connected and present in the here and now. When you are at peace and harmony, free of distractions and limiting beliefs, you are free to be creative.

9. ***Clarity, Responsibility, Honesty, Integrity, and Respect.*** You need to be clear on your intention and direction. You need to

forgive yourself and others as well as change your ways when the old way does not get you were you want to be. You need to take responsibility for your words, actions, and life situation. You need to speak impeccable words. You need to be honest with yourself and others; you need to assert your boundaries so you may earn respect from others. You need to respect others for who they are, without judgment.

10. ***Authentic, Passion, Joy, Fun, and Laughter.*** You need to be authentic and true to your heart; fully engage in the moment; and express passion and joy in your labor, pastimes, and relationships. You need to have fun, laugh, and enjoy life. You need to discern the negative and amplify the positive.

11. ***Accomplishment, Empathy, Understanding, Acceptance, and Approval.*** You need to feel a sense of accomplishment, a feeling that you learn and grow. At times, life does not happen the way you or others expect. You need to have empathy without pity for others and yourself. You need to accept the outcomes of events and accept where you are in life. You need to accept and approve of your physical body and appearance. You need to realize and understand what you learn from every life experience.

12. ***Safety, Trust, Appreciation, and Rest.*** You need to feel safe and secure, physically, mentally, emotionally, and financially. You need to trust that everything always works out in the end. You need to appreciate everything and everyone you have in your life. You need to be appreciated for what you do and who you are. You need to remember what you learn. And you need to know your limits and allow enough time for quality rest.

Your needs and your desire are what are alive in you. It is your fuel that gets you going. If you lack fuel you cannot get going. When you read through that list of basic human needs, did you recognize some that aren't being met in your life? Fill out the wheel of life diagram to see how well your needs are being met. Rate each category on a scale of one to ten, with "one" meaning the need is unfulfilled, and "ten" meaning the need is fully satisfied. Place an X in the appropriate square, and then connect each X with a line. "Flat" spots in your otherwise well-rounded "tire" indicate needs that are not being met, and an area of your life that needs attention.

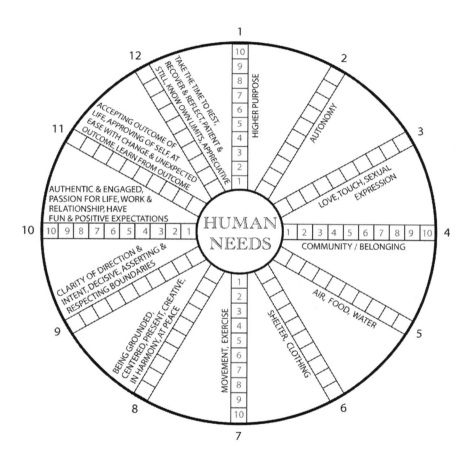

HUMAN NEEDS

1 — HIGHER PURPOSE (10 9 8 7 6 5 4 3 2 1)

2 — AUTONOMY

3 — LOVE, TOUCH, SEXUAL EXPRESSION

4 — COMMUNITY / BELONGING (1 2 3 4 5 6 7 8 9 10)

5 — AIR, FOOD, WATER

6 — SHELTER, CLOTHING

7 — MOVEMENT, EXERCISE (1 2 3 4 5 6 7 8 9 10)

8 — BEING GROUNDED, CENTERED, PRESENT, CREATIVE, IN HARMONY, AT PEACE

9 — CLARITY OF DIRECTION & INTENT, DECISIVE, ASSERTING & RESPECTING BOUNDARIES

10 — AUTHENTIC & ENGAGED, PASSION FOR LIFE, WORK & RELATIONSHIP, HAVE FUN & POSITIVE EXPECTATIONS (10 9 8 7 6 5 4 3 2 1)

11 — ACCEPTING OUTCOME OF LIFE, APPROVING OF SELF, AT EASE WITH CHANGE & UNEXPECTED OUTCOME, LEARN FROM OUTCOME

12 — TAKE THE TIME TO REST, RECOVER & REFLECT, PATIENT & STILL KNOW OWN LIMITS, APPRECIATIVE

The information you receive from this human needs diagram shows the areas of life in which your needs are not being met. You can use this valuable input to set goals to meet these needs. Use the following exercises to start making a plan for meeting each of your unmet needs or goals.

Fertilization

Many people do not know what they need. They never think about their needs and are not very happy about where they are in life. Previous experiences in life are judged with expressed or repressed anger, resentment, frustration, or irritation. Perhaps they believe having needs is bad or selfish, and at best, all they can think of is what they don't need.

The following is an exercise in getting clear on what you need.

Write down all things that have not worked for you in the past and the reasons why you believe those things did not work out. In this list, you may include all your negative experiences, bad habits, negative belief systems, poor self-esteem, what other people did or did not do, and the things that you did or did not do. All those negative words and experiences are fertilizers that can help you identify and get clear on what you don't need and which approaches did not work. Next, use a thesaurus to find the antonyms for each negative experience, and write them in another column. This will make you clear on the opposites, what you **do** need. In this way you will have clarity before you start a new cycle so you can improve on how to do things the next time around.

Prior to meeting my wife, Sue, I did this same exercise. I sat down with pen and paper and wrote down what I did or did not like about my previous marriages and relationships. I had one very short list of things I liked and a very long list of things I did not like.

This long list of what "stunk" in my past relationships was my "fertilizer" or what I refer to as my "shit" list. For me, and probably you as well, repeating a pattern over and over without getting my needs met lead to frustration, irritation, anger, resentment and judgement. If you, as I did, kept repeating a series of dysfunctional or dissatisfying relationships, the list would grow, as would the frustration, anger and judgement towards the opposite sex. The more times we repeat these patterns without "harvesting" the longer the list will get. The problem is that once we are up to our neck in "shit", full of stinking thinking, all we can see is what we do not like and what we do not need. However, the act of "fertilization" in this exercise made me take responsibility and ownership for my past relationship experiences.

If the farmer does not take the waste from the past to fertilize before he plants again, the soil will never be fertile to produce a harvest.

I opened up a thesaurus to find the antonyms of all the negative words that made up my "shit" list. For each stinking experience there were a number of antonyms, so I selected the one I liked the most. When I considered each item I didn't like and figured out the opposite, I realized there were many things I needed in a relationship that I'd never thought about. For example, one of my dislikes was drama, so the opposite of an emotionally dramatic person is someone who is peaceful and calm

Once I converted all the negative, stinking thinking into the opposite I was clearer than ever about what I really needed in a relationship. I added all the converted antonyms from the "shit" list to the short list of what I did like about past relationships, and this made one long list of what I needed in a future relationship. After that, I prioritized my needs, putting the needs that were an absolute must first. Those were the deal breakers that determined if a future partner was a fit right away. This would save me from futile attempts of trying to fit a square peg into a round hole again.

In this way I got clear on everything I would like in a mate, and this became the list of what I desired in a relationship. I needed to find someone who was authentic, calm, peaceful, honest, loyal, and responsible, with integrity. I realized my mate needed to be my best friend. She needed to love what she did for a living and be passionate about her career. I needed to respect and accept her for who she was, and she needed to do the same for me. I wanted to find a mate who loved to exercise, eat healthy, and be fit. I wanted her to be affectionate and loving, and I finally added it would be great if she had a dog. I realized I had wanted a dog, but never had the time to take care of one. When I fell in love with Sue, it was because she had all these qualities. The heading on her Fitness Singles on-line dating profile read; "This is a drama free zone." Her profile matched my list and mine matched what she was looking for.

The underlying lesson here is that you cannot find what you are looking for until you know what you are looking for. If all you can see is what you don't like and what you don't need, you will be toxic with a stinking attitude and repeat more of those bad relationships. Your mind keeps moving towards whatever you are focused on. All my past relationships, good or bad, all the way back to high school, became feedback for what I really needed. All negative feedback became fertilizer that helped me see what was important and get clear on what I needed. All the negative experiences of the past helped me find Sue. All bad past relationships had been my teachers and they had done me a favor showing me what I did not need so that I could get clear on what I do need. When you come to this realization forgiveness comes naturally.

A list like this can be done with any bad or negative experiences of the past. It could be done with bad past jobs, broken friendships, failing to get physically fit, finding peace and purpose in your life or any need. This exercise can be applied to any goal that you have been unable to reach.

It is natural to at first think "shit' stinks and is good for nothing, but good things grow out of a fertilizer. All feedback, positive or negative, is good for growth. Once we learn that unpleasant or bad experiences of the past helped us grow and get clear on what we truly needed, then we can take responsibility for our situation. In this way we are able to forgive others and ourselves to start over in a new spring, clean and clear.

When something in our lives is working the way we want it to, it is fine to keep doing things in the same way. When things are not working we need to fertilize to get clear on what we need and try a new approach. In this way by process of elimination we will get closer to harvest what we desire with each go round.

Goal Planning

Use the feedback from the human needs diagram and the converted needs from the fertilization exercise to turn your unmet needs into goals. The needs that you make into goals are seeds ready to be planted. Write down your goals, using as much detail as possible-- the more specific, the better. Write down how you will feel once this goal is met.

Goal Setting/Commitment (Planting)

Write down the goals you are ready to commit to right now. Write a plan of action (strategy), then sign and date your commitment to reaching this goal. Once you commit to a goal the seed is planted. Now you have to work on the field (summer, water and weed) till you reap your harvest.

Daily Work for a Balanced Summer

ALL OF YOUR GOALS ARE in the summer season from the moment you make a commitment (plant) till the time of harvest. Everything you already started and are engaged in is in summer. Summer is about expecting a harvest, expecting success, and expecting to win. Invariably, winners *expect* to win. If we don't believe, on some level, that we can succeed at something, why even try? If your belief in a successful outcome is not stronger than your belief in a negative outcome, you will be wasting time and energy. Yet most people continue pursuing something they don't believe they can accomplish in one area of life or another. You need to spend more time visualizing, thinking, and speaking of a harvest than you spend imaging, thinking, or speaking of not making it.

Visualization - the Act of Watering

In a relaxed state, visualize what you want. Visualize the solutions to any obstacles, the answers to any problems. Do this on a daily basis. Make the visualization as real as possible by incorporating all your senses: what you see, what you hear, what you feel, and what you smell. By repeatedly pre-playing what you want as a virtual reality in your mind, your mind will start to believe it is true and that it has already happened. Once you are convinced something is true and that you have already done it in the past, it will be easier to do it over and over again. The mind does not know the difference between imagination and reality. Repeating a positive visualization waters and nurtures the seed that was your goal or intent, bringing it to a harvest. Likewise, re- playing a negative experience or belief in your mind will water and nurture the weeds. Whatever you water will grow, what your mind dwells on is what you move towards.

Vision Board

Images are very powerful tools for programming our minds to receive what we desire to harvest in our lives. Get a poster board and make a collage by cutting out and taping pictures, images, and words that represent a vision of reaping your harvest. Place this vision board where you can see it daily. This could be next to your bathroom mirror, on your refrigerator, or on the inside of the door to your home. The important thing is for your subconscious mind to see this image many times every day.

Discernment: the Act of Weeding

Summer also stands for weeding; in other words, separating pure from impure, true from false, and good from bad. Just like the farmer pulls weeds from his fields to ensure his harvest and our small intestine retains nutrition while rejecting waste, our minds, when working in a way that serves us, likewise need to filter or discern what serves us and what doesn't serve us.

When listening, ask yourself; is what you hear true? Is it good? Does the information benefit you? If the answer is not yes to at least one of those three questions, reject the information. When communicating with others, ask yourself the same questions. Is what you intend to speak true? Is it good information? Will it benefit the individual you are communicating with? If the answer is not yes to at least one of those questions, avoid speaking this information. Obviously, mindless gossip needs to be weeded out. When taking part in any activity, ask yourself if this activity brings you joy, if it is good, and if it benefits and serves you. If the answer is not yes to at least one and preferably all three questions, stop what you are doing. When eating, ask yourself if what you intend to eat is healthy and if it will benefit you. This weeding or discernment is ongoing and requires a present and conscious mind.

Daily Work for a Balanced Fall

FALL REPRESENTS REAPING A HARVEST. If you are a perfectionist, if you have adopted a belief system that you are not good enough, or if you feel you are not worthy to receive, you need to change your belief system to one that serves you. If your definition of success is perfection, then you will never quite get there. If you are one of those people, you need to focus on what you learn in each and every moment of your day instead of constantly beating yourself up for not being good enough.

About twenty years ago, I came to the realization that my belief system about my definition of success was not serving me. Every evening as I left work and every weekend, I kept thinking of the patients I had not been able to help. I felt I was not good enough or not doing enough for those patients. I felt guilty for charging them and did not feel worthy of the fee I charged. My definition of success was that every single patient should leave my office free of pain, or I did not have a good day. I needed to be perfect to have a good day. For everyone to leave completely pain free, when seeing up to 20 patients a day, was not likely. If 18 of 20 patients left pain free, all I could think about was the two who did not get better. Consequently, I never had a good day. So I kept beating myself up, tormenting myself by never receiving my harvest. It is true that this belief had made me who I was. The drive to constantly do better or develop a better therapy had made me a better therapist and served my patients. Nevertheless, I never had any peace or sense of accomplishment. I did not approve of my efforts or myself.

Then one day listening to some self-help tapes while driving home from work, I realized that there were many things I did not have any control over. Maybe a patient did not want to get better. Perhaps they got some reward as attention from being in pain. It is possible that they hated their work and their injury became their excuse for not having to go back to work. Perhaps they did not follow my instructions or advice on what to do to get better. Maybe they were not completely honest or telling me everything that was going on in their lives. Also it humbled me to realize there was so much I still did not know about how the human body and mind works. How could I have results if I lacked knowledge or "know how?"

I needed to change my belief and my definition of success. I realized success is not being perfect. If people do the best they can with the resources (knowledge, time, energy, beliefs, finances etc.) they have at hand and always learn from the outcomes then they are truly successful. How could anyone ever do more than his or her best with the resources he/she has at hand? I realized if I always do my best and always learn from the outcome, then I would always grow and improve as a therapist and a man. This definition of success is based on things I can control: my intention, my effort, my attitude, accepting the outcome and learning from my experience.

Today I still expect every patient to leave the visit free of pain, but I do not beat myself up if they do not. Doing my best and learning from every single patient assures that I continue to grow.

Consider adopting a belief system that defines success by always doing the best you can with the knowledge, resources, and time that you have at your disposal and by always learning from your experiences. If you accept this as your new belief, even if the outcome is not what you had expected, you can always be successful, for you can always learn something, and you can always grow. If you always do your best, always learn and grow, then you never get stuck. You keep moving forward always realizing a harvest (what you learned) even if it was not what you had expected. By process of elimination, this approach will make you get better and better at what you are doing, and you will be more likely to reach your expectations. The key to changing the old way of thinking is to catch yourself in the act when it occurs. Practice being present and aware of your thought patterns, and you may notice when that voice in your head says, "You should have done this or that." "Why didn't you do this or that?" "You are a loser." "You are stupid." or anything else that is about second guessing or putting yourself down. When this thinking comes up, take a deep breath and ask yourself, "Did I do the best I could at the time, given what I knew, or given the circumstances?" And of course the answer is always "YES, I DID," (unless you deliberately screwed up). Then you ask yourself, "What did I learn?" Fall is about accepting the outcomes of your harvest for what it is, good and bad, in total, so you may learn and grow from the experience.

Part of accepting outcomes is also tied to accepting who we are, as individuals. Many people believe they have to achieve to be worthy, when in fact the opposite is true; we are all worthy of achievement. One example of this is the individual who says to himself or herself, "When I lose weight I will approve of/like/love myself." But the opposite is true: you cannot lose weight until you approve of/like/love yourself. Approve of your efforts, learn from the outcome and keep changing the approach until you get desired results.

Journaling

At the end of each day, write down in a fall journal what you did and what you accomplished and/or learned today about yourself, others and your environment. No matter how seemingly insignificant or great a learning experience or accomplishment, write it down. It may take some thinking to realize what each daily experience taught you. If you have a fall imbalance this will take effort. As in all things, if something is effortless, then you have already mastered it. Repetition and practice will lead to mastery, and in time this exercise will build insight, as you see your lessons build upon one another. The practice of changing your belief system to one that serves you and journaling what you learned and accomplished on a daily basis will help you realize greater and greater accomplishments with each go-round. Realizing that you always learn, and therefore always accomplish something, will help build self-esteem.

Daily Work for a Balanced Winter

WINTER IS A TIME TO appreciate what you have, remember what you have learned, and be still. It is a time to be in an attitude of gratitude. Write down a list of all things you are grateful for. This could be your life, your health, your mind, your purpose, your profession, your home, daily bread, loved ones, your freedom, your country, established wealth, personal belongings, or anything else you can think of. While lying in bed at night before you fall asleep and when you first wake up in the morning, recite this list of gratitude to make sure you remember it and never take anything for granted.

Read Your Journal

If you are keeping a daily fall journal of what you learned and accomplished every day, you need to remember these lessons to remain balanced in winter. Before you go to sleep each night, read this journal from beginning to end so you retain what you have learned.

Daily Awareness to stay Present

To BE BALANCED IN THE ever-present earth element, you need to be fully aware and conscious in your breathing, your posture, your emotions and your mind. You need to be calm and present at all times under any circumstance. The problem arises with this: we are completely unaware of when we are not present. However the moment we recognize the patterns of not being present in ourselves, we instantly become present. This awareness principle is based on two key concepts

1. Take note when your mind is wandering away from being in the present moment (the task at hand), bored or overwhelmed, disappointed/depressed or worried/anxious.
2. The second concept is to enhance the present moment through awareness of your breathing. This will give you improved thoughts and actions in a calm state of mind.

The quicker you catch yourself not being present, the faster you will be able to bring yourself back to the present moment. And because of this practice, you will find yourself being present, calm, and at peace for longer durations.

To demonstrate this principle, here is an example:

One day you find you are overwhelmed and your mind is racing all over the place. Your mind is franticly screaming, "I have twenty things that need to be dealt with and taken care of right now!!!!"

Everyone can easily agree that this state of mind is not harmonious, healthy, productive, or creative.

Now, following the principles above, you can take a breathing time out and ask yourself:

"Which of those twenty things do I really have control over right now?"

Not, tomorrow or an hour from now, but RIGHT NOW!

Taking a deep breath, you can say to yourself, "Okay, I can control these five things."

Taking another deep breath you can ask yourself "Which of those five things are a priority?"

Another deep breath and say "Okay those three things."

Taking another deep breath you can ask yourself "Now of those three things, which one of those is the highest priority?"

After taking another deep breath you have successfully identified the number one priority and you can say to yourself, "'This is the number one priority that I have control over right now!"

Good! Do that one thing right now, and do not think about the other 19 things.

Simple right?

But let's take this example a bit further, as real life often does for us.

We have relaxed and identified our number one priority, and then the phone rings and someone is telling you there is an emergency that has to be dealt with right now.

Again, here is where we can be aware of our newly found practice.

Take that first deep breath, and ask yourself, "Is this truly an emergency for me and not just their emergency? Another person's lack of planning is not necessary your emergency.

If it is truly an emergency for you, take another deep breath then ask, "Do I have any control over this matter right now?"

If you do not, then there is nothing you can do about it right now, and you can go back to your first priority.

If you do have control of the outcome of this emergency, take another deep breath and ask, "Is this a higher priority then what I was already doing?"

If it is, take a deep breath and deal with your new priority without thinking of all the other urgencies that need to be dealt with. If it is not THE top priority, prioritize it on your list for a later time and go back to your first priority.

These exercises and examples show you how you stay calm and present in the midst of stressful circumstances: one thing at a time, one breath at a time.

You are only one person, and you can only do one thing at peace and with excellence at any given moment.

Resist the urge to say, "I am so busy I don't have time to do my breathing."

In fact, the opposite is true. The busier you are the more important it is to breathe and do one thing at a time.

Four Seasons Communication

FAILURE TO COMMUNICATE IS OFTEN a great source of stress and suffering that ultimately can affect our emotional well-being and our physical health. Most of the time, our communication is very poor; we are unable to make our needs understood or we don't understand the needs of others. Miscommunication leads to conflict, tension, pain, and suffering. In his book, *Nonviolent Communication: A Language of Love*, Marshall Rosenberg details how improving our communication enhances our lives by helping us meet our needs and the needs of others. This way of communicating is truly win-win, giving and receiving, planting and reaping in harmony with the Four Season System.

In the following section, I have incorporated his concepts, as I understand them, into four steps representing the "Four Seasons."

Spring:

If we are not clear about what we need—we are so conditioned to think of others' needs before our own—an imbalance in spring communication is present. People who are imbalanced in their spring communication speak without having a clear intent or direction. When you ask why they said a certain thing, they often do not know. They do not think about consequences and effect. They seem passive, often letting others decide for them, and they have a hard time saying no. Resentment and anger can build up over time as they fail to assert their needs and boundaries.

Another imbalance in spring communication can be found in people who get angry, frustrated, irritated, or put blame on someone or something else because their own needs are not being met. Using anger to force your way might get your needs met by bullying others to comply by fear or guilt, but this behavior often causes the other person to get defensive or counter-blame. By using anger, they fail to take responsibility for their life situation (needs not being met) and fail to communicate their needs without judgment or blaming others.

Without judgment or blame for past actions or events, take responsibility for the life situation you are in right now. Whenever you are feeling disharmony, get present and clear and observe what need you have that is not met right now (What is missing?). Observe how not having that need met feels. The ability to clearly see and communicate your need (and your intent with your communication) is your responsibility. Think about the possible consequences of your spoken word before you speak it.

Practice using impeccable words to clearly communicate your needs.

Summer:

People who are imbalanced in summer communication ramble on without coming across as real or authentic. They talk all the time, a lifeless conversation without connecting and engaging others. This could be a salesperson who talks too much and oversells or a self-centered or insecure hypocrite (hyped up, frenzied, or a phony). "Fake" summers act or pretend to be what they think others want them to be; they are trying too hard.

Another example of imbalance in summer communication lies in people who lack enthusiasm or are unable to express what is alive in them. They lack action, and they are often melancholic or gloomy about life. These people do not talk much, and when they do talk, conversation is slow and reluctant. They lack passion and have a hard time getting their needs, thoughts, messages, and feelings across.

Speak authentically from your heart what is "alive in you." Passionately express your needs and how you feel. Express your feelings of not having your needs met, as well as how you would feel if they were met. When you authentically connect with your heart and passion, expressing your needs and feelings, people will be more likely to engage in your cause and get excited with you.

Fall:

People who are imbalanced in fall communication might **demand** to have their requests met. Balanced communication and interaction happen when the other person wants to do what you ask. Demand is not a win-win; it will either cause defiance or forced compliance. This kind of compliance comes from guilt, manipulation, or fear of consequences or reprisals.

People who are **unable to ask** or request anything from others are also expressing an imbalance in fall communication. These people often assume that others should simply know what they need without having to ask. Or they do not ask because they don't feel worthy and don't want to be a bother.

Ask for what you need. Ask and you shall receive. **A request is a reference of a specific action by a specific person**. If you have followed the previous steps from the other seasons, people will feel very good about meeting your requests. It is important to ask without demands and to empathetically accept whether the individual chooses to or is able to meet your need.

Winter:

People who are imbalanced in winter communication do **not appreciate** their relationships, or they take their relationships for granted. They do not care for the needs of others, or they selfishly **do not take time** to sincerely listen and hear other people's needs.

Another type of winter imbalance in communication is when a person who is exhausted, poor, or depleted and **does not know** his or her **own limits**, but will still **try to meet other people's needs at the expense of personal preservation.**

Be still and quiet; **sincerely listen to others' needs and requests**. Can you support and appreciate other people's needs and feelings, as well as meeting their requests?

In summary, **get clear** on and **state your need**. Express **authentically** from your heart **how you feel** when this need is not met, AND how you would feel if this need was met. **Ask** without demand or guilt trips for a specific **request of help** on how your need could be met. **Listen** to the needs and requests of people you care for. Meet the needs of others if you are truly willing and able. **Healthy communication is a win-win**, it cannot be a way of making one person wrong.

A Typical Day in Four Seasons Harmony

T HE FOLLOWING IS AN EXAMPLE of, or recommendation on, how to stay in harmony with the Four Season Law on a daily basis.

Winter: Waking up

When waking up, do not make the mistake of letting your mind immediately rush into everything you have to do that day or instantly reach for your cell phone. Instead, lie in bed (awake, not snoozing), stretch out your body, and use deep breathing to focus on being present. Take a minute to reflect on all the things for which you are grateful. Being in this "attitude of gratitude" helps you realize what is truly important before you start your day.

Spring: Morning

After you eat breakfast, compose a list of things you need to do, or how you want your day to be. Observe your needs. This can be done in your head or, even better, on paper. Think about what you want out of this day and why. Ask yourself if you have any old "crap" (stinking thinking) that is poisoning your attitude. If so, try to see how your "crap" can actually help you grow. Things are not done *to* you; they are done *for* you. Take responsibility for unmet needs rather than judging or blaming others.

Once you have your list, number what you want to get done in order of priority. Make sure you stay present (do not let your mind run ahead or go back to the past), stay calm, and feel assertive about your needs and what you want to have done. Think of the possible consequences or outcomes before getting started. Always breathe deeply and calmly from your belly.

Summer: Day

Stay present, calm, authentic, and fully engaged in your interactions with others. Express what is alive in you. Communicate your needs and feelings from your heart. Look people in the eye, pay attention to them, and genuinely smile. Focus on the parts of your work that you enjoy so you can truly labor with love. If your mind and actions do not focus on the solutions (watering), then you are part of the problems (weeds). Be passionate and inspire others around you. Maintain a positive attitude and always see the good in every situation. Focus on solutions rather than problems. Focus on breathing deeply from your stomach.

Fall: Evening

As you end your workday and "gather in your crop," ask yourself what you learned today. Things does not always work out the way you intended or expected. If you tend to be hard on yourself, or feel like you never accomplish anything that is good enough, it is good to write down in a journal what you learned and accomplished at the end of each and every day. A harvest will always be realized if you focus on what you learned. This will give you a growing sense of self-worth and accomplishment. You do not always get everything on your list done for the day. Some days you might not even get a single thing done. Unless you deliberately attempted to fail and screw things up, you did the best you could under the circumstances you had. Accept the things you cannot change; accept what is. Learn, let go, and keep moving forward. Breathe in, accept what is; breathe out, let go.

Winter: Night

Remember that your in-box will never be empty. There will always be something else coming up. When the Golden Gate Bridge gets painted, the workers never seem to finish; they just start over again. Likewise, you will never get done; there is always more to do. Trust that you have all the time you need and that everything will happen when it is supposed to happen (if it is supposed to happen).

Make a point to stop working and thinking about work at a certain time. Trust that everything that needs to get done will get done in due season. Turn off your cell phone and don't check voice mail, text messages, or e-mail until the next morning when you compose your daily to-do list. Spend quality time with your spouse, children, or animals. Stay present and still with them, and do not allow your mind to drift back to work, future or past. Use breathing exercises to become present in resting and turn off your mind, which may be spinning about the past or the future. Make sure you get enough hours of sleep.

A day spent in harmony with the Four Seasons like this will help you stay present in each season and every moment, doing the right thing at the right time in perfect timing and peace. A day like this will help you enjoy your journey of continuous growth.

What to Do When Things Go Wrong - It's
Only Failure if We Fail to Learn

S OMETIMES THINGS DON'T WORK OUT the way we think they should. This is inevitable. However, all failure and every ache, pain, or disappointment you experienced in your life is due to a failure to go with the seasons, to do the right thing at the right time. Being thrown off track, or being stuck means that we did not complete a cycle, and we are in denial of, or resistance to, the outcome—what is. This resistance causes tension, aches, pains, emotional distress, and over time, injury or disease.

The Four Seasons System works regardless of whether or not you believe in it. The cycles are a natural law like the law of gravity. The law or principle of the seed is to grow, bear fruit, and multiply. Everything we think, say, do, or believe is like a seed planted. This principle is behind common wisdom expressed in religion and science, such as, "As you sow so also shall you reap," and, "Every action has a reaction." The Four Season System is ever present for our guidance on our way.

We do not learn much from success. When we are on a roll and everything works, we usually don't reflect on how we did it. The greatest learning opportunities come from failure. If used properly, failure and the ability to learn from it, remembering what we learned and applying a new approach, is what causes us to grow. When a toddler is learning to walk, they fall often, but always get up and keep trying until they get it. And adults inevitably cheer their children on, "oohing" and "awing" over how adorable he is as he keeps falling (failing). No one expects the father to grab his toddler and tell him he'd better get it right or quit because his failure is an embarrassment. We accept this failure as part of the learning process. But as we grow older, failure is no longer cute or adorable but rather bad and shameful. We need to be like the little toddler and realize that there are no failures, just learning experiences. When something doesn't happen the way we plan, we need to remember what we learned so we don't have to learn our lessons over and over. Suffering is any experience or outcome that we do not accept. If we do not accept the outcome, we can never learn. The suffering is removed as we stop resisting reality (what is), learn from it, and grow.

According to the ancient Chinese wisdom in the Law of the Five Elements, our bodily pain and emotions work as feedback to tell us in which season we got stuck. Spinning our wheels in the same old track will only cause more tension, pain, and disease. There is a time for sowing and a time for reaping. Time inevitably takes us through the progression of the metaphorical four seasons. There is always a harvest, even though it may not always be what we wanted or expected, and we may not always realize it. Whether we reap a harvest - one we seek or not—depends upon our individual actions in each season. When you use the Four Season System to look within yourself and understand what you did wrong, you can ultimately succeed and be free from suffering.

How to Turn Failure into Success

THE SUBCONSCIOUS MIND SERVES AS a storehouse for memories of our life cycles, both completed (successful) cycles and unfinished (unsuccessful) cycles. The ego perceives the unfinished or incomplete cycles as failures, and they can subsequently become a source of suffering, tension, and disease, particularly if we are constantly reminded of the failures and dwell on them. The true failure, however, is the inability to learn and let go. It's holding on and resisting the flow of life and nature. This resistance causes tension and fatigue in our bodies and minds. Some theories suggest that muscle memory will trigger an increase in tension whenever an individual, either consciously or subconsciously, is reminded of failed cycles (stressful thoughts) of the past. The tension can be triggered by hearing a familiar song on the radio, the smell of a perfume or cologne, a time of year, or almost anything else. Our subconscious mind starts playing these old recordings of unfinished cycles. Reflecting on our past and projecting to our future, we fear things will never change. The more unfinished cycles we have, and the more often we reflect or project them, the more miserable we become. Not accepting what is and not learning from our life lessons will prevent us from letting go, and it will most likely cause us to relive the same experiences (failures) over and over, spinning our wheels until we learn or die.

Obviously we cannot change the past, but we can change the way we react to and feel about it by changing our perception and thoughts. This will enable us to finish a cycle and reap a harvest! But how can we possibly reap a harvest from a crop that ended in failure? A man once asked Thomas Edison if he could observe his work. After spending a month conducting countless experiments on one of his inventions, the observer asked why Edison kept working on the project after failing 10,000 times. Edison looked the inquisitor straight in the eyes and said calmly, "I have not failed 10,000 times. I have successfully discovered 10,000 ways which would not work!" So as you can see, it's a matter of attitude. We can indeed reap a harvest from an experiment that does not work, just as we can from any experience that does work. Learning from our experiences, remembering what we learned, and trying a new approach will by process of elimination bring us closer and closer to discovering a successful method.

If we refuse to accept what life brings us, we either beat ourselves up or become victims who blame others, circumstance, or the world at large. Then we are stuck reliving the experience. Only by accepting what is, realizing and learning (harvesting) from the experience, remembering (storing) what we learned and getting clear on direction, changing approach (fertilizing) for the next go around can we move on and continue to grow.

Do you have an unfinished cycle from your past that you are having a particularly hard time accepting and letting go of? It is very common to find the same pattern of dysfunction in most of your unfinished cycles. These patterns, if allowed to persist, will cause greater and greater suffering, tension, and pain. You may find that certain actions in some seasons come naturally to you. However, in another season, you may have repeatedly repeated the same mistakes.

Think of a stressful event or situation that had a negative outcome you haven't been able to overcome. Ask yourself the following eight groupings of questions to help you analyze where you might have strayed. Question #6 serves as a catalyst for changing failure to success by making us realize (harvest) a learning experience and bring closure to pain and resistance from the past. Question #8 is important to help you remember (store) what you learned, so you will be in a better position to exercise that wisdom in the future. The eight questions will highlight actions you took when you were not in harmony with the nature of life and the season you were in. This will help you realize, learn, and remember so you can change your approach in the future.

SPRING: The Beginning

1. *Fertilizing (Getting clear and benefitting from old waste/poor outcomes.)*Go back to the beginning of your unfinished cycle and answer the following questions:
   - Had you ever experienced this situation or attempted this task previously?
   - If so, did you try a different approach this time, compared to your previous attempts?
   - If your previous attempt(s) were not successful, were you able to take personal responsibility for not succeeding, forgiving other people and yourself before you started again?

2. *Planting (Making a decision, or a commitment; starting the new cycle.)*
   - Before you got started, were you clear on what you needed, why you needed it, and where you were going?
   - Did you set boundaries and assert your needs?
   - When you committed to this course of action, were you calm, clear, and assertive?
   - Were your motives and intentions clear and honest?

SUMMER: The Process

Go back to before you realized that the outcome would not be what you expected or desired, and answer the following questions:

3. *Watering (Positive thinking and attitude)*
   - Did you anticipate a positive outcome?
   - Were you present, engaged, passionate, and authentic in your actions?
   - Did you believe and expect you would be successful?

- Did you focus on what you perceived as good or positive, rather than what you perceived as bad or negative?
- Did you authentically express your needs and feelings from your heart?

4. ***Weeding (The ability to identify and reject what will strangle your harvest)***
   - What obstacles did you face? Did you overcome them?
   - Did you focus on the solution instead of the problem?

FALL: The Outcome

Go back to when you realized that you would not harvest what you desired, and ask yourself the following questions:

5. ***Harvest (Receiving what you've sown, accepting the outcome of your actions, learning from the results.)***
   - Were you able to receive and accept the outcome and move on?
   - Were you able to accept and approve of yourself?
   - Were you able to ask for what you needed without demands or "guilt trips?"

6. ***The "Turnaround" Question***
   - What did you learn from this experience?
   - In what way did the experience make you stronger or better?

WINTER: The Reflection

Once you realize what you learned from your harvest, ask yourself the following questions

7. *Hibernation (Stillness and reflection.)*

- Before starting over, did you take time to reflect on what worked and what didn't?

8. *Storage*

- Did you retain and remember what you learned, so you can try a new approach at your next opportunity without having to repeat the same lesson over?
- Are you able to appreciate the experience, what you learned, and your efforts?

Remember, you have not failed if you can look at any "cycle" (life experience), learn from it, and remember what you learned. The next time you attempt this cycle, make sure to take responsibility for past outcomes by getting clearer on what you really need and by trying a different approach. In this way, your last attempt was, like Edison's example, just another successful way that did not work. The process of elimination will bring you closer and closer to a way that will work. It's not about being perfect. It's about staying present, in "season," genuinely working on learning, growing, and getting better day-by-day. Present awareness of the seasons and what to do or not do, will help you understand cause and effect and lead you to perfect timing.

What we are today is based on our actions, words, and thoughts (planted seeds) of the past. What you think, say, or do right now is who you will be in the future. You have no control over the past or the future; the only time over which you have any control is right now, in this present. As Master Uguay said in the animated movie, *Kung Fu Panda*, "Yesterday is history, tomorrow is a mystery, today is a gift, that's why they call it the present." If our purpose is clear, if our intentions are honest (spring), if we authentically engage in and enjoy what we do (summer), and if we always learn (fall), appreciate what we have, and remember what we have learned (winter), then we are growing. A continuous growth and improvement in whatever you do will eventually lead to mastery.

Once you realize (fall/harvest) that failure is impossible, the pressures of life and the pressure to be perfect are removed. You accept that you are where you are, learning what you need to learn. When you are staying present and calm, thinking constructive thoughts, life becomes free of suffering regardless of your present life situation. Life is a continuum of problems to solve and lessons to learn. Once you accept this as a truth, then the problem you're facing is no longer a problem but rather an opportunity to learn. You can choose to look at your problem as the cause of your suffering or as an opportunity to grow. When you have this awareness your life will be more joyful because you can create and play with ease. Life truly becomes a journey rather than a struggle or a destination, and nothing matters except for the step you take right now. You can still be ambitious, set goals for the future, and work toward them, but when you are completely calm, present, and engaged, you enjoy this moment. You stop seeking perfection, because in that moment you already are. It is like the enlightened man who said he stopped seeking God when he realized God was always with him.

Taking the Journey

LIVING IN BALANCE WITH THE Four Seasons System is an ongoing journey of adjustment and growth. As for me, my journey is still going; I am on my way, but I am still learning each and every day. I am a student of life, and life is my school. My belief systems and faith are reshaping as I grow through my experiences. This is the third book I have written about the Four Season System *, and as I finish writing the third edition of this book, I can't be sure it will be the last.

Only God knows. I realize that I still have to repeat many of my cycles and lessons of life when I'm not learning or retaining. Life is, in a sense, like the movie *Groundhog Day*, where the main character has to relive a day over and over until he finally gets it right. Any life lesson will be experienced over and over until we learn. We cannot run from our problems or hide from our lessons.

I used to think of life as a battle or struggle where the purpose was to never surrender, just like Sylvester Stallone as Rocky Balboa. I would take pride in getting knocked down but never knocked out. As I grew tired of getting my head banged up, I realized that surrendering to what is, and going with the seasons is more like a dance than a struggle. So, as you can see, a belief (believing a thought) can be struggle or ease. A belief can give you peace or make you suffer. A belief can cause stress and tension or harmony and ease. Evaluating whether your belief systems serve you is important as you search for truth and inner peace. I have decided to share my beliefs, not to tell you what to believe, but rather to illustrate how a belief can give you peace and faith.

---

* Previous self published books; Your Life; Now in Season, 1987 and The Four Seasons, 1989

I believe that everything happens for a reason. When things do not go the way I expected, desired, or believed was fair or right, this outcome still happened for a reason. Everything has a purpose, and it is my job to find the purpose of my life events.

I believe there is a God, and I believe God is good, not a sadist that takes pleasure in torturing me or others. I have faith that everything that happens is serving an ultimate good.

I believe God's will is done. I do not have to pray for things to happen. I work on accepting things I cannot change, learning from them, and remaining still, all the while trusting God will always deliver me in the end. How do I even know that what I want is what's best for me? In other words, if God is good, and if God's will is done, then everything that happen is good even though I might not see it at this time.

I believe in not trying to control things that are out of my control or none of my business.

I believe there are only three businesses: my business, other people's business, and God's business.

I believe things are not done to *me; they are done* for *me.*

I believe other people are not a pain in my neck. They are my teachers, if I can only see what they are teaching me.

I believe everyone is my teacher and I am the student. Because I focus on learning, I do not have to worry about being perfect.

I believe it is impossible to fail. The only failure is failing to learn.

I believe I will not die a minute too early or a minute too late, but exactly when I am supposed to. This belief will take away the fear of death.

I believe nothing of any value can ever be lost. I believe my spirit and God are both eternal.

I believe something is true to me when it agrees with my present belief systems. I realize I can change any belief system that does not serve me.

I believe something is true for you and me when we both agree. If you do not agree with me, then it is not true for you. I do not expect people reading my book will agree with all I believe in. And by the time you read this book, some of my beliefs might have changed.

I cannot prove that what I believe is true, but I can make a case that those beliefs will be less stressful and will promote more peace than if I believed in the opposite. It is important for you to align with belief systems that serve you and are true to you. This becomes your religion and it is what is alive in you.

The Four Seasons System is not something you try for a "season." It is a lifestyle for a lifetime, just as you do not brush your teeth once or for a month and then suddenly stop brushing them. By brushing your teeth twice a day, you will benefit from having strong, functional, good-looking teeth for life. The Four Seasons metaphor is in your life whether you pay attention or not. You might as well apply this wisdom and reap the harvest.

The hardest part of life may lie in accepting certain life situations. Not accepting is the greatest cause of tension, pain, injury, disease, and suffering. By accepting, learning, remembering, and trusting (remaining still), a new spring will always come, bringing new life and new possibilities. If we adopt the idea that it is impossible to fail, we can play with the cards we are dealt and still play to win.

In closing, I'd like to share a story. There once lived a very wise, old guru in a small village high up in the Tibetan Mountains. There wasn't a secret of life he didn't know. So one day, some of the kids in the village planned a cruel and evil trick on the old man—they wanted to catch the guru being wrong.

Their plan was to catch a bird and hold it behind their backs while asking the old master if the bird they held in their hands was alive or dead. If he said dead, they would let it fly away. If he said it was alive, they would break its neck behind their backs and hold it up dead in front of the old man's eyes. After catching a bird, the kids approached the old man, and with a nervous stutter they said, "Oh, wise and mighty one, please tell us, is this bird we hold behind our backs alive or dead?"

The wise old Guru took his time to answer, his eyes piercing the eyes of the nervous kids. Then he answered, "The matter is all in your hands."

And so the knowledge of how to use the Four Season System to obtain balance and relieve suffering in your life is now in your hands. May this knowledge help you grow, as well as bring you peace of mind and good health on your journey in life.

About the Author

Tobe Hanson

WHEN I WAS A KID growing up in Stockholm, Sweden, I dreamed of being a professional hockey or soccer player. At fourteen years of age I had the crushing realization that my childhood dream was not to be, and my dad inspired me to start weight training so I'd have another exercise to enjoy. Weight training helped me build both confidence and muscles, but it also inspired me to further investigate the function, potential, and performance of the human body.

I was pondering what to do for a living. When I was twenty years old and attending a lecture, I stumbled across ancient acupuncture philosophy and applied kinesiology. The experience from this lecture helped me realize that enhancing human well-being and performance through holistic healing was the path for me.

I studied acupuncture, Eastern medicine philosophy, alternative medicine physiotherapy, anatomy, physiology, applied kinesiology, reflexology, "Touch for Health," and massage. Upon my graduation in 1983 from the Institute of Alternative Medicine in Stockholm, I had already been a teacher at the school for one year and I was managing the school's student practice as well as my own sports medicine practice. I became a syndicated columnist for *B&K Magazine*, Scandinavia's biggest bodybuilding and fitness publication. The elite bodybuilders, power lifters, and Olympic weight lifters who were my patients, gave me the nickname "the Witch Doctor" because of unconventional holistic methods and immediate results from my therapy.

In 1985, I immigrated to northern California with nothing more than a promise of a job interview at a chiropractor's office and $400 in my pocket. I did not realize at the time of my immigration that I was not allowed to challenge the board of acupuncture in California to get licensed, and so I had to either repeat a three-year acupuncture training in the United States or find another way to practice healing. I chose the latter and started to practice as a certified body worker, using my hands instead of needles and traditional acupuncture. Between 1984 and 1990 I wrote and developed my own material and taught seminars in Sweden, Norway, Holland, England, Canada, and the United States.

My extensive search for a better therapy led me to the development of my own system based on everything I learned about how the human body works.

HansOn Muscle Therapy (HMT), a new and holistic approach to sports medicine, is a feedback-based, customized therapy for pain relief, injury rehabilitation as well as performance enhancement. Since 1991 I have had over 100,000 patient visits, and currently have a four-week waiting list for an appointment. I've grown my practice by word of mouth without advertising, yellow page ads, or even a phone directory listing. Orthopedic surgeons, family doctors, chiropractors, dentists, athletic trainers, personal trainers, acupuncturists, and massage therapists refer patients to me on a daily basis, and my services are frequently sought after by professional athletes from NFL, MLB, PGA, triathlons, and mixed martial arts, as well as college and recreational athletes. I am currently part of the San Jose Sharks NHL medical staff. My work using HMT has a long record of successfully giving instant relief from pain and functional improvement in muscle/joint pain syndromes. I now teach and certify other healthcare providers my HMT techniques and was contracted to teach my workshops to Stanford University's Athletic Training and Physical Therapy department.

Today at 55 years of age when I look back at the road I traveled, I marvel over how everything happened for a reason. To aid fellow human beings in their healing and to inspire growth on both a physical, mental, emotional and spiritual plane is more fulfilling than anything I could ever have dreamt doing for a living. In fact I would not want to be any other person throughout history than me right here or do anything else than what I am doing right now.

Explaining my profession is hard because it is so different and very few understand what I do or know what I am. I am not a physical therapist, even though I use similar methods to evaluate posture and range of motion. I am not a chiropractor, even though I restore joint function and use a derivative of applied kinesiology, a method used and developed by chiropractors. I am not practicing as an acupuncturist, even though I treat acupuncture points and frequently refer to acupuncture philosophy and teachings. I do not practice acupressure in a traditional way. Even though I provided therapy using my hands, I do not practice massage because my patients remain fully clothed through the therapy. I am not a personal or athletic trainer, even though I use exercises to rehabilitate injuries and improve performance. I am not a sports psychologist or counselor, even though I coach my patients in cause, effect, and how to improve performance and quality of life. With the development of the Four

Season System and the writing of this book I am hoping to provide knowledge that will enable everyone to understand cause and effect on human health, performance, and well-being. So what am I then? Perhaps one day, God willing, I could just say I am a HMT practitioner and everyone would know what that is, but for now I simply am Tobe.

Appendix

One Source, One Truth

HUMANS HAVE ALWAYS SEARCHED FOR peace of mind and purpose in their lives. This has been discussed in philosophy, religion, and science, in different centuries and in different cultures, since the dawn of civilization. Great thinkers of modern physics frequently arrive at the surprising conclusion that many of their theories on energy, matter, cause and effect, and the creation of the universe are identical to philosophical scriptures from ancient China, India and Greece that date as far back as 5,000 years in the past. A great many similarities to these theories can also be found within the Bible. In many cases, they all state the same thing using different words. Unfortunately, most dogmatic followers of science, philosophy, or religion fail to recognize these universal truths.

When we lack inner peace and understanding, when we fail to function in harmony with the immutable laws of nature, it becomes difficult to accept reality and take responsibility for our own circumstances. It becomes easier, by far, to simply blame circumstances, and thus our subsequent actions, on external elements. Because of this desire to place the source of our problems externally, we have been searching for solutions to our problems in that same external environment. This is why we develop a blaming, materialistic attitude, and also why we seldom find adequate, lasting solutions. We are too eager to treat symptoms with anti-depressants and pain pills without taking responsibility by looking for cause and solutions.

Science: $E=mc^2$

Albert Einstein introduced the concept that all matter is comprised of energy. Everything in the universe is a form of energy. Matter may change, but the energy it contains—atoms, molecules, and electrons—are eternal. All matter/energy can be concentrated or diluted and could appear as solid, liquid, gas, or ether. Einstein's famous equation, E=mc2, explains a relationship between energy and matter as well as cause and effect: Cause=Effect2.

Philosophy: *Cause and Effect*

Aristotle, the Greek philosopher and the originator of physics, identified four elements in nature (fire, earth, air, and water), which made up all things. He used the interaction between and among these elements to explain the relationship between energy and mass. In ancient Indian philosophy and religion, the word karma was used to explain consequences for our behavior and actions (cause and effect).

Religion: *As you sow, so shall you reap.*

The seed is used as a powerful metaphor throughout the Bible. The potential of the seed to bear fruit and multiply is the divine mechanism of life and holds the potential for unlimited growth. In fact, God's command to the first man and woman was, "Bear fruit and multiply." On the surface, this command seems to imply having children. But its deeper meaning is to multiply and bear fruit in all things, to be alive, to grow spiritually, mentally, and emotionally.

When planting a seed, that one seed grows into a plant capable of producing a hundred seeds. Those hundred seeds, in turn, grow into plants capable of producing yet another hundred seeds each. So whatever you plant multiplies. In a microcosm of the universe, our life's potential represents a seed, a potential that knows no end. The principle of the seed is to bear fruit and multiply. This is what we are meant to do in our lives, to grow and develop our gifts and talents. And a seed does not question its purpose or worthiness. Our life, potential, and talent are God's gifts to us. What we do with them is our gift to God and the world. Jesus spoke to the masses in the form of parables, often about seeds and seasons, to heal people, to set them free by providing them with true inner peace, and to show them the way.

Our instinctive and insatiable curiosity, coupled with pain, suffering, and a lack of purpose and inner peace, causes humans to seek answers. This "re-search" is merely a search for truth, which has already been discovered. Truth is universal, simple, and fundamental. Nature teaches us about truth and the divine harmony surrounding us. In nature, there is no waste—only full potential and unity. When we are wise enough to learn from nature, we see the elements comprising it, including the seasonal changes.

Ancient Chinese Philosophy in the Modern World - Chi or energy

Before contact with Western science and philosophy, the ancient Chinese did not use terms like cause and effect or energy and matter. Instead they used terms like Chi (energy) and li (pattern) as cause and effect, and these terms dated back as far as 5,000 years. The closest interpretation of the word Chi in our Western vocabulary would be life force, energy, or spirit. The Chinese philosophers and physicians taught that everything in heaven and earth is comprised of Chi. This Chi permeates everything and links the surroundings together. They believed this Chi/energy flows around and through the human body, forming a cohesive and functioning unit. Understanding the cause (Chi) and the effect (pattern) led to the knowledge of how to live in harmony within oneself, with one's surroundings and circumstances. By studying nature, the ancient Chinese came to understand the rhythm and flow of Chi and to recognize healthy and unhealthy patterns in humans. With this knowledge, they believed they could teach a proper way to live a long, harmonious, and healthy life.

Traditional Chinese medicine (TCM) asserts that the body has natural patterns of Chi that circulate in channels called meridians. In TCM, symptoms of various illnesses are believed to be the product of disrupted or blocked Chi through the body. These symptoms may also be caused by a deficiency or excess of Chi in the organs or related tissues. Balanced Chi in an individual means life and growth. When the Chi stagnates; injury, disease, and ultimately death occurs. Traditional Chinese medicine seeks to relieve these imbalances to heal the body and optimize its performance. This is done by restoring the circulation of Chi using a variety of techniques, including acupuncture; acupressure; moxibustion, herbs; food; physical training regimens, such as qigong or tai chi; **as well as teaching the proper way of life.** (In other words reading and practicing the wisdom of this book can heal body and mind as well as optimize performance.)

Chi can be concentrated as solid matter, less concentrated in the form of liquid, or, in its most dilute form, as a gas invisible to the eye. Just as Chi outside the body can appear in all three forms of concentrations, the human body is also composed of solid Chi (skin, muscles, tendons, nerves, organs, brain, bones, and other solid structures), liquid Chi (blood, lymph, and other fluids), and air Chi (spirit, life breath/life essence, thoughts, and emotions). Some types of Chi are considered good and some are destructive. The internal Chi, which represents individual health, can be degraded by any adverse external or internal forces of Chi (stress) acting on that individual. Too much or too little of any kind of Chi can be harmful and cause injury, disease, or death. The most common external forces of Chi that can cause injury or disease are physical factors such as impact, trauma, or overuse. Other forms of excessive external Chi are environmental factors, germs, food (spoiled or unhealthy), and climate, and these can also affect an individual's health and well-being. The ancient Chinese also talked about an internal, destructive Chi that affects the mind in the form of destructive thoughts, behavior, and beliefs. In other words, everything is energy and certain forms of energy can break us down while other forms can build us up.

Acupuncture Points

Thousands of years ago, the ancient Chinese somehow became aware that physical dysfunction was coupled with the presence of sensitive reflex points on the body. These sensitive areas were the same or similar in all people who suffered from the same impairment. Moreover, the reflex points varied consistently according to the organ or body function that wasn't normal. This is how the relationships among various internal organs, tissues, and body functions were observed and established. In this fashion, the Chinese mapped several hundred points on the human skin, connected to each other by what they described as meridians that covered the body like an invisible network.

There are acu-points with an exact set of anatomical locations, as well as ashi-points (trigger points) that can occur in soft tissue (muscles, tendons, or ligaments) anywhere on the body. Acu- and ashi-points are not physical tissue in the body; rather, they seem to act like invisible circuit breakers. An overload of any stress, such as trauma, overuse, infection, or an inability to live in harmony with life situations and nature, can cause these circuit breakers to "trip," creating a "short circuit" or blockage.

Western science has found that a change in electrical resistance and temperature on overloaded acu-points can be measured with an ohmmeter or thermogram and can also be seen on Kirlan photography. This overload of the acu-point causes a blockage of circulation and an accumulation of tension in connected muscles, nerves, and organs, leading to pain, injury, and disease.

Meridians

Traditional Chinese Medicine teaches that the Chi is distributed through pathways called meridians. Meridian charts or drawings were used to illustrate this flow of Chi. Those meridians are not physical in nature and cannot be seen by the eye. The body has twelve major, bilateral meridians, each with a beginning and ending location and acu-points along its course. The meridian charts have lines connecting the acu-points to illustrate the direction and flow of Chi along the human body. They believed that disease or injury was caused by blockage or stagnation of this flow. An old Chinese proverb illustrates this philosophy: "There is only one disease, its name is stagnation. There is only one cure, its name is circulation." The ancient physicians believed the human body could cure itself when the circulation of Chi and harmony was restored.

The Chinese named the meridians after the organ or organ system they were connected to. These twelve main meridians were thought to cover the entire surface of the human body like an invisible web. All parts of the body and mind were connected directly or indirectly to each other through this network.

The Twelve Organ Systems

Organ disturbances or pathology determined by the acupuncturist are quite different from what we know as organ pathology or disease in Western medicine. In the West, we use scientific methods to observe the smallest components of the body. We measure and compare those components to a baseline to determine what tissue is diseased (dysfunctional) or healthy. It is fairly black or white, positive or negative, diseased or healthy.

In Eastern medicine, the whole individual is evaluated. Any blockage of circulation will cause a disturbance of harmony and inhibit optimal function and performance. A blockage of circulation will cause symptoms of excess at the blockage and symptoms of deficiency ahead of the blockage. When an acupuncturist says that your liver is weak, it's not the same as your medical doctor alerting you to a liver disease. It means the flow of Chi in your liver is not balanced and its function not optimal. This could manifest as symptoms anywhere along the meridian or in any of the liver meridian's associated tissues and functions. This may or may not at some time manifest itself as a positive blood test for some liver dysfunction. Traditional Chinese medicine, acupuncture, and acupressure are a form of preventive medicine aiming to treat the cause or blockage rather than the symptom, injury, or disease. If your medical doctors have diagnosed a disease, these doctors should supervise all your treatment.

The Western world has difficulty understanding the ancient Chinese philosophical explanation of the organ systems and their functions. My attempt in this book was to explain how the Chinese described and defined the organs because, according to their belief and as described in *Huang Di Nei Ching*, each organ has its own energy, spirit, function, and rank. The *Huang Di Nei Ching* is the oldest known document of medical practice dating back to 2697 B.C. A Western doctor may say a patient's symptoms are in his or her "head" after all diagnostic methods and tests have come back negative. In ancient Chinese medicine there is no separation between mind and body. If the patient experiences symptoms then they are real to him or her and there is a blockage of energy somewhere. In this philosophy there is no separation between body, mind, and spirit, or between an organ system's related tissues, emotions and meridians. Everything is energy in different forms connected as one. Health or balance is defined as harmony between the organ systems, within the self, in our relationships, with our environment or our life situation, as well as with the laws of nature.

Each one of the twelve organs has acupuncture points that are directly related to them. On the front of the torso those organ reflex acupuncture points are called Mu Front points or alarm points. Along the back on the urinary bladder meridian there are corresponding reflex points for each organ called Back-Shu points. Those organ reflex acupuncture points are found to be sensitive to palpation when there is a disturbance of Chi in the organ.

MU-FRONT ORGAN POINTS

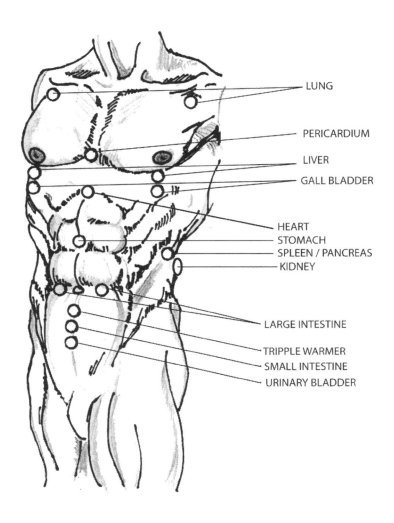

LUNG

PERICARDIUM

LIVER

GALL BLADDER

HEART
STOMACH
SPLEEN / PANCREAS
KIDNEY

LARGE INTESTINE

TRIPPLE WARMER
SMALL INTESTINE
URINARY BLADDER

BACK - SHU ORGAN POINTS

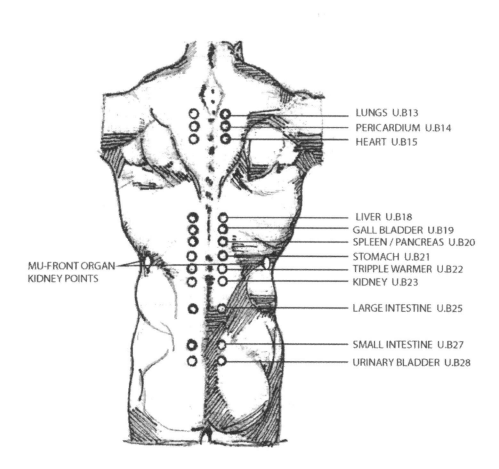

LUNGS U.B13
PERICARDIUM U.B14
HEART U.B15

LIVER U.B18
GALL BLADDER U.B19
SPLEEN / PANCREAS U.B20
STOMACH U.B21
TRIPPLE WARMER U.B22
KIDNEY U.B23

LARGE INTESTINE U.B25

SMALL INTESTINE U.B27
URINARY BLADDER U.B28

MU-FRONT ORGAN
KIDNEY POINTS

Huang Di Nei Jing

The Yellow Emperor's Classic of Internal Medicine (*Huang Di Nei Jing*) is the most important ancient text in Chinese medicine as well as a major book of Daoist theory and lifestyle. The text is structured as a dialogue between the Yellow Emperor and his physician. The Nei Jing explains how disease is caused by not being in harmony or balance with self, others, nature and universe or God. According to the Nei Jing, the universe is composed of a force, Chi, and governed by principles like the laws of Yin/Yang, Heaven/Man/Earth, and the Five Elements. Man can stay in balance or return to balance and health by following those laws as well as understanding and applying this wisdom. Man is a microcosm that mirrors the larger macrocosm. Therefore, the Force of Chi and the principles of Yin and Yang, the Five Elements, and the Four Seasons are part of the universe and recreated in us.

Breathing

This information about breathing is taken directly from the American Medical Student Association's website (AMSA.org), it is an excerpt from the book; "Integrative Medicine" by Dr. David Rakel. ***"Using and learning proper breathing techniques is one of the most beneficial things that can be done for both short and long term physical and emotional health".***

Breathing as a bridge:

It is thought by many cultures that the process of breathing is the essence of being. A rhythmic process of expansion and contraction, breathing is one example of the consistent polarity we see in nature such as night and day, wake and sleep, seasonal growth and decay

244

and ultimately life and death. In yoga, the breath is known as prana or a universal energy that can be used to find a balance between the body-mind, the conscious-unconscious, and the sympathetic-parasympathetic nervous system. Unlike other bodily functions, the breath is easily used to communicate between these systems, which gives us an excellent tool to help facilitate positive change. It is the only bodily function that we do both voluntarily and involuntarily. We can consciously use breathing to influence the involuntary (sympathetic nervous system) that regulates blood pressure, heart rate, circulation, digestion and many other bodily functions. Pranayama is a yoga practice that literally means the control of life or energy. It uses breathing techniques to change subtle energies within the body for health and well-being. Breathing exercises can act as a bridge into those functions of the body of which we generally do not have conscious control.

An example of how life affects physiology:

During times of emotional stress our sympathetic nervous system is stimulated and affects a number of physical responses. Our heart rate rises, we perspire, our muscles tense and our breathing becomes rapid and shallow. If this process happens over a long period of time, the sympathic nervous system becomes over stimulated leading to an imbalance that can affect our physical health resulting in inflammation, high blood pressure and muscle pain to name a few.

Consciously slowing our heart rate, decreasing perspiration and relaxing muscles is more difficult than simply slowing and deepening breathing. The breath can be used to directly influence these stressful changes causing a direct stimulation of the parasympathetic nervous system resulting in relaxation and a reversal of the changes seen with the stimulation of the sympathetic nervous system. We can see how our bodies know to do this naturally when we take a deep breath or sigh when a stress is relieved.

The breathing process can be trained:

Breathing can be trained for both positive and negative influences on health. Chronic stress can lead to a restriction of the connective and muscular tissue in the chest resulting in a decreased range of motion of the chest wall. Due to rapid more shallow breathing, the chest does not expand as much as it would with slower deeper breaths and much of the air exchange occurs at the top of the lung tissue towards the head. This results in "chest" breathing. You can see if you are a chest breather by placing your right hand on your chest and your left hand on your abdomen. As you breathe, see which hand rises more. If your right hand rises more, you are a chest breather. If your left hand rises more, you are an abdomen breather.

Chest breathing is inefficient because the greatest amount of blood flow occurs in the lower lobes of the lungs, areas that have limited air expansion in chest breathers. Rapid, shallow, chest breathing results in less oxygen transfer to the blood and subsequent poor delivery of nutrients to the tissues. The good news is that similar to learning to play an instrument or riding a bike, you can train the body to improve its breathing technique. With regular practice you will breathe from the abdomen most of the time, even while asleep.

The benefits of abdominal breathing:

Abdominal breathing is also known as diaphragmatic breathing. The diaphragm is a large muscle located between the chest and the abdomen. When it contracts it is forced downward causing the abdomen to expand. This causes a negative pressure within the chest forcing air into the lungs. The negative pressure also pulls blood into the chest improving the venous return to the heart. This leads to improved stamina in both disease and athletic activity. Like blood, the flow of lymph, which is rich in immune cells, is also improved. By expanding the lung's air pockets and improving the flow of blood and lymph, *abdominal breathing also helps prevent infection of the lung and other tissues. But most of all it is an excellent tool to stimulate the relaxation response that results in less tension and an overall sense of well-being".*

Excerpt from Dr. Rakel's book Integrative Medicine copyrighted by Elsevier 2003 with permission to use.

Daily meditation on the breath:

This could be done for an extended time or one single breath. The individual pays attention to their breath moving in and out. Hear, feel or mentally watch the air completely filling up the abdomen and the lungs, holding for a second and then completely deflating the abdomen and lungs. Visualize the image of air completely filling up (inflating) and going out of (deflating) a balloon. This will cause a pause in a mind that was racing with thoughts. Complete awareness of a single breath will bring a moment of being completely present. Not paying attention to the thoughts, but rather bringing the attention back to the breath, will bring peace and a connection with the true self that is not your thoughts.

Diaphragmatic Breathing Exercises

Lying Down:

THIS BREATHING EXERCISE SHOULD BE done, while lying on your back in bed before you fall asleep and in the middle of the night, if you wake up and find it hard to fall asleep again. It is also recommended that you do it in the morning right after you wake up from your alarm clock and before you jump out of bed to check your cell phone for voice mail, text messages and emails. Performing this breathing exercise before you start your day will create a smooth harmonious transition from rest to work day.

Place one hand on your chest and the other on your abdomen. When you take a deep breath in, the hand on the abdomen should rise higher than the one on the chest. This insures that the diaphragm is pulling air into the base of the lungs.

1. Inhale: take a slow deep breath in through your nose imagining that you are sucking in all the air in the room until your belly and chest blow up like a balloon, without straining.

2. Exhale: let the air out slowly through your mouth while counting the seconds in your head. As all the air is released with relaxation, gently contract your abdominal muscles at the end to completely evacuate the remaining air from the lungs. It should take 5-20 seconds to completely exhale. It is important to remember that we deepen our respirations through complete exhalation not by inhaling more air.

3. Repeat the cycle for a total of 15-25 deep breaths and try to breathe at a slow rate.

Once you feel comfortable with the above technique, you can incorporate words that can enhance the exercise. For example, as you inhale, you could say to yourself the word, *relax, peace, love, acceptance or gratitude.* The idea being to bring in the feeling/emotion you need with inhalation and sharing it with exhalation.

You can also think about your positive affirmations during inhalation to assist in changing your beliefs to ones that will serve you.

The use of the hands on the chest and abdomen are only needed to help you train your breathing. Once you feel comfortable with your ability to breathe into the abdomen, you no longer need to place them there. The idea with consciously practicing deep breathing is to reboot your relax/recover (parasympathetic) nervous system and to turn off your fight and flight (sympathetic) nervous system. This is of great value for anyone who has a mind that never stops going. At first you may find that your thoughts jump into the middle of your breathing exercises, but as you keep focusing on your breath and practicing mindful awareness, you will be able to turn off your racing thoughts and relax.

Seated or Standing:

You can do this exercise where ever you are when you need a time out from your activities. This exercise could be performed whenever you find your mind racing or dwelling on upsetting thoughts, catch yourself with not breathing correctly or when you are experiencing worrying, anxiety, disappointment, depression, tension or pain.

1. Sit or stand up straight. Exhale fully.
2. Inhale and, at the same time, relax the belly muscles. Feel as though the belly is filling with air.
3. After filling the belly, keep inhaling. Fill up the middle of your chest. Feel your chest and rib cage expand.

4. When your air is fully inhaled, begin to exhale as slowly as possible.
5. As the air is slowly let out, relax your chest and rib cage. Begin to pull your belly in (contracting your abdominal muscles) to force out the remaining breath. Exhaling should take approximately 4-10 seconds without strain.
6. Close your eyes, and concentrate on your breathing.
7. Relax your face and mind.
8. Let everything go; focus only on this moment and the breath you are taking right now.
9. Just one breath can have an immediate impact on releasing tension and improving performance and well-being.

The more abdominal / diaphragmatic breathing is practiced, the more natural it will become to stay internally calm, present and at peace even when surrounded by chaos. The only thing you have any control over, is this moment right now and the breath you are taking right now.

Insomnia

IN MANY CASES WHEN A person has been overstimulating their sympathetic (fight and flight) nervous system over prolonged periods of stress, they will have trouble falling and or staying asleep. This individual is in desperate need of relaxation, recovery and rest but unable to get it, due to being unable to turn off thoughts of urgency, worry or fear.

Insomnia is therefore primarily an Earth or Winter imbalance. Not being present and at peace when it is time to relax and sleep, indicates an Earth imbalance. The mind will race into the future of everything that needs to get done and could go wrong, or the mind gets stuck in the past on everything that should or should not have been done and should not have happened. A restless mind that is not able to fall asleep tends to be either anxious or depressed.

Night time as well as the ability to rest, recover, be still and feel safe, are all attributes of Winter, and rest, recovery and sleep are primarily for night time. A person with Winter insomnia might fall asleep due to exhaustion, but is a very light sleeper who wakes up with the slightest noise or needs to get up and go to the bathroom to urinate frequently. This is all due to excessive fear or a sense of urgency. Any individual that has been in a sustained period of urgency can experience this. Post-traumatic stress disorder (PTSD), suffered by soldiers that return home from combat experiences or individuals that has been in abusive relationships, is a severe example of this condition. Unless this person is exhausted, he or she will have a hard time falling asleep.

Stress is either real or perceived, however even when the stress is perceived, which is the majority of time, it is still perceived as real by the individual with insomnia. Perhaps at one time there was real danger as in being chased by a predator, but the person is acting as if they are still being chased.

According to resent sleep studies we all need 8 hours of sleep per night for optimal recovery and performance. Most people in today's fast-paced society are sleep deprived to some degree. Quantity of sleep, the hours of sleep you get per night is not everything; the quality of your sleep is as important for you to wake up and feel rested and fresh. When the quality and or quantity of sleep is compromised it is like spending more money than you make. You end up in the red and this effect is cumulative. Not getting enough sleep will affect the body's ability to regenerate and repair itself after daily use, abuse or overuse. The more stress someone is under, the more the breakdown of the body occurs, and the greater the need for quality sleep. Sleep deprivation will affect performance, lead to a compromised immune system, injuries that linger and won't heal, disease and premature aging. This a paradox because most people with perceived stress believe things like; "I have too much to do and not enough time," "I do not have time to rest," "I cannot rest until I am done, and I never get done," "I am running out of time," "I am missing out," "I do not have enough," "I am getting to old," "I am in danger," All those perceived belief systems cause either a state of urgency, fear, or both, which makes it impossible to have a calm mind and get restful sleep. This stressful thought, in fact, becomes a negative affirmation, and the more it is repeated, the more real or true it becomes to the person thinking those thoughts. This belief system and state of mind will stimulate the sympathetic nervous system and the release of stress hormones. It will cause muscles to tense instead of relax. How can one deal with their insomnia when they are in a state like this? To be able to get deep sleep a person needs to be calm, peaceful, still, and feel secure and safe.

In some cases, over the counter or prescription medication might be necessary to get some immediate rest. Medication however, will not take care of the underlying root cause of the problem. The person suffering must remove themselves from what causes their stress, change their habits and life style, or in the case of perceived stress they need to change what they believe.

Breathing exercises and affirmations practiced repeatedly over time can help an individual get calm, relaxed and present. This can stop a racing mind that is obsessing on urgency while experiencing worrying, anxiety or fear. Affirmations like; "I am calm, still and at peace", "I am resting in deep sleep," "I have all the time I need," "I trust that everything that is supposed to get done will get done when it is supposed to." To those individuals that need to believe in these affirmations, they will sound like a complete lie. The perceived fearful or anxious beliefs that are keeping them from falling or staying asleep are so strongly rooted that the positive affirmation has to be repeated over and over like a mantra.

Breathing exercises are, in fact, a form of meditation and a way to quiet the mind. Paying attention to one breath moving into and out of your body will bring a moment of being completely relaxed, calm, and present (see "Daily meditation on the breath" page 241?). Deep, slow, relaxed breathing is one way to stimulate the (parasympathetic) relaxing nervous system. When a person with an over-stressed (sympathetic) nervous system is trying to do 15-25 consecutive deep breaths like this, he or she will find their mind drift back to the stressful thoughts and beliefs. The more stressed out an individual, the harder it is to stay present for consecutive breaths without drifting. This now becomes a battle of the mind between the attempt to focus on breathing and/or positive affirmation versus the stressful thoughts, AKA negative affirmations.

Many of my sleep-deprived patients tell me they tried breathing exercises, but the worrying mind took over and they gave up. I tell them just to have a conversation within themselves and tell their mind that they will either fall asleep while doing the breathing exercises or they will continue the breathing exercises all night long. With each successful deep breath, they stimulate relaxation, and the more relaxing breaths they have, the more rested they will be in the morning. With time and practice they get better and better at deep breathing without drifting into the stressful thoughts and beliefs.

Start the breathing meditation over again after each drifting thought, rather than giving up tossing and turning all night. Thinking the stressful thoughts, while tossing and turning will get you even more stressed. Stressing about how late it is, how little sleep you are getting, how tired you are going to be in the morning and how much you have to do the next day is like pouring gasoline on a fire further stimulating the fight and flight (sympathetic) nervous system and the end result being even more tired and tense when it is time to get out of bed. Doing breathing exercises all night without falling asleep, will still promote rest and stimulating the relaxing (parasympathetic) nervous system.

A Wake up Call to get Present

IF YOU STUDIED PSYCHOLOGY IN school, you probably heard of Pavlov's dogs. Ivan Pavlov was a Russian scientist who discovered a conditioned response in dogs to repeated stimulus. He found that if he rang a bell simultaneously as he fed his dogs, he created a conditioned response. After this was repeated a few times, the dogs associated the sound of the ringing bell with food. At this point, the dogs would start to salivate when the bell was rung, even if they did not smell or see their food. Thanks to Pavlov's discovery, classic conditioning became the basis for Behaviorism, a school of psychology.

It is interesting to note, that we as humans have conditioned ourselves to behave in certain ways due to various conditioned stimuli. Not presently aware, we subconsciously react to other people's facial expressions, memories to songs played on the radio, the smell of certain foods and much more. Everything we perceive is compared to our past experiences or conditioning and judged as good or bad, hence our reaction. All those conditioned stimuli are what make us feel the way we do. The problem is that so many of those subconscious conditioning stimuli are perceived as stressful or bad, when in fact they may be harmless. Stress is either real or perceived, but even when the danger is not real it is still perceived as real.

As cell phones became more mainstream, I found that they were a cause of negative conditioned response in most of my patients. When I was working on a patient and their cell phone vibrated or rang, I could feel an immediate tightening of the muscle I was working on. This was more noticeable in overwhelmed patients that were under stress. Those were patients that believed they had too much to do and not enough time, and each ring of their cell phone caused more tension in their muscles.

In a time and society where many perceive so much stress and live with an over stimulated fight and flight nervous system, we need to find a way where we can perceive things in a different light. Stress is mostly perceived and mostly about the future (things that have not happened yet) and the past (things that have already happened.) This takes us away from experiencing the present moment calmly and from doing one thing at the time while realizing that everything is ok right now. Every time we are not present, calm and at peace, we are not breathing right.

The problem is that we don't know when we're not present, because when we realize we're not present, that's when we ARE present. When we realize we're not breathing right, we become present and immediately start to breath right. When we DO catch ourselves not being present, were we not present for three minutes or for an hour? Many people spend most of their day not being present, hence never having peace of mind. It is however, ONLY when we are present that we can operate in excellence, create and love. Needless to say, life would be lived more fully if we could increase time of presence in our daily life.

In other words, it would be good if we could have a form of wake up call to help us get present when we are not. We need to create a new positive response that will help us get present and experience peace.

You can actually use your own cell phone as a way to create a new conditioned response that will serve you. This new conditioning can help you to be calm and get present with peace of mind.

First you need to pick a new ring tone, one you have never used before or associate with someone or something else. This needs to be a nonabrasive ring tone like soft chimes or a bell. When you hear this new ring tone, you need to immediately take one deep diaphragmatic breath before you look at your phone or do anything else. This needs to be done EVERY SINGLE time you hear it ring. In this way, you will condition yourself to get present, calm and at peace every time your phone signals you have a call, text message or voicemail. The beauty of this is that the ringing is random and most likely will catch you at a moment when you are not present, not breathing right and experiencing stress. If for any reason at any time, you cannot commit to take a deep breath when your phone rings, you should turn the volume off. For this conditioning to work, it requires a new peaceful ring tone AND that you take a deep breath EVERY time it rings.

If you are under a lot of stress, overwhelmed and feel you have too much to do and not enough time, you can say an affirmation (quietly in your head or out loud) when your new ring tone goes off and you are taking your deep breath. One of the following affirmations might work for you: *"I am calm and at peace," "I have all the time I need,"* or *"Everything that is supposed to happen will happen when it is supposed to."*

One of my patients, Julie, a 38-year-old mother of three girls that was recovering from her imbalances in "Fall" and "Earth," had healed from lower back pain caused by a herniated disc and improved her low self-esteem as well as intestinal problems of constipation and bloating.

Old patterns are hard to break and Julie still fell into periods of being nervous, anxious and disappointed in herself. As I described before, we do not realize when we are not present. I told Julie about changing the ring tone on her cell phone so that every time it randomly rang, she could use it as a wakeup call to take a deep breath to get calm and present. When she came home and introduced the idea to her husband and daughters, they were all giggling as she took a deep breath to calm herself every time her phone rang.

Then one day when she was unaware that she was in her old self-chastising, anxious, nervous, not present state, her 9-year old daughter yelled out, "Dad, call Mom. She needs to breath."

Julie started to laugh, got instantly present and hugged her daughter.

Loved ones, family and friends can help you break old dysfunctional patterns and condition new healthy patterns.

What Causes Pain?

S TEVE, A THIRTY-EIGHT-YEAR-OLD MAN WITH chronic neck pain and recurring headaches, who wanted to ensure his pain never came back. After I released the tension in trigger and acu- pressure points in his tight neck muscles, Steve said, "Wow, I have not been pain-free for weeks and not been able to move my neck like this for years. How long will this last?"

"I'm not sure," I said, "but let me tell you a story. A man broke his garbage disposal by dropping a spoon down the drain while the disposal was on. He called a plumber to repair it. After the disposal was fixed and the man paid his bill, he asked the plumber how long this garbage disposal would last. The plumber answered, until next time you drop something down there that does not belong."

The broken garbage disposal, headaches, or stiff neck are the symptoms, outcome, or results. Fixing them does not guarantee they will not come back. Unless the cause of a problem is realized and removed, there are no permanent fixes. If we take the time to understand that what we did or did not do caused the situation, and learn how to change our approach, we can prevent experiencing the problem over and over again.

Why do we experience pain in our back, neck, head, muscles, tendons, ligaments, and joints? In my experience, stress is the cause of all injury and pain. Stress is defined as a state of physical, mental, emotional or spiritual strain or suspense. There are five forms of stress, and to understand the link to well-being, it helps to understand the definition of each.

Physical stress comes from direct trauma, such as impact— hitting or being hit by something—and sudden, uncontrolled body movement, as in a whiplash. Direct trauma causes immediate tension and tissue damage, disturbing blood flow and nerve signaling leading to inflammation, and pain. Microtrauma, on the other hand, is accumulated structural strain that causes tension and eventually tissue damage with injury and pain. Microtrauma is caused by repetitive movement patterns, improper movement patterns, and poor posture. We have all at one time or another used, overused, or abused ourselves physically by doing too much. Afterwards, tension and pain remind us of our past action.

Nutritional or chemical stress is another form of stress. Deficiencies, such as poor diet, lack of essential nutrients, and dehydration, will cause stress to our metabolism and affect our immune system. Excesses of toxins, drugs (medicinal or recreational), sugar, and fat will also cause stress to our body functions. All stress will cause tension in our body and eventually lead to disease.

Environmental stress is caused by our surroundings. For example, an excess of bacteria, viruses, or allergens activate and stress our autoimmune system. This external energy could congest and inhibit our lymph drainage, as well as kill or overtake healthy cells to cause disease. A stagnation of metabolic waste products and congested lymph will cause a relative oxygen deprivation in our muscles. This can cause muscular contraction, tension, and pain.

Unresolved mental or emotional turmoil, past or present, is the greatest stressor and cause of suffering. This is seen in anyone who is stuck, repeating a pattern, harboring destructive belief systems and having negative thoughts or emotions (expressed or suppressed.) Accumulated emotional stress causes chronic muscular tension and restricts circulation that, over time, will cause pain, injury, or disease.

And finally, there is the spiritual stress we experience when we are not true to our heart and stop growing and learning as humans.

Here is something for you to think about. Imagine that you were experiencing excruciating pain, and then your phone rang. You had been waiting for an important call for weeks, but that is far from your thoughts at the time when in agony you reach for your phone.

Instead, you are thinking, "Who is bothering me now?" Then when you see the caller ID, you see it is the call you have been waiting for. You immediately get excited! What happened to the excruciating pain at that moment? Did the pain go away or did your mind just go to a different place? And if the mind went to a different place, who made that happen?

All forms of stress cause a buildup of tension in our muscles. An accumulation of tension in certain muscles causes a muscular imbalance, which can lead to uneven wear and tear. In other words, our body gets out of alignment. Muscular imbalance (uneven pulling) causes bad posture, changed joint positions with decreased joint space, decreased vascular circulation, and inhibits lymphatic drainage. This tension causes friction, pressure, compression, excessive pulling and pain. Over time, this can result in dysfunction and degeneration of the joints. Stress also causes tension and contraction of internal organs and blood vessels. Excessive stress will, over time, cause life-threatening conditions. Stress causes tension; tension leads to pain. Unresolved, recurring, or repetitive stress causes an accumulation of tension, which leads to injury, disease, and ultimately death. Stress isn't always bad. If applied gradually, with proper time to recuperate, stress helps us grow physically as well as mentally. For instance, weight training is stressful for the muscles involved; it causes a breakdown of muscle tissue. However, proper quantity and quality of rest and nutrition will allow the body to repair the muscles that were broken down and rebuild them, bigger and stronger than before. Progressive weight training is based on a balance between breaking down (stress) and building up (rest, recovery, and nutrition). This same principle is true for stress to the mind.

"The faculties of the mind are improved by exercise, yet
they must not be put to a stress beyond their strength."
– John Locke

So is stress, or even pain, bad or good? If it teaches you something, it must be good. It is possible to be in pain or experience stress and not suffer. The suffering is only in the mind, based on our interpretation and belief system that assigns it a value of bad or good.

How do we know for a fact that what we experience is bad, or how do we know that what we want is best for us? I'm sure you've heard the expression, "Whatever does not kill you will make you stronger." It's true that out of great despair and desperation often come the greatest solutions. If you are an average skier who brags about never falling, then you are not pushing (stressing) yourself to get better. If, on the other hand, you are a reckless daredevil skiing out of control (excessive stress), sooner or later you will injure yourself. If you are overzealous in your sports or exercise routine, your body will not have ample time to recover, and decreased performance and injuries will halt your activities. If you think being a couch potato is safe and stress-free, think again. Obesity, high blood pressure, high cholesterol, and diabetes can shorten your life. If your work is not stimulating and challenging, you will be bored and depressed, and your immune system will weaken. The anxiety and tension from unreasonable on-the-job expectations or demands can eventually lead to injury or disease. A healthy, well-rested individual will overcome bacteria and viruses to build a stronger immune system. A weaker, tired, anxious, or depressed individual will get sick from the same exposure. So we can see how stress, applied in the right amount, can help us grow and get stronger. Too much or too little stress will bring us tension, negative emotions, pain, injury, and disease. Paying attention to your emotions and physical symptoms will help you learn which stress is good or bad, as well as what is too much or too little. As in all things, we need to strive for balance.

Diagrams and Symptoms Overview

Cause and Effect: As you Sow, so shall you Reap

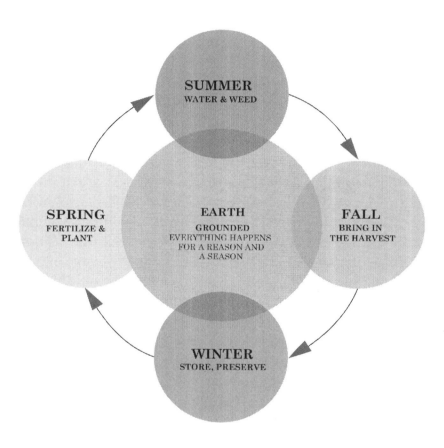

Action: In Harmony With One's Circumstances

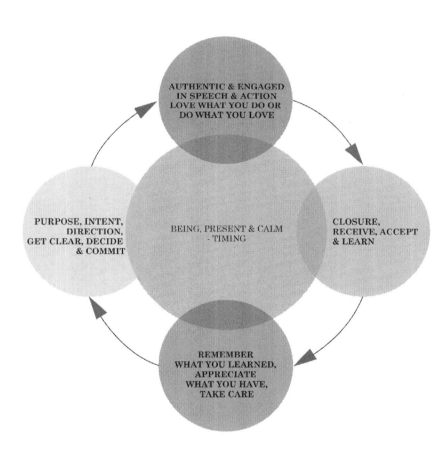

AUTHENTIC & ENGAGED
IN SPEECH & ACTION
LOVE WHAT YOU DO OR
DO WHAT YOU LOVE

PURPOSE, INTENT,
DIRECTION,
GET CLEAR, DECIDE
& COMMIT

BEING, PRESENT & CALM
- TIMING

CLOSURE,
RECEIVE, ACCEPT
& LEARN

REMEMBER
WHAT YOU LEARNED,
APPRECIATE
WHAT YOU HAVE,
TAKE CARE

Emotional Ease
Doing and Being in Harmony with Our Circumstances

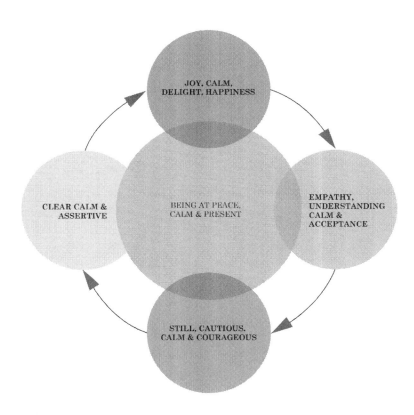

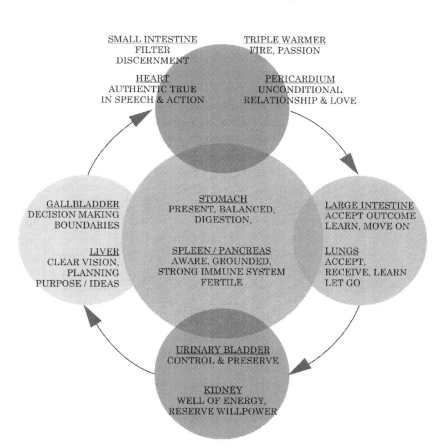

SMALL INTESTINE
FILTER
DISCERNMENT

TRIPLE WARMER
FIRE, PASSION

HEART
AUTHENTIC TRUE
IN SPEECH & ACTION

PERICARDIUM
UNCONDITIONAL
RELATIONSHIP & LOVE

GALLBLADDER
DECISION MAKING
BOUNDARIES

STOMACH
PRESENT, BALANCED,
DIGESTION,

LARGE INTESTINE
ACCEPT OUTCOME
LEARN, MOVE ON

LIVER
CLEAR VISION,
PLANNING
PURPOSE / IDEAS

SPLEEN / PANCREAS
AWARE, GROUNDED,
STRONG IMMUNE SYSTEM
FERTILE.

LUNGS
ACCEPT,
RECEIVE, LEARN
LET GO

URINARY BLADDER
CONTROL & PRESERVE

KIDNEY
WELL OF ENERGY,
RESERVE WILLPOWER

Getting Stuck: Repeating a Pattern

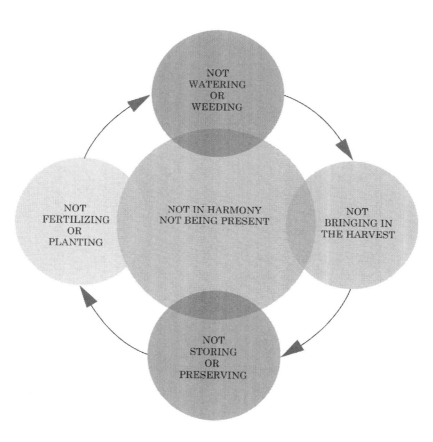

Stressful Beliefs

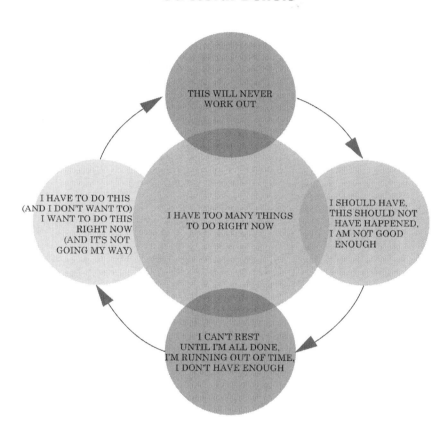

Is it TRUE ? Is it Possible the Opposite is True?

Emotional Feedback
Suppressed or Expressed Emotions

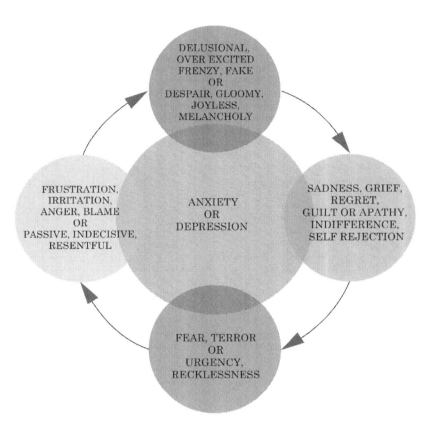

Spring

- Eye problems, conjunctivitis, and other more severe problems.
- Dryness or tearing of the eyes.
- Twitching of muscles around the eyes.
- Tension headaches from the lateral neck into the base of the head (occipital) and temples.
- Migraine headaches often affecting the sight (lights, black spots, etc.).
- Disorders affecting equilibrium (balance).
- Dizziness and vertigo.
- Nausea.
- Pain in the lateral (sides of) neck and top of shoulders.
- Pain between the shoulder blades (right side more common).
- Tenderness in the pectoral region (anterior chest wall, especially the right side).
- Intolerance or craving of greasy food.
- Intolerance and/or addiction to alcohol, often causing anger or rage.
- Fullness and gas after eating fatty food.
- Pain in the right lower ribcage.
- High cholesterol.
- Abdominal pain,Toxic conditions.
- Jaundice.
- Allergies affecting the eyes.
- Lateral (sides of) lower back pain.
- Lateral (sides of) hip pain.
- Pain along the lateral thigh, lower leg, and ankle.
- Medial knee pain at the site of the medial meniscus or medial collateral ligament.
- Twitching, numbness, and pain along the outside (lateral side) of the torso, legs, and feet.

Summer

- High or low blood pressure.
- Decreased circulation in hands or feet.
- Dysfunction of arteries or veins.
- Metabolic disorders (hyper- or hypo- metabolism).
- Hyper- or hypo-thermia.
- Hot flashes.
- Hyper- or hypo-libido.
- Chest pain.
- Inability to open up in love relationships.
- Indigestion.
- Diarrhea.
- Hemorrhoids.
- Spasms of the neck.
- Pain in the shoulder area.
- Pain in the shoulder blade and armpit.
- Frozen shoulder
- Ringing in the ears (tinnitus).
- TMJ (temporo-mandibular joint syndrome), clicking or locking jaw.
- Wrist and forearm pain.
- Pain or numbness in the 3rd, 4th or 5th fingers.

Fall

- Coughing, asthma, and bronchitis.
- Spasm of the throat.
- Pneumonia.
- Allergies.
- Lymphatic congestion.
- Swelling or dryness of mucous membranes.
- Mucus drainage.
- Nasal congestion.
- Dry skin, eczema, psoriasis, and rashes.
- Constipation.

- Bloating.
- Diarrhea.
- Lower back pain or rigidity (lumbago).
- Chest and upper back pain.
- Shoulder and deltoid problems.
- Tennis elbow (lateral epicondylitis).
- Pain in thumb and or index finger.
- Neck pain.
- Tension headaches.

Winter
- Dehydration.
- Disturbances in the regulation of blood, lymph, cerebrospinal fluid, joint lubrication, urine, sweat, and saliva.
- Swelling and edema.
- Sleeping disorders and fatigue.
- Lower back pain and sciatica.
- Bone pain or painful, dysfunctional joints.
- Arthritis
- Osteoporosis or osteopenia.
- Decaying or weak teeth.
- Problems with memory: poor memory, poor retention of new information, interruptions in the flow of thoughts.
- Alzheimer's and dementia.
- Ear infections or hearing problems.
- Pain or cramps in feet, ankles, and calf muscles.
- Cold feet.
- Achilles tendinitis or rupture.
- Hair loss or balding.
- Headaches or tension at the base of the skull or inner corners of the eyes.
- Sinus pressure and headaches.

Earth

- Digestive problems.
- Obesity.
- Headaches and dizziness.
- Sinus problems, primarily pressure in sinuses under the eyes.
- Neck pain from the collarbone to below the jaw and behind the ear.
- Epigastric spasms (problem swallowing).
- Shallow breathing.
- Hiatal hernia.
- Heart burn.
- Acid reflux.
- Hyper- or hypo-acidity.
- Vomiting.
- Gagging.
- Burping and belching.
- Stomach pain.
- Gastritis.
- Abdominal pain.
- Hypo- or hyperglycemic.
- Emotional instability.
- Eating disorders, including anorexia or bulimia.
- Lethargy and depression.
- Obsessive and anxious.
- Stubborn or obstinate behavior.
- Female infertility.
- Autoimmune disorders.
- Blood disorders.
- Sleep disorders.
- Metabolic disorder.
- Hormonal disorders, particularly menstrual.
- Anterior hip and groin pain.
- Front thigh pain.

- Knee pain or joint dysfunction.
- Pain along the shinbone and shin splints.
- Pain on top of the ankle and foot.
- Bunions.

Spreading the Word

Dear Reader,

For over three decades I have been working on the Four Seasons System with a burning desire to heal the whole body, improve inner peace (being) and performance (doing) in order to enhance personal growth and quality of life.

This book has been published with no other marketing than word of mouth. It needs your help to grow and help others. Please help spread the word by sharing its website with everyone seeking to improve the quality of their lives and the lives of others. www.TheFourSeasonsWay ofLife.com.

Would you like to offer *The Four Seasons Way of Life* book to your clients of your physical therapy, chiropractic, massage, acupuncture, life coaching, spiritual, personal training, reflexology, acupressure, or medical practice? If so, please contact us at info@TheFourSeasonsWayofLife.com to inquire about bulk discounts.

If you are interested in the life and growth of The Four Seasons System, follow along on the website. I will update the site with the latest information about *The Four Season Way of Life* book and e-book, as well as the latest development of new products such as an audio book, smart phone apps, educational DVDs, and possible workshops.

I invite you to read my new book titled *Athletes Way to Be - Way of Excellence: Ancient Eastern Wisdom Revealing the Secrets to Modern Day Athletic Peak Performance and How to Be in The Zone.* For more information, please visit: www.AthletesWaytoBe.com.

My sincere gratitude,
Tobe Hanson

References

All of my patients in 31 years of practice

Personal notes from Acupuncture lectures

Traditional Acupuncture: The Law of the Five Elements by Dr. Dianne M. Connelly

The Yellow Emperor's Classic of Internal Medicine: by Ilza Veith

The Meridians of Acupuncture: by Felix Mann

The Power of Now: A Guide to Spiritual Enlightenment by Eckhart Tolle

A Thousand Names for Joy: Living in Harmony with the Way Things Are by Byron Katie and Stephen Mitchell

Non-Violent Communication: A Language of Life by Marshall B. Rosenberg and Arun Gandhi

Integrative Medicine, by David Rakel, M.D.

The Four Agreements: A Practical Guide to Personal Freedom by Don Miguel Ruiz and Nicholas Wilton

The Road Less Traveled: A New Psychology of Love, Traditional Values and Spiritual Growth:

by M. Scott Peck, M.D.

The Way of the Peaceful Warrior: A Book that Changes Lives by Dan Millman